TRANSFORMING
TALES

of related interest

A Creative Guide to Exploring Your Life
Self-Reflection Using Photography, Art, and Writing
Graham Gordon Ramsay and Holly Barlow Sweet
ISBN 978 1 84310 892 4

Writing Works
A Resource Handbook for Therapeutic Writing Workshops and Activities
Edited by Gillie Bolton, Victoria Field and Kate Thompson
Foreword by Blake Morrison
ISBN 978 1 84310 468 1

Classroom Tales
Using Storytelling to Build Emotional, Social and Academic Skills across the Primary Curriculum
Jennifer M Fox Eades
ISBN 978 1 84310 304 2

Storytelling with Children in Crisis
Take Just One Star – How Impoverished Children Heal Through Stories
Molly Salans
ISBN 978 1 84310 745 3

TRANSFORMING TALES

How Stories Can Change People

Rob Parkinson

Jessica Kingsley Publishers
London and Philadelphia

First published in 2009
by Jessica Kingsley Publishers
116 Pentonville Road
London N1 9JB, UK
and
400 Market Street, Suite 400
Philadelphia, PA 19106, USA

www.jkp.com

Library of Congress Cataloging in Publication Data
Parkinson, Rob.
Transforming tales : how stories can change people / Rob Parkinson.
    p. cm.
ISBN 978-1-84310-974-7 (pb : alk. paper)
1. Narrative therapy. 2. Storytelling. I. Title.
RC489.S74P368 2009
616.89'165–dc22
                                2008035926

British Library Cataloguing in Publication Data
A CIP catalogue record for this book is available from the British Library

ISBN 978 1 84310 974 7

Printed and bound in Great Britain by
Athenaeum Press, Gateshead, Tyne and Wear

For Ruth, with my thanks for
not taking me too seriously –
and with my love.

Contents

TABLE OF STORIES   9

ACKNOWLEDGEMENTS   13

INTRODUCTION   17

1.   The Natural Storyteller

Personal stories; Social Stories™; Trance-forming
stories; Language, metaphor and story; The biology
of stories; Healing stories; Breakthrough stories:
The mbala effect – and how to beat it; The natural
storyteller – a summary   23

2.   The Spanish Game: Guided Imagery and Stories

The Spanish game; Seven visualizations;
Interpretations and misinterpretations; How we know
that visualization works; Four relaxation techniques;
Visualization and guided imagery with children;
Visualizing for change   68

3.   The Way You Tell 'Em: The Art and Craft of Oral Storytelling

Fibbers and fantasists – getting started; Stretching
stories; Remembering and 'fixing' stories; Stretching
stories again; Techniques from traditional telling;

All kinds of extra signals; Techniques for focusing
attention inwards; Storytelling and consciousness –
psychological dynamics; The attention bargain... 100

4. Traditional Ways of Storytelling

Traditional stories and storytellers; Fables and
short teaching tales; Dilemma tales; Puzzling
tales... 143

5. Marvellous Miniatures: Making Short
    Metaphors

Jokes and anecdotes; Sayings, maxims, *et al.*;
Aphorisms to analogies to parables; Similes and
smiles; Chaining mixed metaphors; Vignettes; The
koan principle; Allegories and satires; Working with
brief reframing stories; A small cornucopia of quick
reframing stories..................................... 182

6. New Lamps for Old: Transposing Stories

Repeating patterns; Jung's archetypes; The many
forms of universal plot; Memes and fundamentals;
Psychoactive stories; Transposing a story; Nine
adaptable tales; Solution-focused story frames... 224

7. Traps and Treasures: Symbols, Stories
    within Stories and Metaphorical Literacy

Symbols as shared metaphors; Personal symbols;
Working with symbols; Five traditional symbols; Two
symbolic stories; Metaphor – the trap and the hidden
treasure; Stories within stories within stories; A coda –
three interwoven stories in five stages.............. 265

NOTES   310

BIBLIOGRAPHY   323

INDEX   328

Table of stories

Introduction

The Noisy Neighbours.................................... 19

Chapter 1

The Man on the Train................................. 24
Nzilla the Tracker..................................... 25
A Chinese Fable 30
The Tray 31
The Three Girls' Veils 34
The Tailor's Cloth.................................... 44
Snap!... 57
The Ugly Servant..................................... 59
Urban legend – The Furniture Van.................... 61
Lakshmi and Vishnu.................................. 62
Mbala.. 64

Chapter 2

The Enchantress and the Animals.................... 69
Three Hairs from a Wolf's Chin..................... 94

Chapter 3

The Way You Tell 'Em................................ 102
The Vicar and the Grindstone........................ 103

The Rich Woman and the Hat Maker............... 109
The Little Tailor and the Silkie Tale................. 111
The Perfect Storyteller (episode 1).................... 115
The Apprentice, the Honeypot and the Scissors .. 117
The Perfect Storyteller (episode 2).................... 119
The Perfect Storyteller (episode 3).................... 129
The Perfect Storyteller (episode 4).................... 131
The Perfect Storyteller (episode 5).................... 135
The Perfect Storyteller (episode 6).................... 142

Chapter 4

The Pardoner's Story.................................... 152
The Sweet Merchant and the Peasant............... 154
The Wooden Bayonet.................................... 157
The Boy Who Cried Wolf............................... 158
The Fox in the Well...................................... 160
The Spotted Snake....................................... 162
The Four Wise Men...................................... 162
Words.. 163
The Ploughman and the Snake....................... 164
The Man, the Snake and the Fox..................... 165
The Two Otters and the Jackal 166
The Frogs and the Snake............................... 167
The Man Who Died 169
The Two Thieves and the King 172
The Three Wizards and the Tree..................... 173
The Scientists... 174
The Three Artists.. 174
The Tree... 175
The Wonderful Tapestry............................... 178

Chapter 5

Enoch and the Cockerel................................ 184
The Jester and the King................................ 185

The Lachrymose Peeler 191

Horses in Alexandria.............................. 195

The Robinson Crusoe Island 199

Reframing stories:

    Breaking the Diet............................ 203

    Self-Diagnosis.............................. 204

    The Donkey and the Diet 205

    Baklava.................................... 206

    Two Disciples and One Guru................. 207

    The Gorilla 208

    Tom and Yesterday......................... 209

25 quick reframing stories:

    1. Roofs and Walls 211

    2. Crocodiles and Cares 212

    3. The Optimist.......................... 212

    4. The Treasure Hunter 212

    5. Two Existential Riddles............... 212

    6. Simple Arithmetic..................... 213

    7. The Hoe 213

    8. Dog Snuff 213

    9. The Fortunate Dog.................... 214

    10. To Them that Have... 214

    11. The Bean 215

    12. The Emir's Robe 215

    13. The Axe 217

    14. The Abyss 218

    15. German Saying....................... 218

    16. Torture 218

    17. Social Controls 219

    18. Social Proof........................ 219

    19. The Wealth of Kings................. 220

    20. Paving the Streets.................. 221

    21. Pearls 221

    22. Knowing Where the Problem Is 222

    23. Delusions 222

    24. More Delusions...................... 222

    25. Wine Lover 223

Chapter 6

The Milkmaid's Dreams 228
Nine adaptable tales:
   1. The Man Who Became Rich Through Dreaming 238
   2. The Princess Who Died........................ 239
   3. The Talisman 242
   4. The Idol 244
   5. The Blue Jackal 245
   6. The Other Room............................... 248
   7. The Noisy House 249
   8. The Saddhu's Loincloth 251
   9. The Enchanting Bird 253

Chapter 7

The Morning Dew................................. 274
The Tree of Jewels 279
The Golden Bird.................................. 285
The Queen, the Lost Crown and the Storyteller... 290
The Touchy-Feely Show 295
Three interwoven stories in five stages:
   1a. The Storyteller............................. 303
   2a. The Sandcastle and the Chest.............. 304
   3. The Ruined Palace 305
   2b. The Sandcastle and the Chest.............. 306
   1b. The Storyteller............................. 308

NOTES 310
BIBLIOGRAPHY..................................... 323
SUBJECT INDEX.................................... 328
AUTHOR INDEX 336

Acknowledgements

Grateful acknowledgement is made to the following for permission to quote copyright material in this book:

Excerpts from *Birds of Heaven* by Ben Okri, used by permission of The Marsh Agency Ltd. Excerpt from *The Web of Silence* by Fran Stallings, used with permission of the author. Excerpt from *The Hero with a Thousand Faces* by Joseph Campbell. Copyright © 1949, 2008 Joseph Campbell Foundation. Reprinted by permission of Joseph Campbell Foundation (jcf.org). Excerpt from *Metaphor Therapy* by Richard R. Kopp used by permission of Brunner/Mazel US via Copyright.com. Excerpt from *The Feeling of What Happens* by Antonio Damasio, published by William Heinemann Ltd. Reprinted by permission of The Random House Group Ltd. Excerpt from 'The Storyteller' in *Illuminations* by Walter Benjamin, copyright © 1955 by Suhrkamp Verlag, Frankfurt a.M., English translation by Harry Zohn copyright © 1968 and renewed 1996 by Houghton Mifflin Harcourt Publishing Company, reprinted by permission of Houghton Mifflin Harcourt Publishing Company; from *Illuminations* by Walter Benjamin, published by Jonathan Cape. Reprinted by permission of The Random House Group Ltd. Excerpt from *Word of Skill* by Mara Freeman published in *Parabola* magazine, used with the permission of the author. Excerpt from *Therapeutic Powers of Narratives and Stories* by Kedar Nath Dwivedi first published in *Context* systemic therapy magazine 2001, used with permission of the author.

Every reasonable effort has been made to trace and contact possible copyright holders for traditional stories included in this volume or to acknowledge other published versions when appropriate. Most exist in multiple forms or come from very old volumes, and are clearly in the public domain. Like many storytellers, the author has also picked up many tales orally, researched all sorts of different versions and worked with them through many years, so that it is not possible to identify single original sources.

Personal acknowledgements

Thanks are due to the many friends and colleagues along the way who have influenced my thinking, contributed ideas and criticisms or simply told me stories – if I have not mentioned you by name, be sure I'm grateful all the same. However, I'd like to give special thanks to some people who have been particularly influential. Pat Williams has been for me a shining example since my earliest days as a rookie storyteller and her generous responses are deeply appreciated. Mark Tyrrell and Roger Elliott of Uncommon Knowledge first gave me the chance to focus and develop some of these ideas publicly in workshops and in audio form; their 'can-do' attitudes are positively infectious. Mary Medlicott took the trouble to wade through my sprawling first draft and offered perceptive and very useful advice. Staff at Jessica Kingsley Publishing have been highly efficient, imaginative and encouraging. Very special thanks are due to my wife, Ruth Herbert, to whom the book is dedicated, not just for making the time available for me to work on it in the midst of busy family/freelance life but also for insisting that I should get on with writing it in the first place, not to mention her essential encouragement following some daunting setbacks. Without her there would have been no book at all.

In parts of this book, I am clearly influenced by the powerful Human Givens synthesis of organizing ideas, practical techniques and scientifically informed good sense that is currently making such a welcome difference in areas such as therapy, healthcare and education and which very much informs my own therapeutic practice. However, I should like to make it clear that I speak here primarily as a practising storyteller and a long time student of the storytelling art and craft, not as the representative of any one approach – nor indeed of any one tradition of storytelling or story use and transmission. I am, though, hugely indebted to the millions upon millions of anonymous people who have made the oral traditions of the world.

Stories are as ubiquitous as water or air and as essential. There is not a single person who is not touched by the silent presence of stories.

– *Ben Okri (Aphorisms & Fragments)*

Introduction

Stories are marvellous, magical things. They are also, paradoxically, mundane and commonplace – because they are everywhere. You can't live without stories, without telling them and making them. You yourself are a story: a story of how you have been and hope to be, of how you are and how you might be. You can't help it. You dream at night, and your brain tells you stories; you wake up in the morning and hear a sound outside the house, and your mind, in explaining what it is, turns it into a story. You read the paper, and it's packed with stories. You switch on the radio or the TV, and what do you get? Stories and more stories.

This is a book about making and telling stories, and about creating change through stories. You could say that it is for everyone and anyone, since we are all involved in change one way or another and we are all affected by the tales we tell. There's plenty to interest the general reader, but it will be of particular professional relevance to a variety of different kinds of people working in different ways with different kinds of change, from therapists, social workers, coaches and trainers to teachers, lecturers, personnel managers and presenters, not forgetting storytellers and story makers of all kinds. It is a practical book, and so, though not short on opinions and thoughts, especially in the first chapter in which I'll lay out some of the theoretical ground, it seeks to introduce many practical techniques and useful ideas about ways to work with stories.

A quarter of a century working constantly with stories has yielded some interesting realizations. One of these is that there is actually a tremendous amount of knowledge about stories already available, but that much of it is locked up in different places – within areas such as education, psychotherapy, psychology, folklore and entertainment. Because such interest areas tend to be seen as quite different and disparate, knowledge gleaned within each isn't shared as much as it usefully might be. The result is a rather imperfect and incomplete view of what telling and making stories is about.

In education, for example, an enormous amount has been written about the use of stories, and there is a tremendous richness of ideas in literature published over the last century about how to stimulate story making in children and adults. And, despite constant interference from politicians and others, the best teachers have continued to come up with new and imaginative ideas of how story making and telling can survive the strictures of literacy hours and the confines of the curriculum and still deliver creative self-expression and imaginative 'enchantment'. But, whilst the average teacher knows very well that story needs to be taught as part of language development and that some stories provide good morals for assembly or for lessons in citizenship, not so many appreciate the many ways in which story metaphors can be used as powerful instruments for inspiring change, nor how the story work they do connects with their pupils' personal sense of meaning.

That is rather in contrast to the ethos that has been developing in the therapeutic field in recent years, where there has been an explosion of interest in stories and storytelling, and a variety of theories about what story metaphors can do in facilitating all kinds of positive changes. This is particularly true of approaches developing out of the pioneering work of the renowned American psychiatrist and hypnotherapist Milton Erickson. However, this interest and enthusiasm may not be coupled with a full understanding of the range and depth of story material available from world oral traditions. Then again, folklorists and anthropologists can tell you marvellous and fascinating things about tales and traditions but are not necessarily familiar with the insights about metaphor emerging from psychology and therapy. Or professional storytellers may know how to present tales, but may not realize the significance of the fact that stories can quite literally entrance, and so on.

All of this piecemeal knowledge needs to be shared in a practical and accessible way. My aim has been to do that in a way that will make this book a manual to which you can return over and again to try out new ideas.

Stories can change minds and even bodies. But it is important to be clear what one means by a weasel word like change. In fact, any story produces some kind of a change in the people who hear, tell or make it. If you use stories in teaching a class or tutoring individuals, you will hope that those people experience change, becoming more versed in what you are teaching or more aware or more intelligent or more motivated to seek to learn more. If you are telling stories during therapy, your hope is that, by this means, individuals, couples or families can be helped to move towards more effective, less negative ways of being. There are all sorts of other ways in which one can, and perhaps should, have a clear idea about the kind of change one is aiming for – and what will make that change genuine and sustainable.

The Noisy Neighbours

There's an old Chinese story about a man who bought a house he liked very much. He liked the view; he liked the location; he liked the space he had inside and outside. The only problem was – well, the neighbours. On the one side, you see, there lived a blacksmith and he would be hammering and banging and cursing and banging from morning to night. As if that wasn't bad enough, on the other side was a coppersmith and he would also be tapping and hammering and cursing and tapping all day long. Between the two of them, they made sure that the poor man had no peace at all.

In the end, this man became so desperate that he went to the blacksmith and offered him a large sum of money to move elsewhere. And then he found the coppersmith and he made exactly the same offer. He left them both to think it over.

Well, they turned up on his doorstep together very shortly after that and each signed the contract and took his money. Yes, they would certainly be moving. 'Where to?' the man asked. 'Oh,' said the blacksmith, grinning broadly, 'I'm moving into his house and he's moving into mine!'

To get the noisy neighbours to move away rather than just change places, something else has to happen first – something that might open their minds to the fact that other streets even exist, that these might actually turn out to be better places to live, leading to new life directions, and so on. This is one of the prime things that stories can do – communicate new possibilities, illustrate new perspectives, take people to new places in imagination, connect imaginatively and metaphorically with a sense of new meaning and purpose. It is a common factor in good storytelling and story making, regardless of how outwardly different the contexts. Working with a group of adolescents with challenging behaviours may seem quite different from facilitating at a conference or at a workshop with adults, which will in turn seem to have little in common with one-to-one therapy focused on highly personal issues or, for that matter, with the way we communicate with friends, colleagues or a variety of audiences. And yet each situation could very well be concerned, at a fundamental level, with attempts to shift stuck, unproductive, limiting reactions, beliefs, attitudes and thinking, and unlock the potential for humour, imagination, creativity and renewal.

In this book you will find much emphasis on the guises in which stories can provide a new perspective on a problem and possible solution, sneaking into the conscious mind disguised in metaphorical clothes. Stories can show a pattern; they can convey a moral principle without appearing to moralize; they can inspire, lift, entertain and also entrance. And then perhaps more.

As is very well known, Alexander the Great conquered many lands and became the most powerful man in the known world. When he was in Corinth, he decided to visit Diogenes, whom he found squatting under a tree, wearing rags and in obvious poverty. He stood in front of the famous philosopher and asked if there was anything he could do to help him. Diogenes looked back at him steadily and said, 'Yes, indeed, there is. Would you mind stepping aside because at present you are blocking the sun.' Sometimes stories can even move the emperor out of the way.

This is, perhaps in summary, a core perspective of the philosophical and mystical traditions that have used stories for centuries – and that are, indeed, the source of some of the most pungent and incisive tales in world literature: traditions such as Zen, Sufism, and so on. A discussion of such traditions is for the most part beyond the scope of this book, which seeks to provide, as it were, a primer in the language of story and its use rather than advanced poetry. However, it is perhaps inevitable that there'll be coincidences, since lasting psychological change implies a development of personal consciousness and autonomy, which is also an aim of these traditions; also since story metaphors can function on so many different but interlocking levels.

The tales we tell and listen to are indeed marvellous, magical things – if we allow them to be. But a caveat or two should be added here. Stories are complex; we may appear to be looking in the same mirror, but we won't all see the same thing – it depends on eyesight, angle, perspective, self-image, preconceptions and much more. And stories are whole cloth; you can't pick the threads apart without losing that essential integrity – not to mention the lavish embroidery with its complex pattern and the myriad other related patterns invoked by that pattern.

Chapter 1

The Natural Storyteller

Homo fabula: we are storytelling beings
– Ben Okri[1]

There are very many ways to begin a story – and there are probably almost as many ways to begin the story of stories and the telling of them. The conventional way would no doubt be to start at the beginning – which would be fine if anyone knew where and what the beginning was. But none of us was around 40,000 years ago, when human beings first (according to expert estimates) began to develop more conscious and extensive uses of imagination. As that faculty opened up, of course, our ancestors could evolve complex languages – with past, present and future tenses – create beautiful artefacts and, inevitably, tell stories about what they were doing, where they had come from and how the world was made. Stories which, of course, were whisked away on the wind, like all unrecorded utterances, so are not here now for the telling.

But, instead of attempting a pseudo-historical account, I'm going to work backwards from what we can see, feel and hear ourselves to be, right here and now – story making and telling creatures. I hope that this will make much clearer the reasons why stories are so important and central to human life: why they are such vital tools in any kind of consciously engineered change and why and how they work. Hence how we came to be such makers and tellers of tales.

There's an old joke for which I have a certain affection, since it was the first I ever attempted to tell in front of a group of adults many years ago. Here it is:

The Man on the Train

A young guy is sitting on a train opposite a wealthy looking older man, evidently a stray from the First Class section, which has been closed off for some reason. They are the only ones in the carriage and, after a while, the young man asks what time it is, but the older fellow just stares out of the window. The young man has heard the other man speak to the guard, so he knows the man is neither stone deaf nor dumb. He asks again, a little more loudly. You can almost hear, above the clickety-clack of the train, the ticking of the large, half-visible gold Rolex amidst thick but greying wrist hair, but the older man some-how manages to avoid his travelling companion's eye and continues to ignore him. Eventually, the young man says very loudly, 'PLEASE! I ONLY WANT TO KNOW THE TIME!'

The older man finally looks straight at him. 'Look,' he says firm-ly, in heavily accented English, 'let me tell you something. You ask me the time and you know I have a watch and I don't speak to you. Why? Because I am naturally friendly and I know this. I am naturally friendly and inquisitive and generous and, in any other circumstance, I would follow the traditions of my own country, which command me to be friendly and generous and also politely inquisitive. But today, if I tell you the time, what happens? We begin to talk. I tell you all about myself and you tell me all about yourself. We swap jokes, opinions, ideas, the way people do on trains. And then we get to our stop and we get out and I offer you a lift, because I know myself and I know that I am naturally generous and my tradition is generous. And you, being young, will take advantage and accept my offer of a little hospitality at my house. Why not? I am rich and you are poor, so why not? You will meet my daughter, my lovely daughter. She is as beautiful as I am ugly. You are handsome and she will like you and you will talk and you will get on and one thing will lead to another and, the next thing I know, you will come to me and tell me you are moving in together. Now, I have to tell you that I really don't want my beautiful daughter getting mixed up with someone who can't afford a watch!'

What is this man doing? Telling a kind of story, really. One that he has imagined in detail, creating a fantasy based on a certain amount of shrewd observation, a certain amount of self-knowledge and then all sorts of supposition, not to mention emotions of jealousy, suspicion and possessiveness, perhaps. All of which, rightly or wrongly, inform his present decision to withhold a simple piece of information.

Now here's part of a rather different tale, from West Africa:

Nzilla the Tracker

Nzilla was one of the three wives of a hunter, a man who went into the forest each day to bring back meat for the pot – wild hog and fowl, monkey and sometimes buffalo too – a bold man, a cunning hunter, very brave. One night, he did not return from the hunt, but this was a thing that happened occasionally so the three wives were not too much concerned – until he failed to come back the following night and the one after that. Then they were certainly worried.

During the night, one of the other wives awoke convinced that she had seen something vital in her dreaming: their husband lying somewhere in the forest in a pool of his own blood, following a struggle with some wild creature. She was certain he was dead and feared now for his spirit in the wild forest.

Nzilla was a very practical woman and was not inclined to wail and worry, nor to wait and wonder. She also had a great skill she had honed and perfected from childhood on, a skill the very best hunters develop over the years: the skill of reading tracks and signs. More than mere foot and paw and hoof prints, Nzilla could read the bending of a stalk or the crushing of a leaf, smell the faintest scent on the bark of a tree, taste in the air the aura of a creature that had passed that way hours and even days before. With her two co-wives following, she set out to track her husband through the forest, reading the signs here and there and all through the forest – invisible to others but clear as an open highway to her. She led the way until they found their husband, just as the first wife had dreamed. Except that he was not yet quite dead...

I'll apologize for leaving the tale there, but will, I promise, give a full summary of it in a later chapter. For the moment, I want to draw your attention to differences and similarities between the people in these two unequal stories. For example, you could say that the first man is worldly wise and he uses all sorts of guesswork to build up his personal narratives and inform his 'intuition'. Nzilla is perceptive, not just shrewd. She looks carefully and reads and interprets signs and patterns, which are 'out there' to be read. She is intuitive in a different sense, a sense you could say is compatible with logic and, indeed, analogous to an unfashionable notion: real wisdom.

Some vital features of human consciousness in relation to larger reality are shown in both of these stories. In many ways, our senses collude with our minds to create, out of all sorts of hints and suppositions and guesses, the world we see around us. We don't 'see things as they are' but from a partial perspective and through a filter of beliefs, experiences, temporary emotions and instinctive drives, by means of which we make a kind of story from minute to minute, day to day – just like the man in the first tale. Our stories might be accurate in some ways and way wide of the mark in others. At the same time, we can't simply 'construct' the world out of nothingness. There have to be patterns 'out there' to which we can match, signs we can read, just like Nzilla, if we can only learn the skill and separate the signs from the imaginings.

Homo fabula: we are first and foremost storytelling creatures. Much of the way we see the world is built up through stories that we tell ourselves and that are told to us. But the paradox of fiction and narrative making (as I hope to illustrate throughout this book), is that, by means of fibs, it can show us what is true – or at least closer to the veridical.

The joke about the man on the train gives one way of looking at fantasy. It is a little picture of the second-guessing, fiction-spinning, semi-conscious mind at work. Then the second tale – well, of course in real life, sign readers do make mistakes, even if in fiction they can be as perfect as Nzilla and Sherlock Holmes in 'reading the world'. Yet highly practical people whose survival depends on reading tracks make exactly those kinds of intuitive readings and deductions. Interpreting signs with genuine insight is more than possible – and the husband, as you'll find out in Chapter 4, does live long enough to marvel at Nzilla and the other two wives with their complementary life-saving talents.

Stories are all around us in one way and another, from the basic kind of storytelling and 'world making' we are largely unaware of through to all kinds of things we know and accept as being forms of fiction, with various stages and degrees along the way. The more you look, the more you can see the centrality of stories and story making. It might be helpful to identify some of the ways and levels in which story and fiction making affect us, through a patchwork of different angles on the subject.

Personal stories

Remember – a storyteller wants to be all his
characters or knows he's already all of them.
– James Berry

If we meet and talk, I might just tell you my story and you might just tell me yours. If you know me already, your story would probably be about things you've been doing, people we both know, plans you have, jokes or anecdotes or gossip you've heard, and so on. If we've never met, you might well think a bit about which sides of your many-faceted self are appropriate for you to present. Or maybe the situation in which we meet will determine that – you might talk to me a little differently, and (who knows?) more carefully, if we are both at a conference concerning weighty matters rather than leaning up against a bar or checking in for a flight to a Greek island.

We know that we have different selves in the sense that we have different personae we adopt at different times. Our maiden aunt may know a quite different individual from the one who chuckles with chums at the club. We may sometimes be professionals, sometimes amateurs, sometimes just ordinary people doing ordinary things. It feels, of course, as though it is one person who does the 'acting'; all our social laws are based on the principle that we 'become responsible' by a certain age and behave accordingly. But anyone who has been disgustingly drunk or carried away by an infatuation or swept up in an all-consuming anger may have cause to doubt that 'commonsense' conception: there are times when we are definitely 'not ourselves'. The instruction inscribed over the entry to the Delphic Oracle (summarized as 'Know thyself') remains a more complicated task than our laws of personal responsibility may suggest.

The Jamaican-born poet James Berry once signed his collection of Anansi-Spiderman stories[2] for me with the wise words about storytellers and their characters included at the head of this section – words I've valued ever since, even though, as a teller of tales of many kinds, I hope they're not the complete and literal truth! Stories we hear, tell and experience show us ourselves. It's difficult, is it not, to get properly involved in a novel if you can't identify, even if only partially, with any of the characters? Have you ever tried to watch a film in which you hated and were alienated by every single actor?

But, in very important ways, all of us put together a kind of narrative about who we are, the kinds of things we do and like, the capacities we have, the way our pasts have been and our futures will be. It is becoming better accepted in psychotherapy – partly through the trail-blazing work of American psychiatrist and hypnotherapist Milton Erickson and his successors – that it's often the unnecessarily limiting stories and personal metaphors individuals tell themselves that need to be challenged, so that they can progress in dealing with a concern. The man who tells you, 'Winter always makes my depression deepen', or the woman who says, 'I'll never be able to deal with heights, and my mother never could either', are both creating a limiting story about themselves, which might be altered through simple changes in the way of telling. 'Yes, winter sometimes seems to make a person remember what feeling depressed is like.' 'A lot of people wouldn't go around in clothes their mothers wore 30 years ago...' These are examples of quick 'reframes' a therapist might gently deliver, in order to throw a little doubt on the way a story has been told and suggest a different way of constructing the plot.

Reframing is at the heart of the effectiveness of stories. We put together our personal stories largely unconsciously – the tale of what we are, what we can do, the ideas, behaviours, thoughts, emotions and images we find acceptable. All kinds of influences and experiences affect what we become, some of them apparently benign and possibly wonderful, some of them harrowing and even traumatic. But the most central element is how we view those influences and those experiences. This is the frame, the story, the angle. It is more or less inevitably a limited perspective, which may be modified in time by new influences and experiences. The new story that is introduced to us at the right time in the right way provides that influence and experience quickly, extending our perspectives in a way that is unthreatening – since, after all, it's only a story.

Narratives 'out there' mirror the way in which we experience ourselves. We all have an internal narrative – 'Now I am doing this...', 'Tomorrow I will be doing such and such...', 'When I was small, I always used to...'. Adolescents and desperate lovers may take this a stage further, mentally narrating a drama in which they and their feelings take the leading role. After all, there is something comforting about a narrative in which we can make ourselves the central character – with an underlying assumption, perhaps, that a benevolent 'author' will make things come right in the end.

The picture that emerges from modern brain research, evolutionary theory and some contemporary explanations of consciousness is, at first sight, much less comforting. We are anything but a single narrative. Our intentional self is only part of that larger picture – and a relatively small part. Much of what we are is monitored, maintained and fixed by parts of the brain over which we normally exert little conscious control. Various different systems within us proceed more or less regardless of our conscious wishes – the blood flows around our bodies, following rhythms we scarcely consider; our immune systems generally deal with infections without checking with headquarters; our autonomic nervous system, as its name suggests, gets on with things mostly on automatic pilot. Then, of course, our emotions, once believed by romantic thinkers to be somehow noble and elevated and even transcendent, turn out to have their roots in primitive survival reactions mediated by a more ancient part of the brain known as the limbic system,[3] which may show scant regard for the pretensions of our nuancing neocortex, turning us in a moment into fighting fanatics or fleeing fools.

What is more, our much-vaunted intelligence is strictly limited by learning mechanisms that can restrict us to loops of thought and understanding that do not necessarily intersect. The way in which the brain processes and accesses information through chains of neurons that 'wire together and fire together' according to the Hebbian learning principle (first outlined by Canadian psychologist, Donald Hebb) makes it possible that much information and many ideas, memories and experiences remain in separate 'boxes' unless and until they can become linked up by accident or design. Hence we may hold ideas that are in conflict with one another, ignore clues and cues which don't happen to hit the right triggers, and fail to learn from experience which could be relevant – or automatically go into what seem almost like rehearsed role-plays with different people or different situations. And we may forget and fail to apply competences that could be relevant to current situations because they appear irrelevant.[4]

Not entirely unrelated to this, heightened and extreme emotional experiences may set up what Dr Ernest Rossi has named 'state dependent learning, memory and behaviour'[5] which remains quite outside the range of normal awareness. This in turn can lead to troubling psychosomatic symptoms or apparently uncontrollable mental phenomena, such as traumatic flashbacks or seemingly inexplicable panic attacks.

It is perhaps small wonder that there are certain scientists who think of consciousness as a mere by-product, an epiphenomenon. Some fundamentalists go further, reciting bleak magically unreal tales that suggest that consciousness itself may be pure illusion or, at best, an island of occasional and dubious rationality in a senseless, mechanical universe. In this view, stories are merely in the category of 'memes' passed on mindlessly for the survival of the social organism.[6] Yet there are quite different ways to flesh out the narrative.

A Chinese Fable[7]

A man was walking along the street when he tripped and fell over. He slowly and ruefully picked himself up and walked on further, only to trip and fall over again. As he lay on his back looking at the sky and seeing stars that were not there, he said to himself, 'If I'd known this was going to happen, I wouldn't have bothered getting up last time.'

Maybe our intellectual culture has reached the state of this man following his second fall, but there is no very good reason why we shouldn't get up and run with the notion of a fundamental, potentially very effective consciousness, despite (or perhaps even because of) our increasing knowledge of our limitations. There is good and extensive evidence for it. A significant part of that evidence is in the form of stories of many kinds, great and small and from many different cultures, which, like the one above, observe and comment on the mistakes our minds can make in assessing what is possible. What's more, by providing metaphorical mental pictures of those mistakes (and of other more positive experiences too), they make available a flexible, imaginative language through which to interpret and deal effectively with new but essentially similar experiences.[8] Stories, in other words, present an important means of overcoming limitations and developing personal autonomy: very practical wisdom and 'sign decoding' in fact. In so doing, they show the existence of a fundamental human capacity for a deeper awareness.

The Tray

This man goes up to the bar and he orders two pints of beer, three gin and tonics, a glass of red wine, a glass of white wine, five packets of crisps, two packets of peanuts and a bacon sandwich. The barman asks him if he'd like a tray. 'No thanks,' says the guy, 'I've got enough to carry already!'

A tray, of course, is more than just something else to carry. Consciousness at the fundamental level is more than its obvious contents. There is, as psychologists such as Arthur Deikman have put it, an observing self,[9] a fundamental awareness of being aware which is separate from the content of consciousness, whether thoughts or moods, feelings or fantasies. Stories are one of its tools. They can show our selves to our selves.

Social Stories™

A people are as healthy and confident as the stories
they tell themselves. Sick storytellers can make
their nations sick. And sick nations make for sick
storytellers.

– Ben Okri[10]

I switch on the TV. A smoky, dangerous-looking, dark-haired beauty is cocking a small gun. A James Bond look-alike is meanwhile making off in a four-wheel drive. The music is stereotypically tense and brassy and there are quick close-ups of the woman and the man. I automatically guess at anger, jealousy. She's going to shoot him and the bullet will beat the car, however fast it is. After all, he has probably cheated on her, and a girl like that wouldn't take those sorts of things well. Her finger tightens on the trigger – and she fires it harmlessly into the air. It's a starter pistol for a playful race in a super, mutually admired vehicle. They smile at each other with that suggestion of sexual intimacy that the director no doubt worked hard to elicit from the actors. The logo of the car is rapidly displayed. Now it's on to another commercial.

Why do advertisers use tricks like that? Because they work. Even while I am consciously cynical about the absurdity of it, the story gets under my skin and I automatically fill in details. I unconsciously track the action and experience a mini emotional arousal as my expectation is set up – and then cheated.

We are instinctively programmed to learn from exceptions, happenings that don't fit an established pattern. In the ancient past, we needed to be in order to survive. When I reach the point at which I suddenly have to change the story I've been seeing in the images on the screen, I am opened up to suggestion. And the quite irrational suggestion in this case, to me as a heterosexual male (it could well be an ad pitched for blokes since the cricket is on), is that, first, having a car like that goes with getting a girl like that, who will smile at me in just that seductive way; second, the car goes fast and will win 'the race'; and, third, the four-wheel drive in question is a cracking good thing to have and will make me into another James Bond look-alike. The sexual imagery of the gun plays a part in all that too, no doubt – though the advertisers, being clever, put the gun in the hands of the girl, so that, if you are female, you can identify with the way she is taking the lead and being powerful whilst if you are a male, you might experience a certain frisson. The fact that you, perhaps, and I, certainly, are unlikely ever to afford such a car doesn't matter because we are being trained to envy the person who can. Cars need to be enviable to sustain their high prices.

There's a lot to be learned from the way in which advertisers constantly and often very cleverly (if with dubious integrity) manipulate and reframe perceptions. The same very much goes for the political spin-doctors. There's a story dating back to Cold War days. Evidently the British and Russian ambassadors in a certain country decided to settle a dispute by having a race. This was won by the British ambassador and, in London, *The Times* reported the fact quite simply under the banner, 'British ambassador wins the race'. In Moscow, however, Izvestia relayed the same facts a little differently, because evidently 'the Russian ambassador came an honourable second whilst the British ambassador was last but one'.

These days you scarcely need to peep beyond an iron curtain to find similar (and sometimes only slightly more subtle) forms of news manipulation. We constantly hear stories told in terms of fabulous freedom fighters and terrible terrorists, yobbish protestors and valiant campaigners, brilliant and talented celebrities and boring old has-beens with inflated egos. It would be surprising if we didn't fall for some of that some of the time – since, as those spin-doctors, journalists and ad men know very well, you can fool enough of the people enough of the time.

Political story manipulation, advertising narrative suggestion – these are two examples of contemporary use of forms of storytelling to condition us socially to the norms of early 21st-century society. There are many more. Story after story after lurid, emotionally arousing, sensation-oriented story swarms around us, hatched, nurtured, released and then, as often as not, desperately distorted by mass media, which couldn't survive without them. Rationalizations from the perpetrators of this contemporary storytelling ('People need to be told about products'; 'people have a right to be informed/entertained/free'; 'facts don't exist until they are constructed', etc.) are relatively easy to dismiss with a little simple logic, and yet we seem to accept their existence as if they were as necessary as air.

Of course, it is *other* societies and other times that have or had irrational myths and primitive superstitions. We can look with condescension at the absurd tales people in former ages told themselves about the world and apparently believed to be literally true. For goodness' sake, whoever would be fool enough to believe that some of the stars in the sky are people who once lived and had adventures on the earth or that some old guy with a white beard made the world we know in six days and had a day off for a bit of a snooze after that? We live in the age of science and real knowledge and information super highways. We know that 'it's all just quarks and quantum stuff whizzing around in a vacuum and that', as one true believer put it in a recent vox pop I caught on my car radio the other day.

Every age has its dominant myths, stories everyone takes in from their earliest days without even thinking of them as stories. Maybe it is only centuries later that one can appreciate the absurdity of some of those stories. Just imagine, a society where it was believed that happy people were those who slaved madly to get lots of stuff, but then chucked it in the sacrificial skip every so often, at the whim of the capricious goddess Fashion! How silly! And how about a world where everyone worshipped ever more complicated machines they reckoned could solve all their problems, whilst those same machines actually created many of them! Crazy!

The Three Girls' Veils

Three girls stitched and embroidered their own wedding veils, as was the custom in the villages and the lands in which they lived. The first, impatient for the wedding itself, worked hastily and without care, thinking it much less important than what was to come. When she was married, the veil was a riot of unmatched colours and people were inclined to comment on this, but she didn't care; she had got what she wanted. Yet that veil also somehow foretold and typified the years of the marriage that followed, not exactly happy or contented years.

The second girl was a fine needlewoman, the best in the village. She prepared herself for the task carefully, putting together the right shades of thread of just the right superior quality. She also carefully imagined how the design would work, creating and conceiving in her mind a vision of pure perfection. But as soon as she began to stitch, she felt critical of her stitches and she unpicked them and started again. Very soon she was unhappy with the second attempt – and the third and the fourth. This had to be perfect – and indeed it was, when she finally finished it. But by that time the husband she had been be-trothed to had long since married someone else and she was 93. The only use that veil had for her was as a shroud when she was buried.

As for the third, well she set to work and she attended to the work, but not too closely, so that very soon she made a mistake. However, it occurred to her that she could rescue it if she stitched around and about in a certain way and altered her plan just a little. She didn't unpick the stitches and she went on stitching – until she made an-other mistake. Again she adapted the design and worked around the error and made it all come right...and again, and again. Whenever she made a mistake, she made the best of it and worked it into the pattern. When she was married, everyone said what a beautiful veil it was that she was wearing. The marriage was a good one too and if she wasn't happy all the time, she and her husband and their children found ways to be much more often contented than not, to adapt the warp and the weft of their lives to practical and even beautiful designs. The veil she kept all of her days and she never tired of telling people what it was made from: mistakes.

The social 'fiction-fabric' isn't woven only from large issues. There are all sorts of practical values that are conveyed through little stories here and there and all around. 'Be kind to other people.' 'No, why should I? What's in it for me?' 'Well, there's a story about someone who was never kind and do you know what happened to her? There's another story about someone else who was very kind and people wondered why, because it didn't do him much good, but in the end...' It's unlikely that you'll get young children, locked quite naturally into the survival-oriented and strictly limited circle of their own immediate wants and desires, really to appreciate the advantages of being kind or to sit and visualize the very real consequences of being unkind all the time – unless you tell them a story and get them really absorbed in it, so that they can imagine consequences, see the possibilities and understand their own situation by comparison with that of someone else. So, of course, to this day, a significant proportion of the stories we tell our children work precisely around that territory and the better ones manage to convey that sort of moral with a subtlety that hides this intent – or quite possibly introduces all sorts of other ideas metaphorically.

Incidentally, the traditional-style metaphor of the three girls' wedding veils is, I confess, one I concocted with my young daughter Asha, and was originally about the second and third girls, since, in some things, she has a habit of perfectionism and needed to accept her mistakes. She quickly added the first girl of her own accord, recognizing that she could, conversely, be like that too. Adapted in the right way to suit listeners, it seems to work with young and old in conveying some relatively simple morals as well as giving a positive pattern for action. At their best, I suppose, that's the kind of thing TV soap operas and dramas can achieve. It's also what the technique of Social Stories™, now widely used in some special needs education, does very effectively.[11]

Such purposeful storytelling is deceptively simple and easy to overlook. One might immediately associate it with what the Victorians called nursery tales or with pompous preachy stories in general. But there are all sorts of comparable concepts and values that need to be understood and tacitly accepted by people in all sorts of societies in order for those societies to survive and perhaps progress. A major traditional way of teaching those values and concepts is through all sorts of story activities – not just the telling of stories, but the acting of them, dancing of them, ritualizing of them, and so on. This doesn't apply only to stories for children; there are plenty of examples of stories of all sorts that convey useful morals on all sorts of levels and are intended primarily for adults – from simple fables such as those in ancient collections like the *Panchatantra*,[12] reputedly used in the education of kings, to dilemma tales related by African elders, to Balinese dancers and gamelan players telling myths through movement and music, to the novels of Tolstoy or the plays of Shakespeare. And that's not to mention the modern storytelling/conditioning media of film and TV.

As we grow into and become adults, things become more complicated. For a start, we don't want to be told obvious things, such as that it's good to be kind. We know that, or think we do. We also notice that some people manipulate unkindly through kindness, while an action that appears to be kind turns out to be cruel, and that people can indeed be killed by kindness. We begin to appreciate, in other words, that black is at one end of the spectrum and white at the other but that there are all sorts of shades of grey in between, not to mention bright and attractive reds and yellows and blues. This is something we learn through life, but also through the myriad mirrors of life held up to it through stories great and small.

Then again we may learn that those mirrors can be distorting mirrors – or sometimes not a mirror at all, but a *trompe-l'oeil*. We also make jokes and satires and allegories, which, whilst they may turn into marvellous metaphors, are often no more than graffiti scrawled on walls that once looked too piously perfect. After all, some things are done just for the hell of it and because it's a strain trying to be good all the time. And some things are about creating a sensation and shocking and getting attention that way.

However that may be, it's obvious enough that there are very many genres of fiction known and styled as such and many other genres we don't call fiction at all but which grow out of the same soil. All of them, at least for the time of the telling, hold attention and become somehow believable. The question is why.

Trance-forming stories

The unusually deep stillness which can fall upon
storylisteners appears to be a true altered state of
consciousness, the storylistening trance. There are
many coincidences between the handling of hypnosis
and the procedures of storytelling. The kinship
between the two arts is striking.

– Fran Stallings[13]

Many years ago, I was talking to a group of teachers and I mentioned
the urban legend – a particular genre of modern oral story, which is
usually passed on by tellers as having definitely happened to someone
they know or to some friend of a friend or to somebody well known.
The story may be lurid or gory or strange, or just interestingly odd or
funny or silly, but it is usually believed to be true. By way of example,
I told the well-known one about the girl and the axe in the handbag.
(Briefly: young woman offers lift to old woman late at night, but
suddenly suspects the old woman is a man in disguise. She makes
an excuse to get the 'woman' out of the car and then zooms off, only
to discover a handbag on the passenger seat. When she opens it,
she finds an axe inside.) As soon as I'd finished, one of the ladies
present, trembling with emotion, asked me how I knew the story. I
sensed at once that the question was loaded, but I simply explained
again that it was an urban legend and had been recorded in all sorts
of versions over the years. 'No, it isn't,' she said forcefully and with
evident contempt for my ignorance and insensitivity. 'It actually
happened to my brother's friend's sister a month ago in Weybridge
and she's still in hospital suffering from shock!' Clearly, it is not just
children for whom stories seem absolutely true. Why and how can
stories convince so utterly? Why can they be so influential?[14]

An interesting phenomenon well known amongst hypnotists is
false memory. It is very easy to implant a memory when a subject
is in trance. Performers, putative wizards, fake gurus and false
prophets were very probably dining out on this trick centuries
before hypnosis was named and defined in our own culture. Sadly,
whilst the phenomenon of hypnotically induced false memory has
been studied, demonstrated and established by psychologists, many
psychotherapists remain unaware of the fact. The setting of a therapy
session, just like other settings where one individual focuses full
attention on another, tends to be trance-like, so that incorrect beliefs

about experiences may be inadvertently created. So it is, for example, that false memories of parental abuse may arise if the therapist starts with the preconception that he or she will find it.[15]

Telling stories is also a 'trance-forming' activity (the pun can be intentional). When a story is told or read well, the listener narrows attention down, and goes into a world of inner imagery in which outside events become less important. Many common indicators of trance may start to manifest. Brian Sturm, of the University of North Carolina, studied audience members at various adult storytelling events in the US during 1997. He found a consistency in their accounts of their experiences, which, he believes, shows that they experienced aspects of trance during listening.

He identified six categories that emerged from the listeners' descriptions of the story-listening trance phenomenon: realism (the sense that the story environment or characters are real or alive); lack of awareness of surroundings or other mental processes; engaged receptive channels (visual, auditory, kinaesthetic and emotional); control of the experience by someone or something else; 'placeness' (the sense that the listener 'goes somewhere' – often 'into' another space); and time distortion (the sense that subjective time moves at a different speed from clock time).[16]

Typical comments he recorded from participants included: 'I kind of forget all my surroundings', 'I can completely forget about everything else except the story', 'Everything else around you just blacks out', 'I just kind of fall into a different world'.

Sturm is one researcher taking up the challenge issued in the 1980s by storyteller Fran Stallings, who called for people to look further at the connections between story listening and hypnosis.[17] Stallings pointed out, for example, that storytellers, like hypnotherapists, often use paradoxical language devices and all kinds of metaphor to deepen the story-listening trance, drawing parallels between the work of traditional storytellers and 20th-century Ericksonian hypnotherapists.

Yet one scarcely needs research findings to confirm what is relatively easy to verify through direct experience. Speaking for myself, I can recall the look of the desk, the inky graffiti, the scores and scratches I was staring at when listening to a particular story getting on for half a century ago in school – this and the images in the story and that feeling of stillness and calm Stallings mentions in the quote at the start of this section. Very many people, absorbed in a book, find time winging by, hours on the train or plane disappearing whilst the images and the characters in the story seem more real than the living, breathing people with whom one is outwardly sharing a particular corner of the planet. The story is entrancing them, quite literally.

The problem not a few people have in recognizing the connection may well stem from the popular stereotypical notions of hypnosis and the hypnotist, with Svengali-like figures swinging watches or the marvellously sinuous and bewitching cartoon dance of Kaa the snake in the Disney *Jungle Book* film, twisting and turning and telling Mowgli to 'trust in me'. Stage performers, who make people do absurd and ridiculous things that they may well live to regret, reinforce the image. Hypnotists, in many people's eyes, are not to be trusted. Why would any rational person want to go into a trance, for goodness' sake?

The fact is that we do, regularly. Trance is quite normal and tends to happen whenever attention is focused, when perhaps we withdraw from external reality into a private world of memories, imagination, emotions, thoughts, dreams, plans, and so on, or, contrastingly, when we become absorbed in an activity, from cycling to calligraphy to sex. Words like 'hypnosis' (which was a coinage from Greek roots to express an understanding of trance as related to sleep) and the earlier 'mesmerism' (after Anton Mesmer, who introduced to 18th-century Europe a bizarre version based on ideas of 'natural magnetism') appear essentially to be distractions, reflecting misconceptions arising as knowledge about the state was redeveloped in Western culture over the last couple of centuries. Equally distracting are current academic controversies around whether or not 'hypnosis' exists as a discrete and unusual state of consciousness or is somehow 'socially constructed', since, paradoxically, it may well be both and neither of those things.

In a chapter on trance in their book *Human Givens: A New Approach to Emotional Health and Clear Thinking*, Joe Griffin and Ivan Tyrrell point out that 'One of the mistakes that some of those who deny the reality of hypnosis make is that they define hypnosis as the state which is induced by a specific type of induction process they put people through. Then they find that other people who are good hypnotic subjects can be put into a similar state of consciousness without that induction and conclude therefore that induction is not necessary, so therefore hypnosis doesn't exist.'[18]

It's a knot that is entirely unnecessary once one conceives of trance as a common enough condition of consciousness, varying in depth but attainable through a wide variety of means, including story. Griffin and Tyrrell further point out its close relationship to the dream state – how, indeed, many frequently observed hypnotic phenomena (including the 'engaged receptive channels', belief in an illusory world, 'placeness', etc. noted by Sturm) are also typical of dream states. These are essential ideas to which I'll return later, since they are central to an understanding of why we are story-making and storytelling creatures.

For the time being, it's worth reiterating some of the parallels between hypnosis as a formal or informal means of accessing the trance/waking dream state and the oral telling of stories. (Written stories can also work in similar ways, but the parallels are easier to grasp in spoken narrative.)

1. Both hypnotists and storytellers frequently paint imaginary, multisensory pictures in the mind.

2. Hypnotists and storytellers direct attention, moving it away from external reality towards that imaginative world.

3. Storytellers and hypnotists often use paradoxical language that confuses the conscious mind. (For example, the traditional story opening formula of 'In a time not my time, a time not yours, but in someone's time, in a world beyond worlds, in a land beyond lands...', etc.)

4. Storytellers, like many hypnotists, often use altered vocal tones to suggest relaxation or excitement.

5. Storytellers sometimes, like hypnotherapists, embed positive suggestions in narratives. (Indeed, in many traditions, the tellers typically incorporate into their tale-telling wisdom teachings in the form of sayings.)

6. Many stories are highly metaphorical, containing allusions on many different levels. Modern hypnotherapists make extensive use of metaphor, both to induce and sustain trance and to offer suggestions for effective change.

7. It is common for listeners to (and readers of) stories to lose track of time and storytellers often manipulate this phenomenon within their narratives. Typical storytelling devices skate over time, sketch in the passage of time with brief, bold strokes and confuse a sense of time by

switching from past to present tense at vital moments of the action. Hypnotists commonly refer to changes in time sense in order to verify and deepen trance.

The perception of storytelling as potentially hypnotic makes sense of an idea that is fairly widespread in world oral traditions, namely that some stories can heal – another notion I'll return to later in this chapter. It also explains why manipulators, both political and commercial, use stories: in trance, people are much less inclined to doubt. The story becomes real, powerful and, therefore, also dangerous.

Language, metaphor and story

Every failure to cope with a life situation must be laid,
in the end, to a restriction of consciousness.
– *Joseph Campbell*[19]

Stories exist in language of one form or another, even if that language is wordless and relies on gestures, pictures, dances, nods or winks. Language depends on, expresses and maybe even creates a certain kind of time-oriented intelligence. Different languages work in different ways in this and other respects. The great Argentinian writer, Jorge Luis Borges, makes an interesting comment about translation in the introduction to his collection of stories, *Doctor Brodie's Report*:

> Our guiding aim had been to make the text read as though it had been written in English; in so doing, we quite soon discovered that *the English and Spanish languages are not, as is often taken for granted, a set of interchangeable synonyms but are two possible ways of viewing and ordering reality.* (italics added)[20]

There are languages that differ in many more essentials than do English and Spanish, which at least have common roots. Some languages do not have complex future, present and past tenses. Some languages are less sequential. Some languages contain extraordinary numbers of words and expressions for things that other languages simply label as snow or rock or sand or street. Semitic languages, such as Arabic, are structured around metaphor to a degree that can be extremely confusing to non-speakers, leading to all sorts of misunderstandings. When Saddam Hussein famously talked about the Mother of All Battles, he was widely imitated in the Western media to a point where 'Mother of all...' became a catchphrase comedians applied to all kinds of incongruous things to get an instant laugh. Yet he was using a metaphorical idiom well established in the Arabic language, not creating a new and picturesque phrase.

In many essential ways, all language has to depend on metaphor. 'Language is dead poetry,' said Ralph Waldo Emerson. Many of the seemingly ordinary words and phrases we use in language are actually metaphors or similes, which perform a metaphorical function. I may be *illuminating* this subject or *obscuring* it; it might be *clear as crystal* to you or you may not have *the foggiest* what I'm on about; perhaps you reckon I'm *bright as a button* or *dull as ditch water* and maybe I'm *beating about the bush* but I'll *get to the point*. Language, as philologists point out, keeps growing because of the metaphors that continually develop around basic literal concepts.[21] We could think of the many ideas around food and eating, for example – it's a *nourishing* exercise to do that, perhaps, one that could *feed* an understanding. However, the metaphors become 'dead' in Emerson's sense because we stop noticing that they are 'poetry'; they stop *striking* us.

Language is metaphorical on all sorts of levels, both conscious and unconscious. Most of the time for most people, there are halos of association around words and phrases. These may be culturally generalized and quite temporary – it's the business of professionals from poets and novelists to songsmiths, advertising copywriters, pop artists, graphic designers and all sorts more to spot and manipulate this. Metaphors may equally well be personal and subjective, based on unique experiences, false linkages, serendipitous juxtapositions and much more. But, because of the associative mechanism, words can sound the same and yet have different meanings not just in translation but for two people speaking the same language.

Many people first encounter the term metaphor in school lessons about language. Collins Concise Dictionary describes it as 'a figure of speech in which a word or phrase is applied to an object or action that it does not literally denote in order to imply a resemblance'. The word comes from the Greek, the prefix *meta* meaning 'over' and 'above' and the second part from *pherein*, 'to bear', thus (by a process which is itself an illustration of how metaphorical usage develops in language) 'to carry meaning over and beyond'. Metaphor involves transfer of meanings/patterns/shapes, etc. from one domain to another: 'This is like this' or 'This works in a similar way to that' or 'These things share essential qualities with those', and so on. It implies a perception of similarity on some level. Hence pictures, mental images, icons, experiences, memories, places, activities, journeys, games, films, adverts, ceremonies, rituals and many other things 'out there' and 'in here' can all be or become metaphors.[22]

Stories are inevitably at some level metaphorical. They depend on language (spoken or otherwise) which, despite its logical and linear dimensions, grows out of a capacity for metaphor. They express themselves through various kinds of image, bringing together motif, subplot, simile, analogy, all of which are metaphorical. And the whole narrative may, at conscious or unconscious levels, be about something more than the literal facts, for which the story is a kind of meta-language. At the right time, when we have the right concern in our mind and being, when circumstance and events conspire together to make us really needy, the story can become deeply meaningful on a personal level, yielding all kinds of insights. That happens in the same way that a shining light helps the eyes – if it happens to be dark and especially if you are lost in a forest.

But at a fundamental level, metaphor is essential to the way we think and understand and build our worlds. Perhaps an absolute, God-like intelligence would have no need for metaphor, being able to comprehend all things in themselves simultaneously. For any less perfect being, the ability to make and understand comparisons between different aspects of the world immediately increases its range and flexibility. Metaphor can, at best, lay bare some of the underlying patterns of reality.

As reported by Howard Gardner,[23] the philosopher Nelson Goodman invented a highly revealing analogy about what makes good art that resonates in all kinds of ways. We can adapt it here in story form, as a way of explaining what it is about a really good story, like any other 'true' metaphor, that makes it such a very powerful instrument as well as an entertainment.

The Tailor's Cloth

A tailor once had a choice of five boys who wanted to be taken on as apprentices. He set them a test. From a bolt of the same cloth, they were each to cut a fair sample to exact measurements. Each of them set to work very carefully and produced the five samples you can see below. When these were presented to him, the tailor had no doubt about which boy had shown not only suitable skills with scissors and measuring tapes but a grasp of the pattern of the whole cloth that could make him a good tailor. Which one was it?

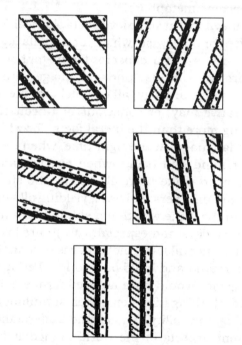

The Tailor's Cloth 1. The 5 samples

Though all are cut from a bolt of the same cloth, only one gives you a clear idea of the whole cloth (see The Tailor's Cloth 2 opposite) and this is what the tailor and his chosen apprentice could see at once.

The story metaphor that has real depth and content doesn't have just one meaning, one sense, one set of realities for which it is a code. It shows you much more of the warp and weft of life, extends your consciousness and awareness, reveals the pattern and makes you, in consequence, more and more able to do and to think and to be.

The Tailor's Cloth 2.
Larger piece showing pattern

How is it that this marvellous capacity to make and understand metaphors has developed in us?

The biology of stories

It appears that long before humans spoke or thought
in metaphor...nature spoke its own language of
metaphor – the pattern that connects. Indeed, the
metaphoric structure of reality in individuals, families
and within and across cultures may be seen as the
expression in humankind of the metaphoric structure
underlying the biological evolution of all living things.
– *Richard R. Kopp*[24]

Just how fundamental metaphor and story are to our biology can best be understood through a look at instinctive templates and then Griffin's seminal work on dreaming.

Simple organisms have very little choice in the way they respond to the world around them. A plant responds to warmth with growth and development but recoils from extreme heat and begins to shrivel, and registers increasing cold by shedding its leaves. That is its range with respect to temperature – and a plant is already quite a complex organism as compared with, say, an amoeba. Human beings can blow hot to warm their hands and cold to cool their dinners; they can bask in the sun and sizzle their sausages on the grill – and lace their drinks with ice on a hot day whilst switching on the air conditioning. This is a complex response that we take for granted, but it grows out of the flexibility of the instincts we have for interpreting temperature. Not that we don't have reactions that are like those of the plant described above – anyone who has put their hand on a red-hot cooker plate knows they didn't have to tell their fingers to get away quick. It's just that we have that instant reaction and then a lot more. We – and other animals, to a lesser degree – have flexible instinctive 'templates', which we use to respond appropriately to whatever we encounter in the environment.

In the 1960s and 70s, French sleep researcher Michel Jouvet established the connection between instinctive templates and the amount of REM (rapid eye movement) sleep a foetus experiences in the womb and after birth. How much REM sleep an organism experiences after birth is directly related to how developed it is when born. Guinea pigs can start running and eating grass within moments of birth; they have little REM sleep. Rats, on the other hand, are born blind and can't move; they spend 95 per cent of their sleep time in REM sleep for a month after birth, by which time they have matured, and their REM sleep drops by another two thirds. In the last three months of pregnancy a human foetus will spend 80 per cent of its sleep time in REM sleep. This drops to 67 per cent at birth and then to 25 per cent later in childhood, at which level it remains.

Jouvet suggested that REM sleep is the time when animals are programmed with the instincts they are going to need for survival. These must necessarily be flexible. A baby bird has to be programmed to recognize a range of vocal patterns, from within which it can distinguish its mother's call. A calf or a puppy or an infant human knows instinctively to seek out something that is like a nipple – which is why they'll all suck fingers and rubber teats quite happily.[25]

Now these basics of biology establish metaphor as essential at a pre-conscious level. A nipple is *like* a rubber teat and a finger. But, while instinct is extremely powerful in itself, clearly learning of one kind and another is a powerful modifier of instinct. (That is now well established. What is still argued about is the relative importance of the nature and nurture components.) Basic instinctive 'programmes' for action have to be, in human beings as in many other creatures, metaphorical. We do not have a predisposition for English or Mandarin Chinese but a 'language instinct' as Steven Pinker puts it,[26] an instinct that usually expresses itself in the learning of the language or languages of the cultural milieu in which we grow up. We do not have a genetic predisposition towards one kind of social organization but a need for belonging to some kind of a group, whether it is a feathered and painted tribe or our academic peers or a bunch of painted and feathered hooligans.

Although Jouvet's work was groundbreaking in explaining an important role of REM sleep, it didn't go far enough since it couldn't satisfactorily explain why REM sleep persists in adults. Joe Griffin's elimination of emotional expectation theory of dreaming provides the pieces of the jigsaw that makes the picture suddenly very clear and distinct and confirms metaphor, and in its turn, story, as absolutely basic to our biology.

Dreams have fascinated people for centuries, and there have been many theories to explain why we dream and what dreams mean. In recent times, mechanistic science has tended to sweep them away under the carpet of attention by labelling them as meaningless epiphenomena, rather in the way that, as suggested earlier, consciousness in general has been belittled and even abolished by some theorists. However, in the still relatively new and exciting theories of dreaming first published in Joe Griffin's 1997 book, *The Origin of Dreams*, dream and metaphor take their proper place as essential elements in the development of human intelligence.

Readers who would like to understand not only the theory itself but the scope and enormous implications of it are referred to *Dreaming Reality* by Joe Griffin and Ivan Tyrrell.[27] Here there is only space for a brief summary. What Griffin realized, as a result of analysing hundreds of his own and others' dreams, is that the strange stories in dreams can be traced to emotionally arousing introspections occurring specifically during the previous day's experience – arousals that remained essentially unresolved since they didn't lead to any actions. In other words, dreams reflect unfulfilled expectations.

Supposing you arrive home on the last train and have to walk along darkened streets through gathering mist. Suppose that loud, loutish drunks are staggering past and there are disconcertingly few other people around. You prepare to run for it or shout for help if necessary, but you arrive home safely. Or suppose that someone you find very attractive seems to be smiling at you in a warm, friendly and inviting way. Perhaps (despite the fact that you are a happily married individual) your imagination choreographs for you various lurid scenarios and your body undergoes a physiological change or two – at least until you realize that the smile is meant for someone else entirely, so you forget about it. In both hypothetical cases, you had aroused expectations, which led nowhere. Your dreams when you eventually sleep may well carry what seems at first sight to be the confused trace of those expectations. But there is a precise logic involved.

Expectations trigger readiness for action and key in to those instinctive templates that indicate ways of acting. When an expectation is aroused, the system is, as it were, on alert. Since no action results, the templates activated by the expectation have to be deactivated to preserve their integrity and effectiveness, and this is achieved in dreams through a symbolic enactment. The brain reaches into its deep cupboard of memories and sensory analogues that will clothe the experience that didn't happen, and it comes up with a series of metaphors to act out the expectations. As these are dreamed, the pattern of expectation is completed whilst the brain is in the 'frozen' state of sleep, so that there is generally no accompanying physical action.

To take another crude example, suppose now that you are working for Melon Associates and you reflect in a moment of stress that your boss has the manners of an ape and a worse bite than a bad-tempered bulldog. As this occurs to you, you consider a confrontation, maybe even a slap in his ugly face. However, this will lose you your job, quite apart from the fact that you are a civilized and non-violent person, whilst your boss trains with weights and does kung fu, so you forget about that one. But, during the night, you find yourself dreaming about tearing a picture of John Bull into tiny pieces whilst chasing a monkey and belabouring a pumpkin with a mallet.

A dream like this one could be interpreted by any Freud-influenced system as relating to the repression of your naturally unbridled aggression, following what might well be a full and lengthy consideration of pumpkins and their symbolism and how your id is expressed in the character of the monkey or the mallet. However, by identifying the actual introspection that gave rise to the expectation and looking for correspondences with the enactment that has just happened in metaphoric form, you can make a far more parsimonious interpretation of what the brain is doing and notice that the metaphors with which it clothed the experience have neatly defused the arousal. (Metaphors are the natural language of the REM state: it both programmes instinctive behaviour and preserves the integrity of that instinctive behaviour, through discharge of unexpressed emotional arousal, in metaphorical form.)

Dreams, then, don't have to be seen as somehow grand and mysterious; dreaming is, in Griffin's words, the brain's equivalent of wiping the slate clean. However, the capacity for metaphor that is demonstrated in dreams is of fundamental importance since, first, what happens in dreams illustrates that the unconscious mind works through association of ideas rather than through repression. Second, human beings have learned to use that same capacity for metaphor consciously, to develop and to use imagination, leading to language and many aspects of culture through which we have continued to develop. Third, and most vitally, metaphor can now be seen to be evident not only in how the basic templates governing instinctive behaviour operate, but also in how they are both maintained and modified through new learning. Thus the puzzle of why REM sleep persists into adulthood is elegantly solved.

So the REM state, the main theatre for dreams, is also seen to be the programming state in which deep learning takes place. This happens not only in sleep and dreams but also in so-called waking states, since at any time of genuine learning we focus inwards, in a state of narrowed attention, which we can call trance. One cannot really learn anything without going into a kind of trance. When one has taken in a really important and vital idea that has a fundamental effect on a deep level, one might find oneself staring for a long time at a crack in a wall or a vista or a space in the sky and tracing the shape of that learning over again. Or when one is simply daydreaming, one shuts out the world whilst imagery concerning past or present or pure fantasy dominates. Or when one has been intensely caught up in anxiety and negative thinking, the world out there can suddenly seem grey and hollow and pointless. For not all trance is positive, and not all learning is good learning.

The fact that instinctive templates have to be flexible means that mismatches will sometimes occur. The more complicated the creature, the greater the repertoire of possible responses available – and the more scope for error. For instance, we do not have one response of 'Let's get the hell out of here! It's a tiger!' but a general response on the lines of 'Eek! It's some kind of nasty, horrible, scary thing and let's get ready to run for it or clobber it!' While this made for a flexibility that had enormous survival value in past ages, it is also a mechanism that is easily triggered inappropriately, since the 'nasty scary thing' might sometimes be only a lost sheep stumbling around in the shadows.

Emotional states such as anxiety, fear and depression are also programming trances, which may lead us to see things through a distorted lens and make connections that are harmful to us, rather than helpful. So how can stories help?

Healing stories

For this is the great error of our day, that the
physicians separate the soul from the body.
– Hippocrates

Many years ago I had a black cat called Shusha. Actually that wasn't the name with which she'd started life. She had once been called Sooty – it was clearly written on the cage at the cat rescue organization she came from. But Shusha seemed to suit her better – it onomatopoeically suggested the way she moved, very quietly, very gracefully, very self-possessed. It seemed also to suggest the mysterious hint of the orient so many elegant cats embody. Presumably these had not been qualities much admired or appreciated by the previous owners she'd escaped from, since Shusha had clearly been kicked more than once. I deduced this from the way she cowered every time I unwittingly approached her, as it were, feet first when she was on the floor. And if I ever tripped over her (which most cat owners find themselves doing with their pets sooner or later), all the tender petting and encouragement I'd given her over the years would be swept away in an instant and she'd look up at me with a contemptuous expression that said, 'You bastard! I knew you were just waiting to do that.'

Technically you could say that Shusha was making a false pattern match. The pattern in her emotional brain said that feet coming your way meant trouble and set up the expectation of being hurt. It was, of course, impossible to reason with her, to point out that the feet belonged to someone else who treated her with kindness and love. These were feet after all – and she was a cat.

I find myself thinking of Shusha when I talk to some therapy clients. There was the lady with the extreme jealousy problem, for example. Her present partner was generally patient, sweet natured and kind, but he also needed time on his own sometimes. He liked to go fishing or for long country walks and he came back from these expeditions refreshed and happy, saying very little about what he had done – which inevitably aroused her suspicions. Sometimes he had to work late, and that could send her into a frenzy. This lady had, you see, been betrayed over and again by a previous partner, who had also abused her physically and mentally. So she would quiz the new man suspiciously and aggressively, occasionally managing to provoke him into an irritable outburst, which, still more rarely, would escalate into a full-blown row. But this was enough to nurture her fear that he would one day attack her. Whilst she knew in her more rational mind that this man was not the same as the other, another part of her was, Shusha-like, looking for the bastard, generalizing from the one example, telling herself a false story, making a faulty pattern match...

Post-traumatic stress disorder (PTSD) is an extreme example of this phenomenon, whereby faulty pattern matching to a highly stressful event occurs continually and unavoidably. PTSD sufferers report all kinds of automatic and uncontrollable reactions, including flashbacks, nightmares and the feeling that they are reliving the traumatic events over and over again. The imaginative mind seems to be on overdrive. Traumatic memories need to be reprocessed by that same imaginative mind, but in a new trance state – one of deep relaxation, in which the trauma can be 'observed' calmly and put into context – and highly effective practical techniques exist for doing so swiftly and safely.[28]

Not so long ago, I was button-holed in a bar by a large, hairy, physically powerful, very drunk man who, you would have thought, would be bold and fearless – and maybe difficult. Having overheard a conversation I'd been having with someone about ways of working with the condition, he at once began to talk to me about his PTSD, which had been diagnosed though evidently not really treated by a learned army psychologist. He had been a soldier, he explained, an ordinary squaddy sent out to Bosnia and he had been captured – thrown to the ground whilst a gun was held to his head for many minutes. In that time, when he had no idea of whether he would live or die, he had seen his whole life passing before him, all the mates who had also been killed, all kinds of things that had happened and could have happened, all of his life. Years later now every day, usually when he least wanted it, he found himself staring at that same gun, feeling the same horror. He needed the drink, he said, plenty of it. He'd left the army, gone into bomb disposal and kind of hoped a bomb would dispose of him one day. It was a moment, for me also, of helplessness. I knew that his need was acute; I also knew that his state and the circumstances in which we found ourselves precluded immediate treatment. Alcohol, the drug of choice in our society, solves few problems and fuels too many. It was an inner state of deep sobriety, calm and focus that this man needed help in finding, as a prelude to changing the false story his emotional brain was telling him over and over again. I managed to tell him a brief tale or two, but he was still partly listening to the powerful yarn his own brain was spinning.

A lot of other conditions, from phobias, obsessions and compulsions to extreme stress, panic attacks and many more, share with PTSD this false pattern matching, the tagging on of extra useless learnings that need to be modified. There are very few spiders in this world anyone needs to run away from and gnawing the nails off fingers can almost never have solved any problems, but people who have done either of these things or indulged in any phobic, compulsive or addictive behaviour will appreciate very readily that willpower and rationality don't often make the difference. You can do something you don't want to do because somehow 'it' wants to do it. Imagination is stronger than will and, until new and more useful imagination comes into play in the area of the concern, the phobia or compulsion persists.

Stories are a very ancient way of soothing and calming and talking to the imaginative mind, providing new and more useful imagination, uncoupling the old associations and putting in place new, more positive ones – given the right circumstance and a bit of a following wind. We hear and see stories all the time through the ubiquitous modern media; only a few of them make a deep impact, often by a process of apparent serendipity. Somehow we have to find ourselves in (or be brought into) a receptive state, perhaps through the skill of the tale teller, perhaps simply by coincidence. I think of the compulsive smoker who, as he drifted off to sleep in front of the TV, had been reviewing his various attempts to kick the habit and the ways in which it always seemed to worm its way back into his life. When he woke up, the night was well advanced, the set was still on and an old black and white film was showing. Sindbad the Sailor had been shipwrecked yet again and had been captured by the Old Man of the Sea. (You may know this episode of the famous Arabian Nights tale – a monstrous though at first sight apparently feeble old villain manages to hop onto Sindbad's shoulders and then refuses to get off, threatening to strangle the castaway with his powerful thighs. Eventually, after days and weeks spent as the old man's mistreated mount, Sindbad manages to buck him off, hurl him over a cliff, regain himself and escape from the island.) As this would-be non-smoker stared in a half-awake state at the frames of the old film flickering in front of him, his gradually surfacing critical mind told him that it wasn't a very good movie, yet on another level it all began to make huge sense. The metaphor in the tale was showing him things about the way his own habit had been working, and when he saw that and observed it and understood it imaginatively, something changed. He had a new power and perception – and in fact he never smoked again. To repeat something I suggested earlier, when we have the right concern in our mind and being, when circumstance and events conspire together to make us really needy, the story can become deeply meaningful...and effective.

Imagination, making for ourselves both true and false metaphors and threading them together in both conscious and unconscious narrative, clearly plays a much more important and central role in the way we think and speak and order our worlds than we are inclined to think. Again and again, the ways in which we imagine our life and its possibilities can affect us right down to the level of the cells from which our bodies are built. And again and again, insight into the ways that life can be and can change arrive wearing metaphorical costumes.

Guy Claxton, in *Hare Brain, Tortoise Mind*, relays part of a 'much-retailed' account by Richard Selzer of the Dalai Lama's personal physician, Yeshi Dhonden, making a diagnosis of a patient in a demonstration at Yale Medical School. Evidently, he holds the pulse of the woman very carefully and gently for half an hour or more, feeling and listening and sensing the problem. After due reflection, he delivers his diagnosis thus:

Between the chambers of the heart, long, long before she was born, a wind had come and blown a deep gate that must never be opened. Through it charge the full waters of her river, as the mountain stream cascades in the springtime, battering, knocking loose the land, and flooding her breath.[29]

Easy to dismiss as flowery twaddle, no doubt – except if you happen to be a doctor and the condition of the patient, as defined by Western medical science, is disclosed to you – congenital heart disease: interventricular septal defect with resultant heart failure. 'Unless he was very lucky,' comments Claxton, 'or had been secretly primed, we may conclude, with the originally sceptical Selzer, that Yeshi Dhonden was listening to the sounds of the body to which the rest of us are deaf.'

What could also be missed, perhaps, because we have been led to expect such 'primitive' and 'strange' forms of language from someone who comes from a remote, very different culture, is the way in which Yeshi Dhonden phrases what he has apparently understood about the woman's condition. What he uses is metaphor. He tells a kind of story. Indeed, this may be how his mind registers and expresses such an insight, which does not come from logical, sequential reasoning but from an intense form of listening and sensing. So, as in dreams (which also occur when logical faculties are on the back burner), the perception is clothed in sensory analogue.

There is no necessary correlation between accurate medical diagnosis and a knowledge of Latin and Greek. These just happen to be the languages our culture has used to express and develop medical concepts, some of which are undoubtedly metaphorical in their own way. One might also profitably compare them to ritualistic words of power or the stereotypical witch doctor's mumbo jumbo; even though they are officially scientific, on another level, what they are doing is inspiring belief on the part of the patients, by convincing them that the doctor is learned. This can have a highly positive effect. To be told by an 'authority', using all the right words, that there is nothing wrong with you can have you walking home on air, even though your partner said the same thing as you sloped off to the surgery clutching your side. But to be told, in the same language, that you need further tests might have all the boom and clang of a death knell.

In a telling passage from an intriguing book about the remarkable methods and discoveries of some South American shamans, who claim as their source communication with what they conceive of as spirits, anthropologist Jeremy Narby points out the fundamental, if hidden, similarities between the language of the scientist and the shaman:

> Shamans say the correct way to talk about spirits is in metaphors. Biologists confirm this notion by using a precise array of anthropocentric and technological metaphors to describe DNA, proteins, and enzymes. DNA is a *text*, or a *program*, or *data*, containing *information*, which is *read* and *transcribed* into *messenger-RNAs*. The latter feed into ribosomes, which are *molecular computers* that *translate* the *instructions* according to the genetic *code*. They *build* the rest of the cell's *machinery*, namely the proteins and enzymes, which are *miniaturised robots* that construct and maintain the cell.[30]

Words are powerful. The curious thing about almost all science is that it pretends to be *entirely* rational. Of course it should be. Of course no sensible person would suggest that science begin to base itself on irrational superstition. The technical terms of the modern scientist are an effective and useful jargon and have led to all sorts of useful discoveries. But they frequently imply a secondary fantasy world in which elements of the body are compared to machines, these being the handy analogues (and indeed obsessions) of contemporary society. Taken to extremes, it becomes restrictive. The body is mechanical to a point, but it is not, in fact, another kind of car or computer or electric screwdriver. Nor indeed can any of these very clever and cunning inventions provide models for explaining human performance holistically *in themselves*, because all of them are much simpler, much less flexible, much less connected to the larger complexities of the universe we inhabit.

One of the dominant false metaphors in Western medical science has been the separation of mind and body. It implicitly compares the two to things we experience as separate: mind, on the one side, like a solar system way 'up there' with its own quite separate and irrelevant orbits; body, on the other, ticking away like a shop full of well-wound clocks, all to be tinkered with happily. It is false because it is inaccurate and increasingly shown to be so.

To arrive at this notion, one hardly needs to stray much beyond what is really mainstream science these days. One of the world's leading experts on the neurophysiology of emotions, Antonio Damasio, has pointed out how very closely consciousness and body interrelate:

> Whether you are immobile from curarisation or quietly daydreaming in the darkness, the images you form in your mind always signal to the organism its own engagement with the business of making images and evoke some emotional reactions. You simply cannot escape the *affectation* of your organism, motor and emotional most of all, that is part and parcel of having a mind.[31]

There is a feedback loop (to use a suitably modern metaphor) between thought and emotion, emotion and thought – and emotional thought and body. Emotion affects and creates thought; thought and the imagery of thought affect emotion; and emotion affects body. It's a continuum.

A whole field of scientific study has developed with the grand and complicated-sounding name of psychoneuroimmunology, a term coined to reflect the complex relation between brain/psyche and the various systems that co-operate within the body – the autonomic nervous system, the immune system, the cardiovascular system, and so on. In the 1970s, American neurobiologist Candace Pert more or less set the ball rolling with her discovery of an intricate system of neuropeptides that move rapidly around the body, connecting the brain to virtually every cell in the body.

But, as psychiatrist Ernest Rossi, who has written extensively on the subject of mind–body communication, has pointed out,

> It took more than a few centuries for humanity to believe and utilise the implications of Copernicus's finding that the earth revolves around the sun and not vice versa. Likewise, it seems as if it will take more than a few decades, if not centuries, for most people to understand and learn to use the mind's ability to facilitate healing at the cellular and biochemical levels.[32]

Yet, while it could seem absurd to suggest that one day you might go to the doctor and, instead of being given some pink pills to take five times a day, be told a story or two, perhaps it's not too far-fetched. Many far-sighted therapists and health practitioners are already finding such an approach helpful.

Two women turned up to see a certain therapist within a couple of days of each other and, by way of building rapport, the therapist told the same short, trivial tale, though with quite different intentions each time.

The first lady, Rosemary, was very proper, 59 going on 95 – her values and demeanour were apparently formed in another era, probably long before either she or the therapist was born. She trusted implicitly the men of medical science (who in her eyes were definitely men – perhaps by no accident the same gender as the God she fervently prayed to in church); they were part of the natural hierarchy.

Melissa, the second client, was almost the same age. She certainly didn't remember the '60s, having been very much there. Quacks and shrinks she mistrusted instantly. The only kind of treatment she had had any faith in was provided by alternative practitioners with 'good vibes' – though she at least allowed the mainstream medicine-men near the temple of her body on occasions.

Now, both women had troubling symptoms the doctors were unable to explain. Rosemary somehow felt she was letting them down. She really ought to be getting better, now that a leading specialist had examined her, but for some reason her body was 'being silly'. Melissa, however, *knew* her symptoms were psychosomatic – she knew the terminology well. She had also been cleared by the medics – but, after all, as she said, what do they know? Problems could easily be created by the mind, real problems. The mind would be aware of that, would it not, long before they showed up on the scans? So how could she stop herself from brewing up her own doom?

The story the therapist told, in its unornamented essentials, goes like this:

Snap!

A woman goes to the doctor and he examines her very thoroughly. 'I can find nothing wrong with you,' he announces bluntly. 'Maybe,' she responds hesitantly, 'it's something psychological'. 'Well, if it is,' says the doctor fiercely, 'you'd bloody well better snap out of it!'

That was a way in, a beginning. Laughing at the arrogant insensitivity of the doctor in the story allowed both of these women to move forward. The first was already almost literally being told to snap out of it by her physicians and by the internalized part of herself that very much identified with authority. The second was doing the telling herself – she had what is sometimes called New Age guilt: if the mind influences the body, then it's all my fault. Both reactions were clearly becoming an obstacle, so the therapist gave the little 'sugar pill' of a light, amusing story.

Snap out of it! If only it were that simple. Physical conditions evidently require complex gadgetry and chemicals that cost a fortune to develop, but as for something that comes from the mind... well, snap out of it, pull yourself together and bounce back! All of which, as it happens, are metaphors but not particularly helpful ones. People can snap out of it – sometimes. People can and do pull themselves together – with the right kind of encouragement and support at the right time and with maybe a hint or two of how to do it. Some people do find it helpful to consider bouncing back – especially if they are, perhaps, sportsmen or thick-skinned politicians, for whom the comparison resonates. But bouncing balls, strange muscular contortions and clicking fingers or breaking twigs may not be useful images to offer to someone already feeling helpless and perplexed.

Analogies, metaphors, stories – interlocking, intersecting, often verbal artefacts – have something in common with medical diagnosis because they are all forms of information. But, unlike the diagnosis, a story may be consciously shaped at its metaphorical, analogical levels, so that it may work its way through the different information systems within the body, carrying the essential information, the pattern of potential healing.

The therapist discovered that Rosemary was a keen gardener and animal lover. They talked about how she worked with her plants and he told her a homely little anecdote about an aunt of his who had developed the proverbial green fingers and swore blind that the 'gift' had come to her as a result of a salutary experience with a drooping clematis. She had, years ago, asked for advice from a local gardening expert, a man who taught horticulture at a college and who fortunately owed her a favour. This man had made an inspection and pronounced judgement on the plant: it had clematis wilt, a condition well known to clematis growers and hard to cope with. She should cut it right back, spray with a fungicidal spray, feed it and wait. The aunt had already checked in the books and listened to gardening programmes and knew that the advice was basically sound, though, as with all experts, there were differences of opinion. She was about to put it into effect when she noticed a visiting tomcat depositing a copious arc of pee on the very plant. This set her thinking. She knew that cat's urine might not in itself poison a plant, but she also knew that animals repeatedly mark the same spot, sometimes more than one animal, sometimes even several when there's a territorial contest going on. So she had put up a fence around the plant and simply watered and fed it and the 'wilt' had gone. From that day on, she had told the therapist, as they admired the very plant, now rambling and abundantly blooming 20 years on, she had stopped listening to experts and started using her eyes and ears and nose, trusting her own senses. Her garden was her own, so bugger those theorists.

Rosemary evidently liked the story, even the brisk language at the end of it. She apparently later also enjoyed some empowering guided imagery, in which she was led to imagine creating a secret garden. In the middle of this, she was told a brief allegory on a traditional pattern. Briefly, it went like this:

The Ugly Servant

There was once a poor girl who was a servant in a palace. She had a scarred face as a result of an illness and was therefore considered ugly. All day long she was bossed around by the other servants, who passed on the orders of the butler, who passed on the orders of the king's ministers, who passed on the orders of the king. All of her life seemed ordered for her until one day, whilst she was carrying out a task which required her to walk down a path through part of the palace garden, she noticed a small door in a wall she had not seen before. She almost passed it by, but curiosity got the better of her and, glancing around guiltily, she turned the handle and pushed the door a little, just so that she could peep in. What she found was a small walled garden that appeared disused. In the middle of it was a dry fountain. She went inside and spent a few minutes looking around and then went out again and got on with her chores, feeling a strange sense of hope.

The next day and the next and the next, she returned to that little garden and, each time, without really knowing why, she tidied up and weeded and worked to set the place to rights. No one else seemed to be aware of the place and, oddly, no one seemed to notice the time she spent there, perhaps because she seemed to do her chores more speedily after she had visited the place. After a time, she began to notice little blue and yellow flowers blooming, which she tended carefully.

After more time, the small garden was blossoming all around and there were rich red fruits on a little tree, which tasted delicious, though she had no idea what they were.

All this gave her a kind of inner confidence and she not only did her jobs well, she stopped cringing in front of the senior servants. This led to promotion, which enabled her to give commands herself, and this she did with fairness and compassion. Promotion led to promotion and she became, at length, a lady in waiting to the queen. In the secret garden one day she looked into the fountain and realized that a stone was blocking it. She removed it and at once the water jetted out, washing all of the scars from her face as it did so, since it was the healing Water of Life. And this she proceeded to use at the palace and elsewhere, secretly healing as and when she could. And she married a nobleman and lived happily, always in reach of the garden.

The two stories provided metaphors that worked for Rosemary. When an image connects with experience, it can unlock learning in that experience and show how it is relevant in other areas of experience. When the imagination is engaged, new behaviour can be rehearsed metaphorically. Rosemary began to take control for herself, and accept and work with the symptoms, which fairly promptly diminished.

And Melissa – well, unfortunately for the therapist's ego, he found himself struggling for inspiration, groping for images about balance and trust and allowing things to happen and wishing that he could allow a story or an image to arrive in his mind that would be appropriate. He noticed his client distracted for a moment by something glimpsed outside the window and turned to see an elegant, athletic cat make a perfect leap from the ground to the top of a wall between two pillars just beyond the window. There was the kind of perfection in it that animals so often achieve effortlessly. 'Wow!' Melissa said with awed admiration. 'I just wish I could do things like that.' 'Yes,' said the therapist, 'and the weird thing is that the cat didn't even think about it.' She later took up pilates and juggling and reported that she found them more helpful than therapy.

Stories and metaphors are not like pills and never could be, though it is a mistake many people interested in using them make, expecting this or that tale to be somehow for this or that condition. It is highly unlikely that you could make them pass the tests of evidence-based medicine. Imagine the scenario as the logically minded Dr Spock look-alike sets up a test that meets the criteria. A series of people diagnosed with similar conditions are each read the same story (it will have to be read or preferably pre-recorded so that there are no variations, otherwise they won't be getting the same thing). Each patient will simultaneously be strapped up to encephalographs and will also have their blood pressure monitored, as well as their pulses and blood sugars and hormone levels and all sorts more. During the hours and weeks following the administration of the story, they will be tested regularly and observed until they either get better or die. Meanwhile, another group will get pills, whilst a third group will get nothing and will also be blindfolded and wear ear muffs so that they don't accidentally absorb any tales along the way. The results might be interesting – if predictable.

Breakthrough stories:
The mbala effect – and how to beat it

Riddle: If I give you this treasure, you'll refuse it like
as not. What is it?
Answer: Good advice.

Returning for a moment to the subject of urban legends, here's one that contains a useful idea or two:

Urban legend – The Furniture Van

A single lady was asked to look after the house of her neighbours whilst they were away on holiday. They owned a lot of antiques and objets d'art, and they were very careful to give her strict instructions about the locks and alarms. She agreed to check the house three times a day and not to let any suspicious characters in.

Well, when a few days had gone by uneventfully, a large furniture van arrived. Two men approached the empty house and rang the bell. The lady, very suspicious and determined not to be duped, listened to the men's explanation. Apparently the neighbours had left a bid at an auction and had, as a result, bought a large 18th-century cabinet. There was no room for it at the warehouse so they had been instructed to bring it anyway. They opened the back of the van to reveal a miracle in marquetry gleaming under French polish and wax. Where was it to be put?

The lady carefully accompanied them into the house, making sure they had no opportunity to 'case the joint' – she knew all about the ways of thieves since she had an appetite for detective fiction. She made sure they couldn't note the code she tapped into alarms and locks, escorted them into the building, watched them hawk-eyed as they deposited the latest acquisition in the hall and then led them out and waved them off, double checking all the locks and alarms.

But the house was robbed, stripped completely bare – by robbers who had had plenty of time to disarm the alarms and open the doors by the time the van came back. They had, of course, been inside the cabinet.

In the Hindu pantheon, two important gods are Vishnu and his consort, Lakshmi. Vishnu is the god of learning and the arts, whilst Lakshmi is the goddess of wealth. Where Vishnu goes, Lakshmi follows. There is a story about the two of them and what they may do for peoples of the world.

Lakshmi and Vishnu

Long ago, there was a certain city where people no longer told the old stories and legends. They had grown hard and callous and only interested in themselves and their own advantage. Vishnu saw the state of things in this place and decided to intervene. He disguised himself as a kathakar, a storyteller, and he went into the market place carrying a vina. This he played upon until he had attracted a crowd of listeners – the divine inspiration of his playing soon had people who had half an ear for such things listening attentively. Then he began to relate story after story for the people, and they listened, completely spellbound and entranced. Afterwards, they told others excitedly about the marvellous teller of tales and related some of the stories they had heard.

The next day, Vishnu was there again and the crowd was much bigger, since his fame had spread. Again, people were struck dumb with wonder and amazement at the images passing before their inner eyes. The next day and the next and the next the kathar (storytelling) went on, until everyone was going to listen to the great storyteller. And, because they listened and because the stories told them all kinds of things about what they might be and how they should act, they began to change and to reform themselves and life became better in that city.

Lakshmi looked down and saw what was happening and she felt jealous at what she saw. She herself went to the city, taking on the form of an old beggar woman. She knocked on a door, which was answered by a young girl who was about to go out to hear the stories of the day. She asked for a little water and the girl, who had learned from Vishnu's tales to be hospitable to strangers, brought her a pot. Lakshmi drank it down and returned the pot, and the girl noticed in amazement that the pot had been turned to gold. The old beggar woman smiled as the girl fetched neighbours to witness the wonder and they in their turn brought their pots, which were duly turned into gold like the first one. Soon people were deserting the kathar in droves and forming a jostling throng around Lakshmi. Vishnu quickly found himself alone.

Since no one would listen any longer, Vishnu took his vina and left the city. Soon afterwards, Lakshmi followed him.[33]

The story has a moral that is as relevant in contemporary advanced capitalist societies as it was when first told centuries ago, but that is not primarily why I am relaying it here. It also provides a fascinating insight into oral traditions of storytelling, to which I'll return in due course later in the book. But the point is, why choose to tell stories to convey important information and ideas? Why not just tell it straight?

People who are told to change rarely do it as willingly or as effectively as people who decide to do it for themselves – or believe they have decided to do it themselves. Millions of smokers have coughed and wheezed themselves into an early grave, despite being told over and over again of the extreme dangers to health that go with the habit – and maybe even because of being told over and over again. Compulsive gamblers, alcoholics, sufferers from obsessions and compulsion generally know very well what they are doing to themselves, but preaching to them or getting them to preach to themselves may not be the most effective way to hack through the thicket of destructive habits because, from where they are standing, they can see no other way to fill the emptiness or need in their lives. For the same reason, we may know very well that the box of chocolates or the hunk of cheese or whatever else takes our fancy will fur up our arteries or turn into undesirable cellulite in unfortunate places, but does it always stop us from having another mouthful? We are up against the Mbala effect, a title derived from yet another story.

Mbala

A zealous 19th-century missionary was visiting an African tribe. He preached to them passionately about the virtues of religion and how they should change themselves and give up their wicked habits of polygamy and tribal warfare and naked dancing and see the one true light and live by the one true moral code in the hope of eternal mercy. His speech was translated by the chief, who had been educated at an English public school. At the end of each translated sentence, the tribe members would all shout 'Mbala!' with huge gusto and apparent enthusiasm. The preacher reached the inspiring climax of his oration and the people were all shouting 'Mbala! Mbala! Mbala!' over and over again, in a rhythmic chant.

The preacher was then shown to the guest hut by the solicitous chief. 'I think that went quite well,' he said modestly to his host.

'Indeed, old chap,' said the chief, taking him by the arm to steer him through the village, along the dusty track and past the cows and the goats. 'Mind, now, or you'll step in the mbala!'

Something inside very many people is shouting out *mbala!* whenever change is mentioned. It is, after all, much easier for any creature to stick with the ways it knows, which have been effective enough to date as 'proved' by the fact that it is still alive. It has been known for centuries that if you want to set up change, whether in individuals or in groups or even in whole societies, you do better to suggest it by stealth. Stories can teach by stealth, not by direct statement. They are, to borrow an image from a marvellous recording by founding director of the London College of Storytellers, Pat Williams on the effects of stories, Trojan horses we take into the mind unwittingly, not suspecting the Greeks inside.[34] Or they are like the deceptive wardrobe in my urban legend. Except that the 'thieves' inside steal away the useless stuff and leave behind a treasure.

The natural storyteller – a summary

Antonio Damasio, hailed not only as an important brain scientist but also as a major theorist of consciousness in recent years, believes that a form of storytelling is basic to the functioning of our brains. He says:

> Wordless storytelling is natural, the imagetic representation of sequences of brain events, which occurs in brains simpler than ours, is the stuff of which stories are made. A natural preverbal occurrence of storytelling may well be the reason why we ended up creating drama and eventually books.[35]

In this opening chapter I have suggested that literature, whether written down or simply spoken, is just one manifestation of a series of basic human capacities for fiction and for metaphor and 'world making', which includes all kinds of less conscious activities, such as dreaming, daydreaming, fear about the past or the future, worry, fantasizing and even lying, all the way down to the moment-to-moment wordless storytelling of the brain that Damasio describes.[36]

Human beings are, as I asserted at the outset, natural storytellers. To summarize, we are storytellers:

- In the way we make our world from minute to minute and from microsecond to microsecond. The world we see and know is a spontaneous 'construction', carved out of the totality of 'what is' by our limited senses and 'explained' to us by the brain as a kind of narrative.

- In the way that we dream. The brain tells us stories about what has happened to us without our conscious volition, spontaneously creating metaphors for our experiences.

- In the fundamental ways in which the language through which we communicate, think and build our conscious worlds is structured and continuously develops.

- In the way we understand ourselves from hour to hour, day to day and year to year. We are a work-in-progress, constantly updating and altering and redrafting the story for consistency – which, paradoxically, we may find less than complete when we look in the mirror of stories.

- In the way that we use the faculty to daydream to 'see' future possibilities, connections between ideas and events, potentials and problems and solutions, read the 'signs' and get insights into the larger patterns of life.

- In the way that, when we remember and reconstruct past happenings, we create a story of how things were from the few vivid fragments our selective memories retrieve.

- In the way that we can create all kinds of difficulties for ourselves through worrying about and imagining what may never happen or by interpreting past events negatively – in effect, embedding problems and unhelpful habits through telling ourselves limiting stories about powerlessness, hopelessness, etc.

- In the way that we may make, or try to disengage ourselves from, the proverbial tangled webs of lies and deceits in all kinds of social settings, and in our thinking and imagining.

- In passing on news and gossip and repeating rumours and speculating about people and events, in all kinds of social interchange.

- In the way that our families and groups and tribes and corporations and cultures explain themselves, and in the myths and legends we live by day by day, whether we are aware of the fact or not. We constantly make and re-make these stories – or have them made and re-made for us.

Viewed from this broad perspective, telling stories surely assumes a central importance in making us what we are. It is, in effect, one of the human givens – the needs that must be fulfilled and the resources that must be deployed if we are to be fully human.[37] Psychological health depends on getting our needs met on a variety of levels apart from the most basic physical requirements for food, shelter and warmth. These include being integrated in, and having a role and status within, a community; having work or other activity that stretches and involves us; giving and receiving adequate attention; intimacy and friendship; privacy and autonomy; having a secure sense of self and of meaning in our lives. When these needs are met, we tend to flourish; when any of them is persistently denied, we do not. Our many human faculties have evolved to meet those needs, including, very centrally, imagination. Our abilities to use and control it led to the development of language and art and science and stories of all kinds, and to the passing on of all of these through cultures. Narrative is very much bound up with that faculty of imagination. You could look at stories and storytelling as a kind of subset of art and science and mythology produced through language, but it is clearly more fundamental. Telling stories shapes and controls and contains imagination in all kinds of ways and makes it work for us.

The story of stories is, then, a story of what you could call another given of human nature that has evolved and continued to develop, to help us to make sense of ourselves and our world. It has expressed and developed itself in all sorts of ways in oral and written literatures through time, from the fabulous creations of early man that survive in cave paintings and decorations, through all kinds of developed mythologies, known and unknown, to the great classics of literature or the jokes and legends we pass on day to day. And then perhaps all the way back in a full circle again to the basic 'wordless' picture storytelling that may be the natural mode of the brain which, Damasio speculates, may well underpin the addictive appeal of much film and TV.[38] Stories can entertain us and take us into relaxing, life-enhancing trances. They also instruct and challenge, show us marvellous solutions and let us glimpse more of what we can become.

Chapter 2

The Spanish Game: Guided Imagery and Stories

Once in a dream, the philosopher Chuang Tzu became
a butterfly flying through a strange dream landscape.
When he woke up, he said he could no longer
be certain whether he was Chuang Tzu who had
dreamed he was a butterfly or a butterfly dreaming he
was Chuang Tzu.[1]

If 50 people listen to the same story at the same time, there will
be 50 different mental representations of that story, 50 different
shadings of subjective meaning and association added to that one
'objective' narrative. How storytellers tell the story – whether they
give a lot of visual clues and include all sorts of adjectives and
comparative descriptions – will guide and shape those imaginings,
though it can never determine them precisely. Everyone brings
different experiences and learnings to bear on the narrative, which
still, miraculously perhaps, draws those chaotically different
images into a kind of fractal harmony through the plot and the
metaphorical resonances.

A story guides the imagination. Thus, listening to a story, reading
a story and even telling and writing a story are all forms of guided
imagery. In this chapter, I'll aim to show that visualization and
guided imagery are close cousins of storytelling, written and oral,

all born out of the basic human need to make and explore narrative meaning at many metaphorical levels. Working with visualization and guided imagery can release the power and effectiveness of the imaginative mind.

In modern culture, we rather take imagination for granted. Amongst the many voices clamouring for improvements in education, there are plenty that stress formal skills such as writing, literacy, numeracy, and so on, because people believe they can see the relevance of these. You will, however, hear imagination mentioned only as an adjunct, usually in the same breath as buzz words such as 'creativity' or 'expression', 'artistic' or even 'scientific' – which themselves are 'nominalizations' (abstract terms with no concrete meaning). Making pupils not only more imaginative but better able to understand, control and use their imaginations appears not even to come to mind. But when you ignore and fail to make deliberate use of a basic faculty, it seems somehow or other to end up using you. That which we do not control tends to control us.

The Enchantress and the Animals

An old enchantress lived in the middle of a forest in a cave. Travellers who met her noted that she had a remarkable way with the animals of the forest, even though she often treated them roughly and even killed, skinned and ate some of them whenever she needed food or clothes. Despite all that, the animals fawned on her and lay passively around the mouth of the cave, apparently accepting their fate. Then a traveller, who had learned, like the enchantress, to speak the language of animals, asked one of them why they did not run away from the wicked old monster, since they were animals and much more agile and fast than she was. 'What,' gasped the animal, incredulously, 'leave our noble queen and protector and her glorious castle? When she has already given us so much and we have so much importance here... Ah yes, but of course you can't see and she did warn us about people like you. You have to understand that we are not really animals at all. I, for example, may look like a deer but I'm really a poet, the parrot over there is a celebrity singer and my donkey friend here is a learned philosopher...'

Psychotherapists and counsellors must be only too aware of just how many clients are the victims of their own imaginations. Sufferers from phobias and fears, people who are desperately anxious or uncontrollably angry, people who regard themselves as failures and undermine their own confidence skills in all sorts of ways, people with some forms of chronic pain, people who even create their own disabilities – all of these and more may have in common the misuse of that one faculty: imagination. Teachers in secondary schools and colleges, watching students go through the system and seeing the extraordinary wastage of potential that occurs year in year out, as able teenagers go off the rails or fail to make the best of their chances, must sometimes have an inkling, too, of the role that uncontrolled imagination can play. And there are many other contexts in which imagination runs a wrecking riot.

Day in, day out, we are subjected to barrages of images designed to promote this or that product or lifestyle choice or company or political party. The image-making industry draws extensively on the input of creative and imaginative people who intuitively grasp how imagination can be stimulated and used, backed up by psychologists with a fair grasp of how to manipulate basic drives. The combination is, of course, extremely powerful. Our general media and the fiction and music industries are frequently indistinguishable from the image-makers. It is, as many have observed, the norm now to appeal to basic motivations once listed as the deadly sins that were a sure passport to hell. If you want to sell, make people feel a bit insecure about themselves and then grab 'em with something that hits those nice brightly coloured buttons of greed for gain, gluttony, lust, anger, pride, sloth, and envy. It works like a dream.

But, in the wake of all that, there are millions of people whose expectations about life have been hopelessly inflated, who become locked into unrealizable fantasies. Imagination is a marvellous thing, a faculty that can be used to achieve all sorts of ends, to solve all sorts of problems, to realize all sorts of dreams. When it is distorted and confused and uncontrolled and mixed up with insatiable appetites or peculiar ideologies or just plain angst, it can equally be a terrible curse. Yet we live in a world and a time in which it is distinctly uncool to point out the difference between a want and a need.

Imagination may be a natural faculty, the given that underpins our narrative-making ability; to be made good use of, it still needs training – or at least guidance. And it needs to be disentangled from swathes of aroused appetites. This is a major part of what the telling and making and hearing and considering of stories can do, focused in appropriate ways. One starting point is visualization, which works with a part of that natural inner storyteller, enabling us to tell ourselves little stories in the picture language dreams also use, or to picture stories told to us in the form of guided imagery.

The Spanish game

There's a visualizing game that has fascinated me for many years. Possibly you already know a version: like a joke or a traditional story, it seems to exist in many forms. Since I first heard it way back as a student, I've come across all sorts of variants used by teachers of creative writing, yoga teachers and meditators and others. A lady I knew who had grown up in rural Spain claimed that she had heard something very similar in her childhood as a piece of folklore, which suggests that it might even have quite ancient origins. This is how it works: you are asked to imagine a short journey and are given minimal clues and cues, so that you form the images in your own way. You are invited to take your time over each image, allowing it to form spontaneously, without much conscious thought. It doesn't matter whether this is done in pictures or in feelings and sensations or anything else that works for you.

So, first of all, it is a forest through which you are walking, but it's up to you to decide whether you are on a path or struggling through undergrowth, whether the route is clear or not, whether you like the forest and enjoy it or dislike it or have other feelings entirely. Maybe it is a deciduous forest in the springtime or an evergreen forest at dusk or whatever else comes to mind.

As you travel through the forest, you find a bottle. I don't know what kind of bottle it is – that is up to you. It could be large or small, new or old, green or brown or clear as crystal or... It might have some content or perhaps not... And you might decide to take it or leave it or...

Somewhere in this forest, you find a key. It could be on the path or somewhere else altogether. It could be a big key or a little one, a silver key or a golden one or one made from rusty old tin. It might be a modern one or it might be an ancient one. There are many possibilities, but it's likely that your image-making mind will choose one of those quite quickly. And again you might take it or leave it or...

Last, you come to a wall. It might be a brick wall or a stone wall or some other kind of wall. But there is no way past this wall that you can see, no way through or over or around it. What could you do? And what could you imagine (or maybe see or otherwise sense really clearly) is on the other side?

That's where the version of the visualization that I know ends, though some go on from there. It is a game, and not one to be taken too seriously. All the images in it are supposed to mean something – the way you see (or feel or sense) them is reckoned to tell how you see those things in life. To give you a chance to play the game without spoiling it by jumping straight to the 'answers', I have put the meanings upside down in mirror writing in a box below.

The wall is death

The key is knowledge

The bottle is love

The forest is life

While the meanings in the box are probably nonsense when taken literally, the game can still show us a thing or two: for example the way the dreaming, fantasizing mind can work beyond conscious intention. If you played the game by the rules and allowed the images to 'arrive' without too much interference, you may well have found this happened quite quickly and spontaneously, almost despite yourself. People differ in this, depending on how they do most of their imagining and how much they consciously use imagination in general: some get clear pictures; others get feelings or little snapshots. But the pictures or sensations or feelings usually arrive complete; most people don't build them up piece by piece, choosing how things are to appear at each stage along the way, like a computer programmer or an animator. Something knows how to make them for us, all done and dusted. Our minds tell us a kind of story. We are (just about) dreaming in a waking state.

This is very interesting when you think about it. In the entirely portable theatre of the imagination, it is possible to create all the effects the movie-makers spend millions creating, all for nothing, all in an instant. But why should one person 'choose' to see a deciduous forest in autumn sunshine and russet colours, whilst another 'decides' on groping through a fairy-tale, deep, dark, evergreen forest, listening to wolves howling? Why do some people 'want' to smash the bottle whilst others 'find themselves' sensing that it contains a wonderful elixir? Why do many people pick up and keep the key, whilst others leave it alone or hang it from a branch for its presumed owner to find? Why does that key have to be ancient and scrolled and golden for some, whilst others go for the modern Chubb or Yale models? Why do some people feel defeated by the wall whilst others peer over it or look for a door with a lock in which to use that key? These are all decisions taken imaginatively, but on the basis of other decisions and assumptions. Ask people why they make those decisions and they will usually come up with a rationalization pretty quickly. But the fact is that those imaginative decisions are not taken rationally.

Imagination draws on association of ideas. The ways in which we associate ideas do not reveal precise universal things to be read impersonally, using a symbol dictionary or a diagnostic manual, which is why the game interpretations given in the box (and indeed a lot of Freudian and Jungian interpretations of association) are misleading. But associations do reveal something, possibly quite a lot of things. The way you see a forest may just depend on whether you were recently in one and what it was like; the way in which you see a bottle may depend on the kind you poured your last drink from; the way in which you see a key could be related merely to how you opened a door five minutes ago. Could and might. But there are other possibilities.

According to Jay Haley, a leading disciple of Dr Milton Erickson, someone asked the great therapist why he didn't ask directly about a particular client's family relationships. This was Erickson's reply:

> That man made his living for 27 years laying floors. Most men can't last 15 years at that kind of work, but he lasted almost twice that long. If I really wanted to find out more about his family background, I might start talking about driving in the desert. I would describe driving along the road and rounding a high point

rising from the desert floor. Suddenly rounding that high point, I would see a rather lonesome ironwood tree. One of the branches had been broken, probably by the wind smashing around that high point.

I would use the image of 'ironwood' because of that man's work history. An ironwood tree with a broken branch. Probably from the wind smashing around that high place. Then I'd talk about the mesquite bushes around the tree. I would learn about his relatives, because a tree doesn't stand alone. 'If I should be the last leaf upon the tree.'[2]

Why would he do it this way, his visitor asked? 'Because when I ask about your sister, brother, parents, you put them into the social frame befitting your education. When I do it in this indirect way, the information is different.'

Erickson clearly understood that the way in which people respond to images tells things about them they might not otherwise wish to show. The Spanish game suggests very much the same thing. The way you move through a forest, whether you are struggling through undergrowth or following a broad open path, whether you skip happily through dappled shade and pools of sunshine or shudder and shiver and wish you were somewhere else might not say exactly how you see life in general at all times, but could say something about how you are feeling now and how you tend to feel and react. But that something has to be 'read' with insight and intuition, not de-coded and ticked off on the answer sheet and frogmarched into some dubious interpretive framework.

We are metaphorical creatures, storytelling beings, and the Spanish game shows a side of the natural storyteller in action. You make the images in a visualization for yourself, inside your head – though even minor clues from the presenter of the visualization may affect it, as may the context in which you do the visualizing. Although I did some of the storytelling for you, the images you made were your own, because we can't ever be told exactly what and how to 'see'. Our images reflect our unique experience and patterns of learning and the ways in which we tend to group meanings together. There are all sorts of ways that we group meanings and some associations we have are bound to be spurious and temporary; others may be echoes of conventional received attitudes and ideas, whilst yet others are nearer to the nub of what we feel ourselves to be. We don't just think and imagine randomly; thoughts and images group themselves into patterns, schemas, maps we use to form more maps and schemas and patterns.

For a little more insight into this, here are some more visualizations you might like to try – as few or as many as you feel like, and just see what comes into your mind. Of course, if any of the images has strongly negative associations for you, you might prefer to leave it alone and choose others.

Seven visualizations

It is helpful to linger over each sentence and allow images to 'arrive'. These need not be visual, despite the term visualization, since some people start from ideas and feelings, others from tastes, smells, sounds, textures, etc.

You could think about whether your images 'mean' something to you in some way, or whether they are simply random associations. How do the questions and other phrasings in the instructions influence you, if you find they do? It can also be interesting to try the visualizations on other people, to find out how differently we all see things and to compare notes.

1. The market

Imagine for a moment that you are in a market... It can be a big market or a little one, a familiar or an unfamiliar one, a market in your own country or a foreign market. You might like to notice a few stalls and the kinds of things that are being sold, smell a few of the smells, taste a few of the tastes and generally explore...

Is there something particular you are looking for? Do you have several different things you are looking for? If that is so, do you have a list? Or are you simply browsing? Are you in a hurry or taking your time? What unusual thing will you notice in the market? What kinds of people are in the market? How long will you spend in the market? Do you like this market?

2. A room of your own

You are designing a room in which you will spend some considerable time. You are able to make this room exactly the way you want.

You can adjust the size, the shape, have it furnished however you like, have as many windows with as many views as you choose, and so on. You can have whatever facilities you like. You must, however, provide the room with all you will need for this indefinite period of time, bearing in mind that you will spend this time alone. List what you will have in the room in whatever order items come into mind. Take your time.

3. Box and contents

You find a mysterious closed box. It may be small or large, new or old, anything that comes to mind. You may like to take a minute or two to get a clear notion of this box and what it is like, where you might have found it and in what kind of circumstance. What colour is it and what shape? How will it feel when you touch it? Are you curious about the box? What other kinds of thoughts and feelings do you have about it? Without opening it, what do you imagine could be inside it? Now, how will you open the box? Is it easy or difficult? And, when it is finally opened, what will you find inside?

4. Going for a ride

You can choose whatever mode of transport you like – a car, a bike, a horse or whatever else seems appropriate. You find yourself going through a completely unfamiliar town. You will look out for three landmarks in order to make first a right turn, then two left turns. After that, you will arrive at your destination. Since the town is imaginary, you can make those landmarks take any form you choose and then check them out in close detail as you pass them and make the turnings. When you arrive at your destination, can you get a feel for what it is like?

5. The meeting

You are going to meet an important person, whom you respect. This individual may be an actual person or an imaginary person. Where will you be meeting? Will the person be sitting or standing when you meet? What are you wearing for the meeting? What sort of things will you say? What kinds of things will you leave this meeting remembering?

6. The crowd

You have to stand up in front of a crowd of people and say something you suspect will not be popular. What kinds of people are in the crowd and where are they gathered? What are you wearing? How will you make yourself heard? Are you standing or sitting? Are you on a platform looking down or in a pit looking up or is the arrangement entirely different?

7. The journey

You are going on a journey. It could be an exciting journey, though there may also be some dangers. You will be able to decide, for much of the time, how you will travel and at what speed, but at other times you may have to trust to whatever you imagine is provided. Where will you be travelling to and what kinds of things will you see? Will you meet people along the way? Will you travel alone or in company? What kinds of places would you like this journey to take you to? How long will the journey take and how soon would you hope to return?

Answering the following questions may help you get each visualization into a little more focus.

1. Is this an interesting image – or can you make it more interesting somehow?

2. What associations come to mind with respect to this image (or series of images)?

3. How differently might another person experience this visualization?

4. How differently might you or someone else experience the visualization at different times?

5. What (if any) insights does this give you about

   (a) how you think about certain things?

   (b) how you feel about certain things?

   (c) the meanings things hold for you?

   (d) how one thing relates to another for you?

(e) skills to be learned?

(f) needs to be met?

6. Were there any surprises and discoveries quite apart from these?

7. What words or phrasings in the visualization text might have influenced you – or were jarring and irritating?

8. How might you develop and extend this visualization creatively?

9. Are there particular uses that come to mind for this visualization?

10. How easily are you able to form, sustain and even refine your mental images and, if you do, do you combine sights, sounds, tastes, aromas and textures or do you favour one particular sense or two?

11. Can practice help you develop and improve your ability to imagine, and what physical states seem to favour this?

Interpretations and misinterpretations

A woman I know used to visit a psychotherapist trained in an influential psychodynamic approach. Since she is a very punctual person, she would usually have to spend some time in the therapist's waiting room, where there were various chairs. When the therapist came to fetch her, he would invariably quiz her in a fairly aggressive way about why she had chosen to sit in a particular chair that day. Once in the consulting room, there was the awkward hurdle of another choice of chairs, followed by more questions. 'You know,' she told me, 'it got to the point where I would make up a reason, just to satisfy him, but he always seemed to feel that the choice meant something.' Evidently the therapy sessions were not entirely successful.

This kind of spurious 'psychologizing' and covert domination is what many people mistrust in the therapy/counselling industry. It is almost playing to stereotype. Maybe there are hidden reasons sometimes for sitting in a particular chair. Maybe there are hidden reasons sometimes for why one trips on a paving stone, but if you think too hard about them you'll probably miss the next one and fall down a manhole (which, of course, could be a much-too-Freudian slip). People can get just too self-consciously taken up with interpreting. A lot of the time we just tripped. A lot of the time we just sat.

It is the same with imagining. Some of it just is. Yes, it connects with our 'meaning networks', but not necessarily in ways that are useful or necessary to examine. It is certainly something to keep in mind when interpreting any imaginings, including the visualizations you might have just done. If we glare at someone and insist that the chair they sat in or the clothes they experienced themselves as wearing in a fantasy about a market or the way they related to the behaviour of a king in a story has a 'serious significance', we are likely to get an answer intended simply to get rid of the glare. If we ask leading questions, it is very easy to implant ideas about the kind of responses that will be appropriate, since people compliantly visualizing are in a highly suggestible state. Thus, we get back what we have given; the image becomes a looking-glass, not a telescope.

This is one reason why it is important to consider how any image is presented – the verbal and body language used, the way it is underlined with this or that emphasis and inflexion, etc. It is why one of the questions you were asked to ask yourself after doing the visualizations concerned the language used and whether it was jarring or irritating. So, although I would now like to consider some possibilities for meanings that may have come out of the visualizations, and for the wider uses each visualization might have, these are set out without any pretence that they are the only ways to interpret each image or to use the scenarios.

1. The market

Interpretations: This image may work in quite different ways for market lovers and market haters and, if you were going to offer it to someone else, it might, in some contexts, be useful to find out how they feel about markets first. (In fact, this applies to all the visualizations. It isn't helpful, for instance, to suggest someone is strolling in a lush garden, if the person suffers badly from hay fever.) Reactions to the market may say something about how you (or someone else) relates to crowds, how you/they feel about being in groups, the kinds of things you/they are interested in, whether you/they prefer the mundane or have a taste for the exotic, and so on. The way that the questions are asked clearly helps shape the visualization. Looking for something in a market might just provide a metaphor for some current concern or problem or may indicate more general interests and focus. Something unusual may be revealing, but note that, if you do the 'why-this-chair?' approach described above and make a big thing of it, either with yourself or with another person, you'll probably trigger a false response. It is generally best to be relaxed about it all, and simply to allow connections to emerge.

Uses as a change metaphor: The market metaphor might be appropriate for someone needing to make choices, and to stay focused whilst being aware of a number of different possibilities. Someone who needs to develop social poise could become aware, via its use, of how visible one can be in some ways and invisible in others, all in the same place. A group of people with a common aim might need to cultivate an ability to avoid distractions. In each case, and many others, the metaphor could be elaborated differently by a creative therapist or teacher or trainer, with various kinds of image and suggestion woven into the narrative.

2. A room of your own

Interpretations: People often pick up on the fact that a room can easily be a metaphor for self, so that in designing the room you might be setting out a version of yourself. This is relatively true, since many people do think in this way and, indeed, are encouraged to do so by lifestyle programmes. This particular room seems to involve a period of virtual imprisonment, but you have enormous imaginative scope in adjusting this. Do people choose things that are only about personal comfort or do they emphasize channels of communication (phones, doors, etc.)? How far is a choice of decor a matter of display and how far a very personal, 'inner' choice? Many of the choices made could reveal priorities. The visualization would also suggest how many basic needs a person is aware of and would cater for in their design. Incidentally, this would clearly be a visualization to avoid or to use with caution with claustrophobia sufferers.

Uses as a change metaphor: This might suit a person who needs to organize and take control and develop a sense of autonomy. Another person might need nudging towards widening communication, through images of windows, phones, even secret escape routes and magic doors for special visits; in a visualization the rules can be reinvented constantly. Others may need to break out of the confines of 'walled in' thinking, perhaps by being encouraged to create a room without walls. The image is a flexible one and can be adjusted to suit many different temperaments.

3. Box and contents

Interpretations: A box could be about possibility. This kind of image changes when people are in different emotional states. There is no specific meaning associated with the colour given to the box, but both colour and shape could have significance in individual instances, which might emerge through open questioning or through considering associations. Some people are excited about opening the box; others are apprehensive. Some are achingly curious about what is inside it; some are unconcerned. There are people who see the box as a sexual metaphor, whilst others describe it as somehow mystical and yet others think of it as an interesting puzzle to solve. This may well affect how they imagine the contents.

Uses as a change metaphor: A person who finds possibilities hard to imagine can sometimes be helped by an exploration of the box image, with a lot of concealed encouragement and hints about opening it. The feeling of opening a box and dealing with locks can be liberating. Conversely, someone who is too ready to leap to assumptions about its contents might be asked to concentrate on opening the box stage by stage – a metaphor that works as well for men who are inclined to rush the sexual act as for men or women who are inclined to narrow down life to obvious options.

4. Going for a ride

Interpretations: Driving a car or riding a bike or a horse could be felt to be about control of self. Many car drivers think of their cars as an 'alter ego', which may be one reason that road rage is easily evoked by apparent discourtesy from other drivers. Advertising of cars very much stresses this kind of identification, so the metaphor has much reinforcement. For some, however, all machinery tends to stand for the brute stupidity of things, whilst others treat cars with the reverence once reserved for sacred icons and statues of the gods. Bikes and horses may evoke similar or contrasting emotions. In the visualization, there are specific instructions about a second important element, the unfamiliar town. How cautious is a person? How much do they rely on maps and instructions? How willing are they to make the town in their own particular way? What sort of destination is chosen and does it show a sense of self-importance or a vivid imagination or simply a realization of a fear or disillusionment?

Uses as a change metaphor: The main elements need to be separated out. The mode of transport will suit some people very well, but not others. Guided imagery about controlling a vehicle or animal through unfamiliar territory may work well for a person controlling an addiction such as smoking.[3] Controlling a car (or bike or horse) is self-conscious at the learning stage, but becomes more and more unconscious with repetition, so that we can drive (or ride) without thinking about it. Landmarks in a town can be metaphors for particular associations that have previously triggered the undesired habit and much can be made of passing the landmarks without stopping at them. The town can also represent any other new behaviour to be explored metaphorically.

5. The meeting

Interpretations: Maybe it is difficult to find the right balance in addressing a person we genuinely respect, since it is too easy to be fawningly sycophantic or overfriendly or cockily assertive. Respect easily triggers other more primitive emotions, associated perhaps with status and recognition. This image could partly be about how much people respect themselves and expect to receive respect back. Someone might notice they are wearing something inappropriate, as would happen in some dreams. However, the questions, at the end of the guided imagery text, about clothing, could be triggering the feeling that what you are wearing or how you are seeing the person is in some way important.

Uses as a change metaphor: This image is an interesting one to explore, either alone or with assistance, as a preparation for an interview or a viva or something similar. It can be helpful to unpack a nominalization like respect: interviews, vivas and exams are not just about respect; interviewers and examiners are not necessarily respectable in the literal sense, but may, however, expect to be accorded a degree of respect. Being clear about what one feels to be genuinely respectable might provide a touchstone.

6. The crowd

Interpretations: Public speaking is commonly feared and disliked, since the majority of people do not often have to do it. Some who are obliged to do it reach for a joke or a disarming smile and hope to bow out quickly, without anyone really noticing. Others, however, revel in the attention. As well as directly bringing up feelings and thoughts about public speaking, this visualization may reveal attitudes to popularity and social acceptance, and how far one is prepared to stand out against the majority and for what reasons. Again, there are leading questions at the end.

Uses as a change metaphor: This image can be used effectively when someone is developing the skill of public speaking – or speaking out. It is a means of testing out the gains against what could go wrong, preparing for the best rather than relying on just expecting the best. The image could also be used to encourage reliance on individual perceptions of truth rather than crowd-pleasing.

7. The journey

Interpretations: Many activities in life can be seen, metaphorically, as journeys, and there is a lot of imagery in common use around this – moving on, fellow travellers, taking steps, getting ahead, keeping on track, following the signposts, going on detours, taking the wrong turning, and so on. In this particular visualization, there is both choice and trust. People who are too self-reliant are sometimes wary of the transport they have to trust; people who rely too much on others may dither over the choice of transport and various other decisions. The questions that shape the rest of the visualization could be answered in many ways and would, like other questions in other visualizations, be answered differently at different times.

Uses as a change metaphor: Journey imagery is endlessly flexible and can be adapted to suit all sorts of concerns. If a person is moving away from a particular set of habits or from a particular negative relationship, they are travelling partly under their own steam but also partly obliged to trust to an unknown new way of being.

How we know that visualization works

Many books have been written on guided imagery, and plenty of research now shows the verifiable effects it can have. The bulk of it concerns how imagery can be used to enhance future performance, probably reflecting a cultural bias towards goals and achievement. There have, of course, always been stories around, about people who have used forms of imagery for this end, with spectacular results. For example, George Hall, an American soldier, was captured and interned for a long time in Vietnam. He was a keen golfer and, to keep himself sane, he played a round of golf in his head every day, carefully concentrating on the playing of each hole, and every single drive and putt, in his mind. Shortly after he was released, he played in the New Orleans Open and scored a 76 – right up there with the fully practised professionals.[4] Anecdotal evidence of this kind is probably enough to whet the appetite and arouse the interest of many – and, maybe, even the greed of some. Visualization is now widely used by sports coaches and by life coaches too. However, the effects would be unconvincing to serious scientists without formal studies. And these exist in abundance.

In one rather neat little study, one group of participants was involved in a physical exercise programme to improve finger strength whilst a second group, at set times and for set periods, simply imagined doing the exercise; a third group did no exercise at all. The result was a 30 per cent improvement in 'finger fitness' for the first group, none at all for the third but an astonishing 22 per cent improvement in actual finger strength for the second group of participants, who hadn't moved a muscle. In some extraordinary way, the brains of those people had fooled their bodies.[5] PET scanners – devices that indicate which areas of the brain are activated during various physical and mental tasks – have made it possible to measure the actual effect that imaginary rehearsal has on the brain. According to one of the world's leading researchers on brain rehabilitation, Ian Robertson (who quotes the finger strengthening study amongst others in his fascinating book *Mind Sculpture*), the studies show that 'imagining is not so very different from actually making the same movement, as far as the brain is concerned'.[6]

It is some leap from this kind of easily measured practical task and muscular performance to general visualizations affecting complex social performance, but it is one that is very possible to make. For example, 'Social Stories™' is a method developed in America by Carol Gray for working with children with autistic spectrum disorders. The approach is increasingly used in work with students at special schools or by special needs specialists in mainstream schools, and its use has also been extended to other pupils who need to develop and master new behaviours and strategies.[7] In a typical scenario, a story is developed which takes a student through what he needs to do in a particular social situation or activity. For instance, an autistic boy who frequently disrupts his school dinner queue with his outwardly bizarre behaviours is taken through a 'story' in which he acts in an appropriate fashion and does things other children would do. As the story progresses, each phase of activity is clearly imagined, described and rehearsed in concrete detail, focusing on and emphasizing positives and generally ignoring negatives, to give effective reinforcement. The story creates for him a substitute for the 'script' that other children unconsciously absorb, understand and generalize as part of their development. Social Stories™ can be created for a wide variety of concerns and for use with widely differing ages and abilities.

The term 'story' here does involve a certain amount of licence – it might well be a first-person monologue consisting of a series of statements about what the subject should do in this or that situation, although some Social Stories™ are third-person narratives. What is worked on is specific, referring to particular activities and preparing the mind and brain to engage in them effectively according to 'the rules' – autistic spectrum experts suggest that this kind of literalism is necessary, since metaphor can be difficult for people with these conditions. However, not dissimilar approaches have been used successfully with stroke victims. The visualizations are a little like those that sports players are trained to use, because these too concern activities with distinct rules in a strictly defined context, albeit allowing for variables within that context. But a substitute script absorbed in this way can gradually be generalized, by a metaphorical process, to different contexts – 'If it works in this way here, it could well work in a similar way over there'; 'This activity here, with which I am familiar, makes a template for the activity over there, about which I know nothing but which appears similar'. This, in fact, is how we naturally learn all kinds of social and other skills.

Therapists who make use of trance commonly encourage metaphorical as well as literal visualization of new, desired behaviours. Carl was a man who was unable to pee in the stalls beside other men, a relatively common complaint, though as far as he was concerned it made him very odd. His therapist had him turn taps on and off in his imagination, enjoy the remembered elation of watching waterfalls and fast rivers and recall what it had been like to dam and then unblock streams as a child in the company of other little boys. Harriet, who loved adventurous travel but was now in a severe funk, believing she would never find the right kind of confidence and mental order in time for final university exams, led an imaginary expedition through a jungle, dealing with all the many hazards as they came up one at a time. The added advantage of metaphor here is that, as well as serving to generalize the learning, it can get past superficial reluctance, and communicate directly to the receptive, unconscious levels of the mind the way that new behaviours or activities or habits will work.

The examples given so far have been future-focused. Guided imagery also has applications for both past and present, but these are less easy to study in a rigorous way. An effect can be monitored and measured over time: you can do your imagery now and measure its effects tomorrow and the next day and the next, comparing them with the effects achieved by others who didn't do any. Whereas measuring the effect of imagery on people's understanding of their own pasts and how they interpret their own concerns depends on subjective reporting, which is notoriously awkward and vulnerable to bias.

However, a particular visualization technique now increasingly used in the treatment of PTSD (and therefore a means of assessing the impact of imagery on past behaviour) would lend itself to scientific testing. This method is variously known as the rewind technique, the fast phobia cure and the VKD (visual kinaesthetic dissociation technique). It was originally developed by Richard Bandler, one of the co-creators of NLP (neuro-linguistic programming) out of an earlier technique used by Dr Milton Erickson. It has since been used widely and highly successfully in a refined form by human givens therapists.

Some informal preliminary research on it was carried out with a group of 30 clients seeing an occupational counsellor for trauma symptoms. Afterwards, 40 per cent rated the technique as extremely successful and 53 per cent rated it as successful. None rated it as poor or a failure.[8] Since then, a protocol for a randomized controlled study has been produced by an academic psychiatrist (a prominent researcher in the PTSD field), and the Human Givens Foundation, a charity established to widen knowledge of and expertise in the human givens approach, has been coordinating attempts to raise the necessary funds.[9]

Recent research by Joseph LeDoux and others has made much clearer the brain mechanisms involved in fear conditioning. It may also, as psychologist and Human Givens co-founder Joe Griffin has suggested, explain why a technique involving imagery would be likely to resolve PTSD.[10] Emotion is faster than thought; fear, we now know, shuts down the capacity for complex thinking and calls for immediate action – fight or flight in the classic description. The amygdala, an almond shaped mass of nuclei located deep within the temporal lobes and controlling, amongst other things, autonomic and emotional responses associated with fear, acts somewhat like a watchdog at the gate barking whenever there is possible danger. The adjacent hippocampus normally interprets the signals and gives them context, communicating with the neocortex, which interprets and stores memories for future reference. ('Well done, Rover. Yes, it's wolves on the prowl. We'll watch out for them and record the sighting.' Or perhaps 'Don't be silly, dog, it's just a shadow.'). But very high emotional arousal associated with traumatic events alters the circuit – the neocortex is inhibited so that clear thinking becomes difficult, whilst the hippocampus no longer 'talks' effectively to the amygdala because of the action of the stress hormone, cortisol. ('Oh my goodness, what! Oh dear me...for God's sake keep barking, Rover. I'll call the cavalry!') As a result, the fear can reach inappropriate levels and may continue to be triggered when the traumatic happening is over.

Most commonly, when we eventually calm down and things return to normal, there is an automatic correction as the context is appreciated. ('Didn't we get in a panic, Rover? There, there now. Yes, it was wolves and it could have been nasty, but they ran away when I waved my flaming torch around. Not every shadow is a wolf anyway. I reckon we can stoke the fire and sleep easy now.') However, PTSD sufferers, many of whom have suffered extreme and deeply disturbing trauma (equivalent to a prolonged wolf pack attack if you like), apparently don't go through this sorting out phase; the traumatic memory remains etched in the amygdala, the barking doesn't stop for long. It is as if the original event were somehow still present, always ready to beckon the sufferer back through a time-warp, into those terrible moments. The merest hint of the original event, a distant howl, a scratching, a shadow, anything that matches the pattern of the original experience, is enough to drag the consciousness back yet again.

To carry out the rewind technique, therapists deeply relax trauma sufferers and then guide them, as if they were a character in a video which is being rewound, in going quickly backwards through their trauma. Next the trauma is experienced as if in fast forward on a TV screen. After going backwards and forwards like this a number of times, in a calm state, Griffin suggests, the inappropriately prolonged inhibition of the hippocampus ceases so that the context can be recorded and coded properly as non-threatening. The client is aware of being in the present moment dealing with what is only a memory. The barking stops.

This powerful, past-focused technique, which is easily testable (no further troubling symptoms are experienced), strongly draws on human storytelling capacities. Often, indeed, the technique is particularly successful if individuals are invited to embellish the imagery in their own way, perhaps turning frightening individuals into ludicrous caricatures of themselves or adding in an action they wish they had made at the time.

There are plenty of ways of using guided imagery to enhance the present moment. For example, there is the special place technique, described in the next section, an apparently simple yet hugely powerful method of using imagery to access deeply relaxed states. There is also that intuitive interpretation of current trends and concerns which may occur after doing the kinds of visualizations presented earlier in this chapter. Or some people, myself very much included, find that it is possible to have a stock of images to bring to mind at moments of need. For example, at moments of potential stress in front of audiences, I summon up an image of clear, placid water, which for me instantly brings back effective and useful feelings of calm.

But imagery and 'inner storytelling' is not just a kind of mental gadgetry. There is something unexpected, marvellous and on occasions humbling about the ways it can work, the purposes it can serve. Sam was a keen and accomplished sportsman and much of his sense of meaning centred on his sport, which he had played from an early age. Now in his mid-40s, he had suffered episodes of sometimes disabling, though not clinically severe, depression, arising after the death of his father. However, his biggest concern was his loss of form in his sport and frequent outbursts of uncontrollable anger. He went to a therapist hoping to recapture his skills and self-control, which he did very effectively through a combination of relaxation, visualized rehearsal and various cognitive techniques.

In his final session, interpreting the therapist's instructions in his own way, Sam went into a profound trance and became absorbed in a kind of dream in which his father and another man played important roles. The other man turned out to be someone he had not thought of in years, but who had been an influential role model in his early sporting days. This man, emerging suddenly in this semi-waking dream, had all of the qualities of self-control, focus, humour and maturity that Sam was seeking, whilst Sam's father was there too, reassuring him in various ways. The experience and the memory of this very vividly imagined interaction served as a healing metaphor that worked with enormous effect. The depression and the anger disappeared and Sam's sporting performance went on getting better and better. The healing may have come out of the therapeutic work and associated practical tasks, but the metaphor came from the treasure vaults of Sam's own dreaming, associating, storytelling mind.

Four relaxation techniques

Guided imagery works best if people are relaxed. It is helpful, therefore, to know how to relax yourself and others. The following basic relaxation techniques can be done sitting comfortably in a chair.

1. Breathing

The key to relaxation is slow, steady breathing, with a longer out-breath than in-breath and with the breathing done from the diaphragm. Some people find counting helpful – inhaling to a mental count of seven and exhaling to a count of 11 (a technique known as 7:11)[11] or, if preferred, using the ratios of 5:9 or 3:7. Others prefer simply to focus on extending the out-breath without counting at all. It can be helpful to put your hands on your tummy and feel the way the diaphragm expels the air when you breathe out and then how the tummy swells as the air is taken in. The out-breath stimulates the parasympathetic nervous system, which controls relaxation. When it is stimulated, relaxation is automatic. It is interesting to compare this with the procedure used in war chants like the famous Maori haka, adopted by the New Zealand rugby team; here the common feature is a long in-breath suddenly and rapidly expelled. The in-breath stimulates the sympathetic nervous system, which awakens the body and gets it ready to go – what you'd want if you were going into battle. In relaxing, you are doing the complete reverse.

2. Body scan

This is a technique, well known to yoga practitioners, in which the attention is directed systematically around the body. You might start from the toes and move through the feet to the calves and thighs and upwards through stomach, back, chest and shoulders, down along the arms to the fingers, back up to the neck and head. You might equally start from the fingers. Or, if you know about muscle groups, you can work through these. The point is simply to become aware of the sensation in each part of the body and then to leave it and move on elsewhere. Some practitioners suggest tensing and then relaxing each muscle group as you go; others say that the focus should be on simply noticing and relaxing, using the steady breathing described above. The technique can be done lying down, if you prefer.

3. Sensory awareness – the 'three things' technique

This method is often used in preliminary meditation work and is comparable to a technique used in Gestalt therapy. It resembles the body scan in that you systematically direct attention, but this time to sensory information and imagery. In a comfortable position of your choice, you fix attention on one spot and then mentally note three things you can see in the periphery of your vision. You then close your eyes and mentally note three things you can hear. Opening your eyes, you go on to note three bodily sensations. Then you might repeat the cycle. As you run out of things to see, hear or feel, you substitute things you can imagine in each category. In some versions of the technique, touch and smell are included, so that all five senses are worked through.

4. The special place visualization

The special place technique is one of the simplest and yet most powerful visualizations possible. Versions of it crop up in very many relaxation and self-hypnosis cassettes and CDs.[12] It has been used to great effect by all kinds of people with diverse challenges to face – performers of endurance stunts, people preparing for operations, musicians, actors and public speakers, for example.

Imagine for a moment being in a very peaceful place, somewhere you feel very calm and secure and centred. You may like to recall a particular place you know or to dream up somewhere completely imaginary, perhaps using elements of different places. What sorts of sensations will you have? What kinds of sounds might you hear? Will it be warm or cool? Are there any aromas? Do you notice particular colours and shapes? You may want to spend some time exploring this space.

It is even more powerful when you 'relax into' this technique by imagining yourself approaching the place and taking 20 slow steps towards it or down to it. As you take each step, you count it to yourself and tell yourself you are becoming more relaxed with every step you take.

This technique is widely used because it widely works. By thinking about how it works, it is possible to understand a lot about the power of a visualization and hence also of the power of the vividly imagined story. When you go into the special place and imagine it as vividly as possible, you are summoning up memories of previous experiences of spontaneous relaxation and calm. It is then impossible not to feel at least some of the relaxation previously experienced. In a sense, the imagination is tricking the brain/body continuum. You might know that you are mentally conjuring up the feeling of warm water against your body or the sensation of cool air against your cheek, but somehow, to the brain/body, the warm water or the cool air is actually there. The more you imagine, the more deeply relaxed you may become. You are tapping into a relaxation resource. Imagination can tap resources.

Visualization and guided imagery with children

All of the visualization techniques discussed so far work just as well with children as with adults. The rewind technique is highly effective for dealing with children's traumatic and life-threatening experiences. Children can also learn to use guided imagery to improve their own performance in various skills as well as to promote healing in the ways discussed above. And children are especially receptive to stories, which for them can be very real experiences, seen, felt and vividly experienced.

There are, however, some distinctions between working in this way with adults and working with children that should be flagged up. For example, a lot of children don't expect to sit still for long. It might, of course, be good to train children to cultivate relaxation and calm repose, and there are certainly cultures in which this has traditionally been done. In fact, 30 years ago, even in this culture, short periods of quietening down and relaxing the body in preparation for acting out guided fantasy were considered a normal part of a school drama lesson, and children were also regularly exposed to forms of visualization as part of creative writing work. Nowadays, students are more likely to be asked to 'plan out' or 'think out' than vividly to imagine an activity – to be, if you like, sequentially intentional in what they do rather than glimpsing the whole pattern. You can't show your working for the inspectors, if it is in the mental theatre.

This is a case where, adjusting the popular phrase, it is unfamiliarity that breeds contempt. If I do a visualization with a group of unprepared children, I may get blank incomprehension or nervous giggles and restlessness. However, if I present it as an exciting story they can tell themselves through their imaginations, and go on presenting it with as much panache as I can manage, I find the response generally rapid and very good. Experience with telling stories and doing workshops for many hundreds of children, in large groups and small ones, has convinced me that almost all children can be drawn into the story trance eventually, given reasonable circumstances and support, and given reasonable skill and conviction. Almost all children, whatever their backgrounds, have extraordinary capacities for concentration, stillness and imaginative focus that are drawn on far too little in modern education. Very few adults retain the capacity to sit in a relatively uncomfortable position on a wooden floor, keeping their attention on the story they are hearing and imagining it in detail to the point where the floor and the room disappear for minutes or even hours. Very many children (in fact the vast majority) can do exactly that – even children labelled as having problems with concentration and attention.

Children don't have to sit still to imagine, in any case. Neither do they necessarily have to close their eyes. Many young children can be in an imaginative world with their eyes wide open, whilst moving around and doing something else. Children are not short of imagination. What they are increasingly short of is a purposeful programme for stretching imagination and focusing it as they grow up. Teenagers will often initially reject the idea of listening to a story and, even more so, doing a story visualization, again because of unfamiliarity. Yet, very frequently, they will rapidly drop the barriers and almost greedily drink up the stories and images, like people arriving at an oasis after a long trek in the desert.

Here is a short visualization that young children enjoy. (It also appeals to many adults who like fantasy scenarios and I have used it effectively with older children and teenagers too.) I have given just the 'bare bones' and it is not intended as a script for reading aloud. The language needs to be adapted to suit the age group. You may find it useful to experiment with it as a story, as a 'picturing challenge', as something to act out in mime or dance or whatever appeals to you. It might be helpful afterwards to go back to the list of questions presented with the earlier visualizations.

The golden staircase and the magic door

Imagine that you are walking in some open place you would very much like and enjoy and even find beautiful. As you walk, you suddenly come upon a marvellous golden staircase. Does it go up or down? Is it plain or decorated, straight or curved? At the top or at the bottom is a magic door, though you may not be able to get a clear image of it yet. If you go to the end of the staircase, however, you will be able to open the magic door. How slowly or quickly will you do that? Because the door is magic, there are many possibilities, so what will you find beyond the door?[13]

Visualizing for change

Out of a misty dream
Our path emerges...
– *Ernest Dowson (1867–1900)*[14]

To conclude this chapter, here is a traditional story in which the parallels with more formal guided imagery can be seen very clearly. It can be used, for example, in appropriate cases, as a preparation or backup to the rewind technique when working with fears and phobias, and it has many other healing possibilities as a metaphor. It is told here at some length and with a little literary artifice, yet it's a story that equally benefits from being told aloud – which leads us neatly on to the next chapter.

Three Hairs from a Wolf's Chin

I don't know exactly where and when it was that this happened – it's a tale passed on down the years, just as I'm passing it on now. And if it didn't happen the way I tell it to you now, it happened in some way.

There was a girl...well, a young woman some might say, but we'll call her a girl. She lived in some far off and remote northern land in a village on the edge of a great forest. Sometimes the cold winds of winter would howl amongst the pines and hurl crisp, cold snow that froze instantly on all the rocky outcrops; sometimes that wind would carry a different howling, the distant, mournful, chilling howling of wolves.

Now this girl was married young, as girls were in those lands, but not in the way that some of her friends had been made to suffer, to toothless men smelling too much of old meat and tallow. Her husband would have been her own choice even if her family hadn't selected him. She was proud of him. He was a fierce, fearless young hunter, but still capable of tender loving affection and understanding. The two lived in happiness. Soon they would have children and life would go on getting better.

But it did not. Not without trials and troubles at least. Something happened to change things. On a hunting expedition, the wind veered suddenly and viciously, blowing straight from the heart of the Arctic, the snow piled in wiping out all the trails and the young husband was separated from his fellows in a remote part of the forest. They came back without him and for seven weeks there was no sign of him as more and more snow crowded the air and blocked the forest trails. The girl mourned him daily, trying to keep a little flame of hope burning, praying to whatever gods or higher beings she and the other villagers believed in to protect his spirit. She asked the village shaman, a man who could see strange things beyond this world, if there was magic that could bring him back, but he only shook his head. 'You will see him again soon enough,' he insisted. 'Trust and wait!'

Well, that old shaman was just about right. One day, when the snow at last was melting and the warm spring sunshine was conjuring sudden small blue flowers out of the earth amongst the livid patches of green, her young husband marched back into the village, wild and dirty and strange and half starved, but alive. There were mighty celebrations in the village that night. At the feast, haltingly and with little of his old style and swagger, he told the story again of how he had survived, digging himself a lair in the frozen earth and the snow, roofing it with branches and managing to kindle a fire which he kept going as he could, venturing out to hunt and gather wood when and where he could – but always wary of the wolves. Now that he was alone and weak and they were half starved as he was, he had needed to take extra care. At night he had hardly slept lest the fire died down and they should find him there, helpless, unprotected, unguarded. More than once, they had been close, very close... He shuddered and stared and left the story unfinished.

Life went back to its old pattern – or that's what it was meant to do. The family and the village gave meat and other foods in plenty to the couple, since of course he would need time to get back his strength before he could hunt again. The air was warmer by the day and the bright birdsong filled the branches of the trees. But the young husband couldn't quite escape from the nightmare he had lived. Daily he kept watch outside the house, flinching at the slightest hint of a howl or even the yelp of a village hound, always on the lookout for the wolves that lived now in the depths of his own dreams. As for tenderness and affection, he had little enough of that left, so it seemed. The girl felt almost inclined to keep away from him – in the way you keep your distance from snappy dogs if you've any sense.

But still she didn't allow her hope to burn out completely. She went to the shaman again, feeling somehow angry and cheated. 'You told me I would see my husband again!' she hissed defiantly. 'But this is only his body, his shell. What has become of his spirit? What demons have stolen it away?'

'It is there,' the shaman smiled, 'and then it is not there, not yet. There is something you must do now to help me to make a magic that will give us the power to bring him back.'

'What must I do?'

'You must go into the forest yourself and you must come back with three hairs, plucked with your own hand from the chin of a living wild wolf, which you must not harm in any way. Those three hairs will give us the power we need.'

The girl came back from that shaman troubled and scared. The request was impossible, just a way of putting her off. How could you take hairs from a wild pack creature and live? Yet as she thought about it and watched her husband twitching and starting and fighting invisible foes, determination hardened inside her.

She went to that forest, by pathways that were clear enough now in the spring sunshine, pathways she'd learned well as a child. There was a part of the forest called Wolf Walk, because it was said the wolves often passed that way, on their way from their lairs in the craggy forest slopes to their own hunting. Here she climbed a tree and she waited and watched and watched and waited, through the rest of the day. In a large woven basket she'd carried on her back, she had meat in plenty. She hung that over a branch. Coiled up and attached to another smaller basket was a rope, which she now unwound and hitched over a branch, ready for use. Some of the meat she put into the smaller basket.

It took her by surprise. She had been staring so long and so hard, so expectantly that the merest shadow of a cloud moving over the furthest part of the forest had startled her more than once. But now, when the wolf arrived, loping noiselessly and cautiously through the bushes, it was on the path immediately below her before she registered it with a strange shock almost of familiarity. The wolf stopped suddenly, looked up at her, directly at her and gave a long, low growl. Not far away, another wolf gave a brief half howl, then another followed suit. Maybe this wolf was supposed to answer too, but it didn't. It froze, looking up at her suspiciously, its yellow eyes bright and wide, pink tongue peeping amid clouds of steamy breath, a glimpse or two of sharp white teeth under black gums. Everything was very quiet for a while, so that you could notice the sounds a more gentle evening wind made in the tops of the trees.

Then she began to lower the small basket. The rope made a soft sawing noise as it slipped over the branch, with occasional high pitched squeals. Slowly, slowly she let it down and the wolf watched, fascinated, sniffing, cowering for a moment when the basket slipped and jerked suddenly downwards, but then curious again, drawn by the enchanting smell. As it plummeted the last few feet, the wolf fell back, startled, shrinking down on its haunches, teeth bared. It stayed like that when the basket had settled and the rope was still – cautious, unsure, waiting for a minute, maybe two. Then very slowly it began to edge forward, stopping, freezing, checking again, its ears twitching, its nose too. Every so often, it would glance up at the girl in the tree to see what she was doing, growling, fierce. Then it reached the basket. A quick dart of the head and it came out with meat in its jaws, which it gobbled quickly. Then more, then more.

When she judged that the meat was all gone, the girl hauled on the rope and the basket sprang into the air. Shocked in the middle of a tasty mouthful, the wolf did nothing for moment. Then it leapt at the swinging basket, snapping at it furiously, but it was out of reach. It watched as she filled the thing again and lowered it down. Again it approached cautiously, less cautiously but still wary. Again it ate until the basket was taken away again – and filled again so that it could eat again. Each time she lowered the basket, the girl climbed down the tree a branch more, until the third time she was just about close enough to smell the wolf as it turned from the empty basket and looked questioningly up at her. 'No more today,' she smiled, shaking her head. 'Tomorrow. Come again then.'

As if it had understood, the wolf gazed at her for a moment, then wheeled around and slunk away into the shadows.

It did come back the next day, and the next and the next. Each time, she expected other wolves to arrive with it, but they didn't. It was always alone with her. Each time, she edged a little closer to that wolf, even daring to climb right down to the foot of the tree on the third occasion. Still it offered no threat, leaving the empty basket for her to carry away and disappearing into the forest when it had eaten its fill. The next day, she climbed down from the tree sooner and stood closer to the wolf, the next closer and the next closer still, until finally she could stand and watch it eat, just as if it were one of the village dogs. Then she sat down.

It suddenly occurred to her to do this. Up to that moment, she had always been wary, ready to run for the tree or to defend herself with a stick she carried. Now she plumped down on the soft, damp, mossy forest floor, defenceless. The wolf did too, not far away from her, close enough to touch, sitting and staring admiringly at her, clouds of rank wolf breath vanishing into the sharp spring air. It was quite a moment when she did touch that wolf – not on its chin of course, just a little smeary touch of the wet, black nose as it sniffed the hand she proffered. But it was a touch. After that she knew that she and the wolf were friends.

It was three more days more before she could think about getting what she needed. By that time she could sit with the wolf for half an hour or more, stroke it and even tickle its paws, a thing the creature had quite an appetite for. All the time she would glance at the muzzle of the wolf, the sharp teeth, the little fuzz of almost white hairs down under the chin. Quite suddenly, without really planning, she decided to do it, to risk everything. Still she prepared the ground carefully, starting a minor tussling game with the wolf, a play fight that had to be judged sensitively – not too rough, not too fierce, not the kind of struggle that would wake up those angry, dangerous instincts, just the kind of harmless romp in which a little tweak could be hidden. It worked. As she found the small chin hair clutched between her fingers and transferred it carefully to a leather pouch she wore, she felt a strange thrill of excitement and racing of the pulse – which she suppressed, just as she calmed the wolf down now. The other hairs would have to wait.

Two more visits it took before she had them. On that last occasion, as she stood up with the last hair secure in the pouch, the twilight had almost become night and the moon was peering through the tall pines. She wanted to race away, run straight to the shaman, insist on the magic then and there. Instead, she took her time, saying goodbye to the wolf and bowing her thanks. The wolf looked at her long and hard, its yellow eyes seeming almost to glow in the gloom. It watched her as she walked away carrying her empty basket, then, almost sorrowfully, slunk away into the forest. She turned to see it disappearing into the gloom and felt a tear well up in the corner of her eye.

But when she confronted the shaman, she felt proud. 'Here are the three hairs you asked for! Now please can you make the magic that can bring back my husband?'

'How did you come by these?'

She told him and the old man smiled, showing his gapped yellow teeth. 'Yes, I can make the magic now,' he said, throwing the three hairs into the fire, where they shrivelled up with a brief smell of scorch, muttering what the girl took to be words of power. 'But I still need you to make it work.'

'What must I do now?'

The shaman smiled again impishly. 'It takes skill, care and patience to tame a wolf so well that you can take hairs from its chin. Now you have learned those skills, you must use them again. After the wolf, your husband should be easy to tame.'

That's the magic the girl used and it worked very well.[15]

Chapter 3

The Way You Tell 'Em: The Art and Craft of Oral Storytelling

How long is a piece of string?

> *– Anon.*

Why bother to tell stories to people who can read? It's a simple and perhaps simplistic question, but it warrants an answer here. Storytelling and story writing are a continuum. But telling stories has some distinct qualities and some particular advantages and these need to be spelt out, since it is very easy to confuse the telling of stories with the mere recitation of the written word – a mistake very frequently made by the media. I have various cuttings from newspapers around the country, reporting public appearances I've made at libraries and festivals and public sites as a professional oral storyteller, and describing how I 'read' my stories to the children. Ask in any bookshop for storytelling audio and you'll be referred to CDs and tapes of famous actors reading scripts. There are even professionals who act the part of storyteller fairly convincingly, reciting what are essentially unvarying monologues that make no concessions to time and place and people.

There is no doubt a role for that kind of thing, but this is not the art of oral storytelling, as has been practised for centuries in traditional cultures throughout the world. Once, some villagers in a remote part of the developing world were given a television set. After two or three weeks, they gave it back. 'We prefer our storyteller,' said the villagers. 'But the television knows far more stories than your storyteller,' said the exasperated donors of the goggle box. 'That may be so,' said the villagers, 'but our storyteller knows us.'

Oral storytelling, in its true sense, could usefully be redeveloped and extended in our modern culture, if we focus on its special qualities and advantages. Some of these follow.

- Telling a story enables you to pace that story perfectly for the individual listener or the group. It is possible to take extra time over one part of a tale, to draw the listener(s) in, to a greater extent, or to abridge another section because you sense that attention is flagging. In other words, you can make your storytelling highly time-, place- and people-sensitive. No recited or written tale can do this.

- Telling a story freely allows you to bring out a different emphasis in a tale to suit the occasion and listener(s), whereas recited and written tales do not have this flexibility.

- Many brief tales have tremendous metaphorical depths, yet they may be skipped over quickly on the page, just because they are short, and the full meaning is not absorbed. There is a cultural bias towards instant understanding – if you don't get it instantly, there's something wrong with you or the text is stupid and obscure. A skilled telling holds up a tale for long enough to let it register; it makes it live in the imagination so that it is far more likely to be heeded both consciously and unconsciously.

- Telling stories is an imaginative interaction in which listeners actively participate. The way a story develops on a particular day depends a lot on the quality of the rapport established between listener(s) and teller. Hence surprising things can happen, unexpected by either teller or listener(s). And surprising and new things can keep on happening with retelling.

- Storytellers get to know a story much better and from many more angles than do story writers, because they may very well tell it many times over and incorporate it into their lives, rather than writing it once, or drafting it two or three times.

- When a traditional or anonymous story is told, the teller does not have to identify with it in the way that a writer would regard a story as somehow representing him or her. The teller is merely passing the story on, not attempting to fix it in perfect form, so attention can move away from form and towards content.

- As already suggested in Chapter 1, telling stories is naturally trance-forming, tending to stimulate the activity of the 'right brain' which works more through context and association of ideas than the more linear 'left brain'.[1] This has many advantages in one-to-one and small group work and also in presentations to larger groups.

You probably already know a version of this next story, but anyway...

The Way You Tell 'Em

A man is visiting some soldiers, who are guarding the frontier. When it comes to evening time, they have a strange way of entertaining themselves. They gather around in a bar and have a drink or several, then one of them jumps up in front of the others and shouts out a number – 39 maybe, or 52 or 71; it doesn't seem to follow any particular pattern. But the result is always the same – they all fall about laughing.

Now the visitor is very curious about this and wants to know what's happening, so he asks the barman, who explains that they're telling jokes. Since they know each other very well and there are no new jokes coming along, they've exercised the military taste for efficiency and streamlined the process of joke telling by giving all the jokes specific numbers. You say the number and the gang remembers the joke and they all laugh.

Well, the man is very impressed and impatient to have a go himself so, the next time there's a bit of a lull, he shouts out '49!' There is a deathly hush and they all stare at him blankly. The man looks at the barman and whispers, 'What did I do wrong?'

'Just watch me,' the barman whispers back. Then he leaps up onto the bar, fixes the upturned faces with a significant sort of look and he spreads his arms dramatically as he bellows: 'Come on, now, fellas, listen to this one! You're gonna really love it. 49!' Huge guffaws and everyone is chortling and slapping the barman on the back and buying him drinks. Eventually the visitor gets to talk to him and he says, 'So what's the difference? I said 49 and you said 49.'

'Yup,' drawls the barman, 'but, you see, it's the way you tell 'em.'

Everyone is a storyteller. But it could be irritating to buy a book to find out about telling stories and then be told that you are already a natural storyteller, so just get on with it. Most people interested in developing their storytelling abilities want to know more about techniques, ways of learning, tips about getting it across, and so on. So this chapter is about some of the art and craft of storytelling – the way you tell 'em. And it's about the way you tell 'em where, since many stories can change their meaning and effect according to situation.

Fibbers and fantasists – getting started

The Vicar and the Grindstone

According to an English legend, the people of a certain village held an annual lying competition. Champion liars won a large grindstone to display in the window of their cottage and this was much coveted. One year, a new vicar had recently taken up residence in the parish. He noticed the gathering on the village green and joined the listeners, smiling pleasantly at the thought of witnessing a quaint rural custom. But his benign smile faded to be replaced by an increasingly sour frown, as one after another, villagers got up and spouted complete nonsense – journeys to the moon, walking under the lakes, strange and impossible creatures and all sorts more. Eventually he jumped up in front of them all and cried, 'Stop! Stop this at once! This is outrageous. You are all telling lies! This is wicked! This is evil! Lying is wrong. I myself have never told a lie in all my life!' Well, the villagers looked at each other and they agreed unanimously on the results of the contest. They gave the new vicar the grindstone.[2]

As I said, everyone is a storyteller. Think of how we make excuses, part true, maybe, part white lie or even all black fib. Just about everyone has done it for good reasons or bad. You could find your mind racing, to make that excuse credible, to convince, to make it feel really true... Lying and excuse making are just two everyday activities in which one uses the 'fiction spinner' without thinking of it as being formal storytelling. A sure-fire way of getting people of all ages to tell each other stories is to start from the skill of fibbing – or, if you prefer, fantasizing. Here's a game I call Tall Stories – or, for young players, Fantastic Fibs. It is a game designed for two or more people and also works in quite large groups.

Tall Stories

Someone is the storyteller and the partner or group listens as the storyteller briefly describes something that 'happened' to them that was, literally, fantastic or at least a little unusual. It can be completely made up or else be based on an actual event, with some exaggeration. It can be stated in one sentence or several. (The kind of fiction will vary with the age and/or sobriety of the people involved. Children are usually perfectly happy to talk about flying to the moon or bouncing off the Eiffel Tower; adults may want to be more plausible – or, at least, to invoke popular fantasies like levitation or UFOs.) Then, to try to find out how much of the tale is true, the partner or group asks a set number of questions (say seven, initially) of the 'But how did...?' 'Why did...?' variety, which encourages the storyteller to elaborate further on the fiction. Direct questions about the truth or falsehood of the narrative are strictly forbidden. The questions generally make the story grow – it becomes more elaborate as the teller is forced to add detail and 'logic'. After a period of time (or a set number of questions), the story can be retold, incorporating the extra details. I often get listeners, not tellers, to do the re-telling, allowing them to add their own new details as they do so, which is a good illustration of how stories grow.[3]

It struck me early in my use of this game that it represents very well in external form what happens within the fiction-spinning mind. Good writers do it consciously, of course. They dream up an idea or an image and then they bring in the critical, question-asking bit, which says, 'But how? Why? Where?' Children often enjoy it for the sheer pleasure of telling a whacking big whopper.

Adults may find the game works best for them if, as a variable, there is the possibility that the story is literally true and, in this form, the game resembles some that have become radio and TV panel games in the past.

As well as being a good lead-in to telling stories, this game teaches several important things about stories and the telling of them:

- that you can be wild and wacky and invent something 'off the wall'

- that you may then have to make conscious use of your fiction-spinning mind, to justify and develop the story

- that the story can become more interesting and plausible as you do this

- that there is such a thing as story logic, which it is essential to exploit and develop if you want your story to work

- that it is possible to be critical about stories and yet enjoy the fantasy involved at the same time

- that one can, to a degree, trust one's natural storytelling capacity to throw up ideas – as long as you are prepared to run with them

- that almost any story idea can be made to work if you let it.

Working on storytelling skills in this way often releases inhibitions. The rules of the game forbid anyone from directly contradicting any statement, thus stimulating trust and a sense of acceptance, allowing experiment.

Playing Tall Stories can also, incidentally:

- encourage resilience and 'mental bounce' (*If I can make you believe that, I can make others believe in me too*)

- help develop the skill of seeing something through to its end

- inspire confidence

- improve social skills and general empathy (*I see what you might be thinking and can respond in advance to that*)

- improve verbal fluency.

And then there is the powerful 'as if' element. Suppose you are someone who has lacked confidence in certain social settings. Try telling a tall story about how you once knocked 'em flat with an impromptu performance at a party or at a meeting, and how everyone was hanging on to your every word and action. As you do this and answer questions about it, you are likely to be imagining how it feels to be confident in such a situation. You are, in effect, rehearsing that behaviour for possible future use. Once you have imagined something, you have set up an expectation. Expectations tend to realize themselves if they are possible and realistic.

Wicked Whoppers

A variant of the Tall Stories game is Wicked Whoppers. It works in the same way as Tall Stories, but this time the storyteller has to invent a rumour about someone not present – a family member, friend, acquaintance or even a celebrity. When questioned about its veracity by the partner or group, the storyteller must advance compelling reasons for believing it to be true. Again, the questions have to start from the assumption that the rumour might be true. Comments such as, 'You can't believe anything people tell you', 'She was lying to you', 'They made it all up' aren't allowed. Instead, questions need to be of the open variety: 'What makes you believe that?' 'How did that affect him/her?'

The Wicked Whoppers game helps us, in a fun way, to take a deeper look at why we might believe something. Do we often claim a story is true because we implicitly trust the person who told us? Why do we trust that person? What are his/her credentials for truth telling? Were we given concrete evidence? How else did they convince us? Someone using storytelling skills needs to know how to make a story about someone else credible. The game rehearses all this. Also, people commonly imagine all sorts of things about other people, a habit (some might call it an appetite) all too often fed by the media. It can be deeply damaging. This game, suitably adjusted, can provide a relatively safe environment in which to challenge such imaginings in a gentle way.

There are times when it is necessary to have some conception of how characters in a tale might think and feel and act, and to enter into their personalities and think as they might think – just as there are other times when one stands outside and observes and comments on them. That is part of narrative skill. The third game, Being Joe Bloggs, is about using and developing role-playing skills in the context of a story.

Being Joe Bloggs

The storyteller becomes either a named character in a story well known to the group, or else a character type (for children, perhaps a giant or a prince or princess or a wizard; for adults, maybe a lawyer or dustman or politician or bus driver). The storyteller makes up an episode or entire story, and tells it from their character's perspective and then answers questions from the group about their role – why they did this or that, and so on. If appropriate, the storyteller can be encouraged to adopt the mannerisms and personality of the character or character-type. Being Joe Bloggs allows people to act out and think out a role in a way that doesn't involve going on stage and making a display. It also gives them permission to explore different attitudes and reactions, because they don't have to be themselves. Most people find they have a 'script' ready – they have some idea of how to play the wronged innocent or the classroom bully, even if they have never been called to do so before. Role-play is a form of storytelling that makes use of the human capacity to take in and absorb whole patterns more or less unconsciously. Like Wicked Whoppers, Being Joe Bloggs also enables people to rehearse success in a chosen area.[4]

The guitarist and composer Bryan Lester tells the story of a close professional associate of his who was asked many years ago, in the era of the Beatles, to hear a promising young guitarist. He was ushered into the cosy front room of a small semi-detached house in Manchester, given a cup of tea and told that the budding genius would make his entry shortly. Meanwhile, a record of the Fab Four was placed on the turntable. With the first loud clang of the guitar chords, a small figure burst in, sporting a mop wig and brandishing a cardboard guitar. This apparition proceeded to gyrate around the room, miming playing the instrument and mouthing the words, whilst the parents cooed admiringly, "E's good, in't 'e?' Being Joe Bloggs can help someone develop a more realistic picture of what they actually need to do to achieve their goals.

Stretching stories

Stretching stories, making them grow in interesting ways and come to life, is one of the most basic skills of the storyteller. Detail is what makes the story work, drawing listeners into the narrative. It is also what can make it founder and struggle. Most of us can recall glazing over as someone goes into a blow-by-blow account of a visit to the doctor or an insignificant conversation. We need to know what to put in – and what to leave out. The game Embroidery is an enjoyable way to practise this.

Embroidery

Someone tells a short story. This may be a new tale quickly learned from a brief outline (such as some of those presented in Chapters 5 and 6) or it could be one already known. The storyteller tells one sentence, after which the partner or group asks up to three questions about the narrative so far. Questions must be relevant to the story. The storyteller must answer the question and return to the narrative as smoothly as possible, taking the action forwards in another single sentence. The partner or group asks questions again, and so on. To make it more exciting as a group game, a time limit of five minutes can be set for the telling of the tale. The teller tries to get to the end of the story within that time, whilst the partner or group tries to stop this happening through the questioning. The game can be varied by allowing the storyteller more sentences at a go or by increasing the number of questions that can be asked between them.[5]

The art of embroidering a narrative is such a central element of fiction making that it always surprises me when teachers to whom I have explained this game treat it as a passing curiosity. Good detail is entirely functional, never merely decorative. It helps readers or listeners to imagine, to enter the story-listening trance that lets them 'go with' the story. The game is also a means of showing that stories are essentially flexible patterns, not set pieces – but also that stories can remain essentially the same, and yet can be dressed differently at different times and for different purposes.

The Rich Woman and the Hat Maker

An attractive and very rich (but still perhaps too thrifty) American woman was invited by an English lord to Royal Ascot, so of course she would have to have a hat – an original, different, stylish and expensive hat. For this, throwing her usual caution to the wind, she went to the most original, different, stylish and indeed expensive designer in town, who listened as she explained her requirements – the colours she liked, the shapes, the patterns and above all, the *simplicity*. Meanwhile, he looked at her closely, studying her profile, the tone of her cheeks, the colours of her eyes. Then he went to work.

The rich woman watched in amazement as he took some crimson silk ribbon and began to twist it here and tie it there and loop it around until in a few minutes he had made an extraordinary, original and very stylish yet very simple hat. 'Something like this?' he said as he placed it carefully upon her head.

'Something exactly like this!' said the rich lady, looking at herself in the mirror. She knew that she looked stunning and was positively purring with pleasure at the effect. 'I'll take it!'

'That will be seven hundred pounds please,' said the designer.

'What!' said the woman, remembering her habitual ways at last, 'I'm not paying that much for a ribbon!'

The designer promptly took back the hat, untied the knots and unlooped the loops and finally presented the woman with the original length of ribbon. 'The ribbon,' he said, 'is free. Please take it!'

Remembering and 'fixing' stories

Donald Alistair Johnson was a storyteller in the South Uist tradition. In an old field recording, he is very clear about the importance of really living the story:

> You've got to see it as a picture in front of you or you can't remember it properly... I could see if I were looking at the wall there, I could see just how they were – the people – how they came in – and how this thing was that and the other.[6]

Many people would have little difficulty in recalling a dramatic and dangerous incident from their own lives or how it felt when they first fell in love, despite the fact that many years have since gone by. Details may blur and confusions may arise, but the essentials still stand out. On the other hand, what we did yesterday morning or even how we drove back from the supermarket an hour ago can be a hopeless blur.

The difference has to do with levels of attention. A dangerous and dramatic event rivets and narrows our attention, mobilizes all sorts of automatic physical reactions, hones our responses ready for fight or flight. We are on alert – and it pays to store the memory, in case the situation occurs again. Each time we recall the event, a little of the original feeling may come back – though our memory of it, like all memories, will subtly change over time, depending on our 'framing' of it and various other factors. Traumatic memories, like cherished ones, are returned to again and again, albeit for different reasons – retold, in effect, like stories.

It is slightly misleading to compare the learning of stories with extreme, survival-oriented learning or other emotionally loaded experiences, since, with a narrative, one wants not only to 'feel' a tale through one's emotions but also to stand outside it sufficiently to note and record its pattern, so as to be able to retell it. But to learn stories and to learn them well, it is best to make use of the natural attention capacities of the brain. Go with the story, get into the story, travel with the narrative, make the story your own – these are all instructions commonly given by experts on telling and learning tales. In essence, they are saying, you don't learn, you experience – you enter into the story trance and then the story is something that really happened to you and you can reconstruct it. You have to be engaged by it and also by the way it is told.

But there is perhaps a strand or two more to it than simply the 'seeing', because it is possible to sense a tale as if you were right inside it with the events happening all around you or, alternatively, to observe the tale from the outside, as a watcher and commentator. Probably an effective storyteller does both, sometimes almost simultaneously. One way or another, the result is vivid and arresting mental imagery that sticks.

There is a lovely little story in *The People of the Sea* by David Thompson, a book which centres on the Silkie or Selchie legends well known along the western coast of Scotland and the northern coast of Ireland and in the various islands between and beyond. Here it is, in my summary. (In the book, the long story mentioned is fully told.)

The Little Tailor and the Silkie Tale

In a village there was an old man, who was a great storyteller, known for the telling of one particularly long story. Indeed, he was famous for the telling of it, since it was his best tale, and people would come from far and wide to hear him. Now, there was a little travelling tailor who, whenever he came to the village, would ask the old man to tell him that story. He evidently wanted it for his own repertoire of stories, with which he would regale the people of the villages he visited – travelling tailors were known in those parts for their skill as storytellers and it was almost the expected thing that they would tell a tale as they worked. However, the old man steadfastly refused, whatever encouragement whether by way of reward or rivalry the tailor would offer him – this despite the fact that he happily told the tale when the tailor wasn't there and he begrudged it to no one else. Then the tailor stopped visiting. One night the old man began to tell his story and he told it better than he had ever told it before. He held his audience in rapt attention for over an hour and, at the end of it, they were all awe-struck and in the deep silence of vivid imagining. But, in the mind of the little tailor, there was simply pure glee. For he had sneaked up into the loft before the storytelling had started and now ran out of the house, shouting, 'I have it! I have it!'[7]

I recall being a little awestruck myself when many years ago I first read this story because, at the time, I was attempting to become a teller of tales. A mere travelling tailor (not even a professional!) had been able to recall an hour's worth of narrative and be certain that he 'had it' as soon as it was done, whilst I at that time had to concentrate hard to remember 15-minute stories. But time went by and, not so very long after, I listened to a Scottish traveller storyteller from a family steeped in tradition, stumbling, not as it happened particularly eloquently, through a story that lasted about 45 minutes. Not particularly eloquently – but with conviction. I realized afterwards that the story had been very real to him and he was telling us about something he had more or less seen with his own eyes – all of which made the story real and entirely riveting to his listeners, myself very much included. So I 'had' that story, which I'd never heard before nor have seen written down since, and can tell it to this day.

Once a story becomes real to you, you tend to remember it. And the more you remember the more you are able to remember. But memory is not, as in popular thinking, like a film in a personal library of multisensory DVDs. Press the right button and bam! Up jumps the memory, all perfectly etched and recorded and you watch it all through. That's how it feels, so that's how it is. Memory researchers and theorists have long ago discarded this notion – as have courts of law, which now refuse to accept testimony from witnesses who have been hypnotized in order to enhance their recall. Memory of events is notoriously unreliable and easily influenced by suggestion. It involves re-making the experience, putting it together anew from an assortment of associated fragments. Memories are not there to be reaped at any time in just the same form; when we reconstruct them, we subtly change them. Experience and the mechanisms of association are constantly working on and sculpting new shapes and new patterns from the material of memory.

Although memory is unreliable because it constantly changes, it is not random; it is self-organizing in various different ways. The billions of neurons within the brain organize themselves by processes of association into networks that 'wire together and fire together', according to the 'Hebbian learning principle', first outlined by Canadian psychologist Donald Hebb. We remember not just separate little unrelated bits but series and sequences of bits that 'belong' together – or rather, things that have been brought, consciously but more often unconsciously, together by all kinds of internal and external processes. We constantly use and update these patterns to relate to and organize new experiences and new learnings.

Studies of the stories and songs of some tribal peoples have suggested that narratives have themselves been used as mnemonic devices. In *The Songlines*, Bruce Chatwin described the way songs were used by Australian aboriginal peoples to navigate their way across what were, to outsiders, 'featureless' deserts – but, to them, peppered with sacred sites with mythological significance.[8] A Canadian anthropologist, who had worked with native American peoples in the far north of his country, told me how he had once travelled through the Rockies with a young native American who had been educated in all the old tribal lore by the elders. This man, who had never been in that part of the world before, would every now and then take a detour from the main road to visit certain sites hidden away. How did he know about these? Through the stories he had been taught, which contained, in a kind of fabulous code, a map of the area. And yet the tribe he came from could not have lived in that part of America for hundreds of years. Stories, my anthropologist informant opined, should not be tampered with excessively since we do not know what maps they may contain.

That, of course, is a salutary warning to anyone inclined to think all tales are up for grabs or intent on ransacking tribal mythologies for 'multicultural materials'. Stories have all sorts of aspects and one should never glibly assume total understanding. On the other hand, it is possible to be too much in awe of oral traditions and oral memory. Jazz pianist Hugh Ledigo told me this anecdote about a young composer who was studying in Germany around the beginning of the 20th century. To make ends meet, he wrote arrangements for the brass bands that were very popular at the time, and employed an old copyist to write out the parts neatly. Local legend had it that this old craftsman had once worked for the great master, Beethoven. The young composer was awed and fascinated and, one day, he asked the old man what the maestro was like. The old man looked up over the small gold-rimmed spectacles perched on the end of his ancient nose and seemed to be peering into the depths of his memory like a seer staring into the glowing embers. Eventually, he said, slowly and deliberately: 'Ze backs of hiss hands vere very hairy.'

There are many ways of aiding the processes of story memorization. While it is probably best to develop your own methods, here are some hints, tips and techniques that many people have found useful.

Pay attention

Give the telling (whether heard or read) your full attention but in a relaxed way, allowing it to 'enchant' and to fire your imagination. Don't make too much effort to 'think' and 'understand'; allow the story trance to happen. Stories are meant, first of all, to be fun. Paying attention is the first part of the storytelling 'attention bargain' involved in storytelling – which I'll explain later.

Have a good idea of the basic structure

When you are reviewing a story and your memory of it (especially in the earlier stages of developing story skills), it can help to make a skeleton of it, which you'll 'flesh out' in your own way. The elements that get removed in this process are probably those that have been added to a tale in the telling and in the repetition, and are the variable elements you may also want to vary. Many very long stories turn out to consist of a series of separate episodes that can be thought of as separate short tales, so that the task of memorizing becomes much easier. Some people like to write down key points. (There are some stories with brief skeleton summaries included in Chapter 6.)

Make multisensory pictures

Some people like to explore a tale through the imagery of sight, sound, smell, taste and touch, to create vivid multisensory 'pictures'. You could also pick particular images from each stage of the tale, to create a kind of map of the story. Studies of memory have shown that imagery is particularly useful for tying together ideas. Popular books on memory, such as those by Tony Buzan, generally recommend use of multisensory imagery to embed lists of facts and all sorts more.[9] Stories, though, are readymade imagery, so it is rarely necessary to introduce extraneous images to anchor them. Exceptions would be lists or a sequence of events that needs to remain intact. Generally, images from within the tale work best, though some people find that, for example, mentally positioning these images in order along a road they know or in different rooms of their houses visited in sequence helps them to get the tale mentally mapped.

Allow it to make sense and then more sense

It is a good idea to tell stories to which you respond imaginatively and emotionally and/or which make good sense to you, but also to allow more sense to emerge over time and repeated telling. Few stories have just one point; the best ones have multiple levels of interpretation and reference, and can be seen in many different ways over time, as they connect with different experiences and perceptions.

Review the sense

It also helps to fix a tale if you review the senses a story might have (so far as you can see) and the situations in which you might use it. You might want to consider alternative meanings and metaphorical uses, while still staying open to reinterpretations over time.

Keep lists

It is helpful, when learning to tell tales, to keep a list of stories you can tell and their possible uses, and to add to it regularly. You can also group these into categories – although it is best to keep these flexible, since stories will – and should – leap out of category from time to time. Rigid categorization can be restrictive.

Be alert to the mood

Consider the mood and 'feel' of a tale and its likely emotional effect. This is an important part of its impact and an essential factor in deciding whether to tell a story at a particular time to a particular person or group. Some stories allow a lot of scope for the kind of elaboration that can calm people down, getting them imagining clearly, and relaxing as they imagine. Other stories can be exciting or disturbing or challenging or puzzling. All of these moods have their place at the right moment. A skilled teller knows how to adjust a story, playing up mood elements as and when appropriate.

The Perfect Storyteller (episode 1)

Once long ago far away, in the days when powerful people could listen with concentrated attention and imagination and pigs could fly backwards, there was a king who had not one, not two but a hundred storytellers, each of them skilled in the art and the craft of telling stories, each of them versed in a thousand tales, each of them different in their different ways with different voices, different eyes, different ways of telling different tales. This king, you see,

---

loved stories, adored stories, lived and breathed stories. So much so that he decided to become a teller of tales himself.

What had stopped him doing that before? Time, of course. There had never been time. He was a monarch, with a monarch's duties and responsibilities. Stories were how he had relaxed and enjoyed himself. But now...well, he would become a prince among tellers, once the secrets of the very best ways of telling stories had been conveyed to him...

(to be continued)

Stretching stories again

Stretching stories, to repeat, is one of the most basic but essential skills of the storyteller. It is really very natural to embroider stories in the telling. A good storyteller knows not only how to do this, but also how not to do it – how to control the use of detail to get particular effects. The golden rule of all embellishment of stories is that it helps to make the story come to life for the listener(s). Embroidery that loses the audience in its detail or draws excessive attention to its own cleverness is not generally useful in oral telling. This next game is a more advanced form of the Embroidery game presented earlier in this chapter.

Reverse Embroidery

The aim of this game is to teach control of detail in a fun way. It requires a storyteller, audience (one listener or more) and referee, whose decision is final. The storyteller attempts to prolong a short story – say, a fable or joke or a brief anecdote, which must be known to the referee or listeners – for five minutes or any other desired length of time. The storyteller tries to string out the tale by adding details in as many ways as possible, introducing extra histories and all kinds of information about incidental characters, scenes, events, etc. However, the audience may challenge any embroidery that appears irrelevant and the referee stops the clock whilst the storyteller attempts to justify its use. The referee can accept the explanation or uphold the objection. If it is accepted, the storyteller scores a point. If the objection is upheld, the audience scores a point. If the story doesn't last the allotted time, the storyteller loses. If it does last the course, the storyteller gets an extra point. At the end, the storyteller and the audience add up their own points, and the winner is the one with the most.

Both of the Embroidery games are from my booklet *Yarn Spinning*, which includes a variety of games for developing the skill of elaborating stories.[10]

Shaping the meaning

The Apprentice, the Honeypot and the Scissors

A tailor received a large pot of honey as a gift from a relative in the country. He needed to go out shortly after its arrival, so he looked sternly at his apprentice who would have to mind the shop (and whom he didn't trust to leave the honey alone), and said solemnly, 'Look at this pot carefully. It looks very much like honey, but beware because it is actually deadly poison.' So saying, he placed the honey pot on a high shelf. 'Make sure no one touches it!' he added fiercely, as he walked out of the shop.

The apprentice watched him until he was well out of sight. Then he took his master's very best scissors and hid them under his robe. Next he ran along the street, shouting loudly, 'Stop thief!' But once he was in another street, he suddenly calmed down. He found a hardware shop and sold the scissors for as good a price as he could get. He then hid the money away in a secret place, well away from the shop. Next he returned to the shop and ate up all of the honey. When he had done that, he lay down in a back room and slept until shortly before he knew the master was due to return. (There were no customers, so he was undisturbed.) Just before his master was due, he went into the shop, where he lay on his back, moaning and groaning loudly and clutching his tummy and attracting a crowd of people from neighbouring shops, who clustered outside the door and began to call out to him, asking what was wrong.

The tailor came back at last, saw his apprentice writhing on the floor, and glanced immediately up at the shelf. He noticed at once that the pot wasn't there. Looking closer, he saw the empty pot beside the apprentice...

This Arabian folk tale has a clever denouement and I will complete it shortly. But at this point I would like to ask you with whom your sympathies lie. The tale is told here in a fairly flat way, as far as possible sticking to the facts. Nevertheless, perhaps the tailor's mistrust and slightly pedantic manner has already prejudiced you against him in favour of what seems merely rascally behaviour on the part of the apprentice? Or maybe the completely unprincipled behaviour of the lad makes you hope he gets his come-uppance.

How would it be if we began the story like this?

> There was once a kindly old tailor who wanted to give a rough local lad a bit of a chance in life, so he took him on as an apprentice. Every day, he would carefully and patiently show him the essentials of his craft, but the lad paid scant attention, preferring to finish his duties as early as he could, so that he could play cards with the other apprentices of the town...

Or like this?

> There was once a country boy who had five sisters and six brothers and a poor old mother, who was widowed. So he went to town and got himself apprenticed to a tailor, so that he could learn a trade and make some money and help his family. The tailor gave him barely enough pay to survive on, but, by dint of carefully rationing himself, he managed to send home a few copper coins each week, which was some help, though the family still suffered terrible hardship...

Quite obviously, if either of these brief blocks of text were added to the tale, you would be likely to see the story differently. I'll leave you to decide which opener you want to go with, but here is the missing bit of the story.

> 'Oh, oh, oooooooooh!' groaned the apprentice, writhing and thrashing around. 'Master, I'm so pleased that you've come back, so that I'm able to confess before I die.'
>
> 'Whatever do you mean?' asked the astonished tailor.
>
> 'Oh, master!' the apprentice howled between spasms, as the crowd fell silent so that they could catch what he was saying. 'The most terrible thing happened. Whilst you were out, I had to go to answer a call of nature and a thief came into the shop and stole your best scissors. I saw him as he left but I was too late to catch him, even though I pursued him for as long as I could. So then I came back here and I knew how cross you would be with me and I thought about the terrible thing

I'd allowed to happen and I decided that it was better to end my life. So, master, I have eaten all of the terrible poison that was in that honey pot and I am now waiting for it to take its effect. Oh, oh, ooooooh!'

Well, the crowd was very sympathetic when they heard the story and the tailor was stymied. The apprentice got away with it. Should he have done?

Although we know intuitively that there is more than one way of telling a story, we rarely spot the manipulation that makes us go down one track rather than another, in our interpretation of it. The way in which a story is told can shape its meaning.

Techniques from traditional telling

The Perfect Storyteller (episode 2)

The king called all the storytellers before him and told them to get together and to discuss and analyse and boil their knowledge down to principles he could learn and stories he could tell to perfection. 'I wish to become,' he said with enormous emphasis, 'the very best among you. Spare no expense in preparing for me a manual that will show me all the most important and essential elements in this art of yours...'

(to be continued)

Traditional tellers of tales typically use a variety of techniques and it is possible to learn from them, even if your context for telling is entirely different from what you might associate with the traditional. Here are some useful devices to consider.

Standard openings

Once upon a time... is just one of many traditional formulas used to begin stories, and has been more than a little over-used, of course. So it may not often be appropriate, except for very young children or for satirical purposes. Other openings that are less familiar to many, and therefore have a fresher feel, include *It was not in my time and it was not in yours, but it was in someone's time* (Celtic) or *My story is long and slippery as a snake. Listen well, for, if you only see the head or the tail, how will you know what the body is like?* (Egyptian).[11] This second, rather baroque, way of beginning shows another strand of effect worth studying: it is a metaphor and it takes you straight into metaphorical ways of thinking; you need to go into a mild trance to make sense of it. All kinds of images could be substituted for the head and tail of the snake opener. For example: *I'll tell you this story and I'll tell it as briefly as I can, but, you know, if you only go down the main street, you'll never know how people live in a town, so maybe we'll take a few side turnings along the way.* You can probably improve on that.

Ways of beginning a story can be as prosaic or as modern as you like, and it is worth building up a stock of 'ways in' that you find work for you. For example, take this simple phrasing: *There's a story I heard and it's a very good one, I think. It's one I like to tell from time to time because – well, it seems to say a few things, but it's just fun to listen to anyway.* This sounds almost gauche but it is setting up expectation, keying the audience for some good sense, yet also playing down the 'significance', so that things don't become too self-conscious. In fact, it is doing many things you might want an opener to do, including announcing the fact that a story is about to happen and giving the listener(s) time to adjust to the mode of story listening.

Here are some traditional and not-so-traditional models from my own repertoire:

- *Long and long and long ago, in a world beyond worlds, in a land beyond lands...*

- *Long and long ago, long before I was born and when you were just a twinkle in the eye of your great great great great grandfather's best friend...*

- *Beyond seven powers and seven seas, when monkeys spoke in rhyme and pigs could fly...*

- *I'll tell this story short, though I could tell it long. But, if I told it long, it would take all of today and all of tomorrow and half of next week, so I'll stick to the main bits...*

- *There's a story they tell and I'll tell it to you, if you like...*

- *This story's worth listening to, I reckon...*

• *If this means something to you, that's good. And if it means nothing at all, that's good too because...well, what's the point of getting all tied up in meanings?*

It is also worth bearing in mind that there may be quite a lot of advantages in not having an opening at all, so that your listeners suddenly find themselves in the middle of a story, without suspecting.

The preamble

The preamble is a story about the story or a series of vivid images not necessarily essential to the story but intended to bring the hearer into rapport with telling and teller and to create expectancy and interest in the story. A traditional preamble might be: *There was once, long and long and long ago, a king who asked his storyteller to tell him the best story he knew. That storyteller thought long and he thought very hard and he racked his brains and pondered... At last he remembered a story he had heard many years ago. And as he thought about that tale and pictured that tale and brought its pattern into his mind, he realized that this was the story he should tell...* (This can be extended and improvised on until the audience really wants to know the story.)

A more modern version, in a one-to-one situation, might be: *I was talking to X and she was telling me a story she heard from Y one time and apparently he always said it was one of his favourites. There was something about the story that always brought him back to it. He was one of those people who have a real fund of stories – you know, anecdotes and yarns and jokes and all sorts of tales of this and that. But this was his favourite, though she was never sure why...* (Again, there can be many variations and extensions – and the effect may well be heightened if X or Y is famous or has high status to the listener.)

This type of preamble sets up the notion that you are about to get a very special story, so of course you want to listen. That is a major point in a preamble: giving listeners more time to settle in to story listening mode than a short opening formula does.

But now consider this traditional type of preamble: *Long ago there was a mountain and it stretched all the way from the earth to the sky. It was the tallest of tall mountains, but it's not the story of the mountain I'm telling you today. Because with each day that passed, the roots of that mountain were gnawed away by mice, one little grain at a time. And when the children of the children of the children of the children of the mice had gnawed away and gnawed away and gnawed away and the children of the children of the children of those mice had done the same thing and the rain had washed and worn it and the wind had hollowed it out, that mountain became less and less and less until there was only a large stone and that stone was taken and used as the cornerstone of a house. But it's not the story of the house I'm telling...* This shaggy-dog style meandering can go on through various transformations, to end up with the hero or heroine or circumstance that begins the tale proper. This idea can also be adapted for modern use. The aim is to set up expectations and tell mini-stories that set the main story against a broad and even breathtaking (if entirely improbable) tapestry of time. For a moment, you are destabilizing things, so that the hearer is in a confusion and wants to grab on to something firm – which turns out to be the narrative. However bizarre that narrative may be, it will sound almost conventional by comparison and the story listening trance can develop.

The rule of three

This is the deliberate giving of three examples or details or facts, creating a rhythm and an expectation. The rule of three also features in the structure of typical fairy-tale plots in which there are three brothers or sisters, three tests or adventures, three golden apples, and so on. Like most rules, it can be broken to good effect, once it is understood.

Listen for the many ways in which speakers on radio and TV, in lecture halls and meetings, as well as salesmen and advertisers and many more, make use of this rule or natural rhythm. Vocal cadence is usually used to 'frame' the three. Try it for yourself with the following sentences and notice how rapidly a description based around three can build a mental image.

- *He is as strong as an ox, has the temper of a wounded bear and the sensitivity of soggy sandstone.*

- *She is as mean as a spider, as pinched as an old powder puff and about as charming as a room full of second-hand-car salesfolk.*

- *That potion tasted as sweet as honey, yet as sharp as the sharpest ice and it was as refreshing as a good night's peaceful sleep and sweet dreams.*

- *It won't cost you more than you'd spend on a bottle of good wine; it's more exciting and stimulating than a bungee jump; and it will change your life for ever.*

- *You can trust me because, first, I make a point of always speaking the truth so far as I am able; second, I can categorically say that I detest all liars and cheats; and third, ask anyone and they'll tell you that I'm as honest as the day is long.*

- *Not only should we abolish poverty, we must abolish poverty and we will abolish poverty.*

(Gordon Brown 2008)

You might also try making up some of your own.

List technique (pedal point)

It appears from the evidence of some narratives originally passed on orally, as well as from studies of living bardic/minstrel traditions, that listing has been a technique worked on and developed over centuries. At its most basic, it means holding up a story whilst listing (say) the many attributes of a character or qualities of a place. Though it blatantly flouts the rule of three, this technique may help to 'tune an audience in' and build more rapport. (There is a contrary use of the technique sometimes employed by politicians, who essentially want to avoid answering a question, so they begin to list achievements of their party/government until questioners and listeners forget the point.) In more sophisticated form, great stories like the Irish 10th-century tale 'The Voyage of Maeldun'[12] or 'The Chamber of Statues'[13] from *The Thousand and One Nights* are essentially lists of strange wonders.

List technique is rather like what musicians know as pedal point – when, on an instrument like the piano, you put the sustain pedal down and play a series of chords or motifs against the same underlying note or chord. The music is, in a sense, static at that point, yet the 'aural space' is being somehow filled. In the same way, when you hold up a story to make lists, it appears that the plot is not moving on. In fact, just as in music, you are building feeling, playing with expectancy and even teasing the ear. And, as in improvised music, you might be subtly working with audience mood, tuning them in more, building up the listening. There is far more to the art of listing than is immediately apparent.

Pacing devices

These are a traditional means of enabling a teller to skate over parts of stories or to move a narrative along whilst leaving detail to be imagined: *I could make my story long, but I'll try to keep it short* or *If I were to tell you all the things that happened along the way, we'd be here all day, so I'll leave them out.* A simple version that works in both a traditional and modern context is *And the story goes on and the story goes on...* One can even choose to appear cynical about the tale, with a version such as, *Well, you know what these stories can be like. Next she does (this) and then she does (that).* Look out for other examples of such bridging devices.

Runs

A run is a piece of standard, often poetic, description, which can include pacing devices, which may be dropped into a story where appropriate. Many traditions include such standard devices. It is useful to build a stock of them and practise using and varying them creatively in different stories and different contexts.

She was as lovely as the morning or the moon on its 14th night. Her eyes sparkled like the stars or the frost on the grass on a winter's morning and her hair was dark as the midnight, yet shone like the sun. This conventionally poetic description (built on the rule of three, described above) will fit many a female beauty in a folk or fairy tale – though it might be less likely to work if your audience lives in a place where frost is unfamiliar and people never go out at night!

Here are some more tradition-based models:

- *That old beggar was thin as a reed and ragged as an old sheet and you would have thought a puff of wind would blow him from one side of the road to the other.*

- *It was (further/longer/stronger/heavier/lighter, etc.) than I could tell you and twice as far as you could tell me...*

- *It was a palace finer and more wonderful than could ever be written down in a book or painted with brush on a canvas or even told by a golden-tongued teller of tales...*

- *It all happened much faster than it takes to tell...*

Endings

Just as there are traditional ways of starting a tale, so there are also traditional ways of ending, and it is useful to build up a stock of them. The intention is to end the story trance, perhaps with a paradox. Some examples are:

- *If that story's not true, I walked all the way from hell this morning and my boots were wrought in the pure hell fire.*

- *I was there myself at the wedding and I told them a tale myself. And the gifts they gave me were these: ice cream in a red hot cauldron, wine in a fisherman's net and this story. And the ice cream melted and the wine ran through the net, so all I got was the story and now I've given it to you.*

- *And that's my story.*

All kinds of extra signals

You could know a story marvellously well, have all sorts of devices in mind for elaborating it and be very well versed in traditions of all kinds – and yet be totally and completely boring and uninteresting as a teller. What is more, someone with very few of those skills in place might instantly engage people and get them right inside their stories. Why is that?

Remember the tale in this chapter about joke telling by numbers? The barman also says 49 – but he says it very differently from the way the visitor does, with all kinds of extra signals, so that the guys in the bar all laugh. Whenever a tale is told, whether or not it is heard will depend a lot on those extra signals. So here are some of them.

Body language

We say a lot through the ways we use our bodies, the postures we adopt, the facial expressions we make, the general expressiveness of our gestures and movements, and so on. This is well known but easily forgotten. A story can be communicated as much by the variety of body language with which we underline it as by the words we use. It can also be entirely subverted by incongruous body language that reveals our lack of conviction and confidence. Laugh lines around the eyes and mouth, a general sense of mirth or even a hint of a suppressed giggle, a glance to the left or right to suggest that you're saying something you don't want 'them' to overhear, can cue expectations of humour that people may otherwise miss entirely. These were all skills exemplified in the camp, gossipy humour of the late Frankie Howerd, for example.

Rapport skills

Whole books have been written about how to develop rapport through non-verbal cues.[14] We need to match our body language to the mood of the listener(s). It is counter-productive to intone a tale with perfect confidence and conviction to someone whose whole body language suggests lack of confidence and doubt; you are challenging the reality that person inhabits. They will probably find you overwhelming and threatening and be more preoccupied with those feelings than with the tale you are telling. Far better to mirror and match the person's body language at the outset and lead into the tale in a more subdued way. In presentations to large groups, on the other hand, exaggerated confidence may be appropriate and even help build rapport, since one is playing the part of the leader/chief/king/exemplar and setting the group mood. However, public speakers also well know the advantages of displaying at least some vulnerability and humanity.

Use of space

Many people do not appreciate that where you are in relation to the person or people you are talking to is vital. Sitting in a tall chair behind a large, imposing mahogany desk, looking down on someone sitting on the other side, is the well-known strategy of bosses desperate to sustain their appearance of power, but is hardly likely to build trust. In one-to-one communication, giving a person enough space to feel comfortable and taking care not to impose is useful. Subtly playing with those parameters, intuitively knowing when to move slightly closer or slightly further away, simply by leaning forward or back, can sometimes be highly effective in creating rapport. Similarly, with a smallish audience, one might sit or stand still for a time, then move forwards, make oneself appear a little larger, then shrink down small, and so on. The point is to use the body as your means of communication, if you spot that an audience, or particular audience member, needs this kind of response. (Working with groups of small children, I've often crouched right down or even lain on the floor to draw particular children into a narrative.) Done excessively or without awareness, however, this is distracting and irritating.

Eye contact

This could be assumed under the general category of rapport skills and body language, but eye contact is a sensitive area and needs especial consideration. It might be expected that, to convey confidence and competence as well as to command attention, you should look people fully in the eye. Indeed, a person who fails to meet the eye may well be dismissed as weak or shifty. However, staring straight at a person whilst telling a story can be uncomfortable for them, causing self-consciousness and interrupting their imagining. (It should also be borne in mind, if working in a therapeutic setting, that people in acute mental distress often find eye contact extremely difficult and threatening.) When people are really engaged by a story, their eyes are generally less focused, as they are partly occupied with internal images suggested by the tale. In one-to-one telling, you might start by looking directly at your listener but then make your own gaze less focused, suggesting the story trance. Similarly, with a small to medium-sized audience, you can play with eye contact with individual audience members whilst building up the rapport, but look more into an imaginary distance as the tale progresses. This is not a rule, merely a hint, and the best guide is experience.

Vocal tone and cadence

Another factor often not paid sufficient attention is that of vocal tone and cadence. Everyone has a unique timbre to their voice but can develop their natural qualities with a little thought and practice. However, cadence and rhythm are often what go wrong for people telling stories. Some people talk too much on the throat or too much in the nose and this can create a tone that is tense and irritating to listen to. When we speak, we also sing – there is a rise and fall to the voice. If this is done in a way that is repetitiously rhythmic, with regular descending notes at the end of sentences, this generally suggests tedium and lack of energy. The best advice for getting it right is to relax, breathe effectively, imagine you are talking to a friend or group of friends, and vary the rhythm of your sentences to maintain interest – if this isn't intuitive, the only way to learn this is to listen to how people who sound interesting speak, and pick up their rhythm initially by imitation. Good speakers don't speak at one pitch constantly, know when to whisper and when to shout, and generally use all the resources of the voice.

Speed of delivery

There is an optimal speed of delivery for a given story at a given time, regardless of the size of the audience. Slow languid telling can bore people at times but create a mood of delicious calm and relaxation at others. Rapid, energetic telling has the potential both to enliven and excite listeners and to lose and confuse them – all depending on context. Indeed, talking too fast is a common fault of many speakers, including highly experienced ones; it is easy to be carried away by the speed of one's thoughts and ideas, when tense and aroused. Most experienced tellers of tales, like many lecturers and public speakers, know how to adjust speed of delivery and try to monitor themselves as they speak. Incidentally, acceptable delivery speed does vary widely across cultures; speakers of the same language may be used to an entirely different pace. People from Dublin, for example, may deliver their English with a much more rapid barrage of ideas and images than, say, the average Londoner.

Timing

Comedians, actors and other public speakers often refer to the importance of timing and it is vital in storytelling too. Good comedians, for instance, know exactly when to leave a long pause and how to manipulate silence – a skill that can, in all sorts of storytelling, be as essential as actually speaking. Many people fear silence when they are speaking, and yet a long pause can be extremely eloquent in itself, playing with the vital element of expectancy. Again, the best way to learn is to observe those who speak effectively – and those who don't.

Energy

Speakers who have what I term 'energy' don't jump up and down or bounce around constantly. Rather, they convey, simply by a combination of many of the things mentioned above and perhaps by their very presence, the feeling that what they say will be interesting and important and relevant. This can be learned to a degree, for example by listening to a teller and then reproducing the energy of the original telling, in the same way that cats learn by copying cats. But if the material is not intrinsically exciting and interesting to you, you are unlikely to be able to sustain a feeling of energy for long. Being inspired is the best way to be inspiring.

The Perfect Storyteller (episode 3)

Off went the storytellers and they talked and they swapped tales and they compared methods. The scribes amongst them wrote down ideas and stories and advice and tricks. Days and weeks went past and the court tellers would go out and speak with the tellers of tales in market places and the spinners of yarns sitting by firesides and the travellers telling travellers' tales and the hermits telling stories to themselves. More notes were compiled and edited and scanned and trimmed and then finally stitched and bound in gold-embossed leather in three magnificent volumes. Amidst great pomp and ceremony, the books were presented to the king, mounted on velvet cushions that sat on golden trays...

(to be continued)

Tapestry

This is a term I based on a wonderful old Chinese fairy tale you will find at the end of the next chapter, in which an old woman weaves a marvellous tapestry, adding to the basic pattern all kinds of incidental happenings and making the very best of a variety of small accidents, so that, in the end, the tapestry comes to life. I use it to describe the way in which you can be constantly aware of the situation in which you are telling a tale and actually make use of things such as interruptions, engine noises, discomforts, warmth, cold and all sorts of things which may otherwise distract an audience. Weaving in incidental happenings and conditions to the basic fabric of the tale is an essential storytelling skill and can only occur if you have a flexible sense of the tale, not a memorized inflexible script. It helps to make a telling unique to, and in harmony with, people, time and place.

Stringing

This is another term I dreamed up to describe the way in which material is sequenced. It comes out of the image of stringing things together and applies particularly to sessions in which a number of different tales might be told, but has relevance to all sorts of storytelling situations. I noticed many years ago that, at sessions in which many different people get up to tell stories (as often happens in adult story clubs), there were almost always peak moments, with particular tales going down especially well. People present would often rush to compliment the tellers of these tales, without noticing that the ground had been thoroughly prepared and the stage set by other tellers, good and bad.

One tale influences the reception of another. The ideas and metaphors presented in different tales or in general 'conversation' may be complementary or may clash. Similarly, the mood created by one story can be enhanced and developed by another – or dispelled by it. The art of putting the right tale after the right tale (or after the wrong one) has to be intuitive and depends on being in tune with what is happening. I describe it as stringing because the implication is of something you do actively and which is involved with connection.

All the suggestions in this section are meant as hints to absorb over time, as your experience grows. A piece of advice that has long resonated for me as a teller of tales came from one of my musical mentors, pianist and composer Keith Cole. He once told me that good improvisation is, in effect, a series of more or less accurate mistakes. Same with good storytelling, I reckon.

The Perfect Storyteller (episode 4)

But the king looked at the volumes in horror. 'What is this?' he said sternly. 'I thought I told you to boil it down. This would take me half a lifetime to read, let alone to practise. You must cut it down!'

The crestfallen storytellers went off and they gathered together and they talked and they bargained and they argued, because, of course, each of them thought this or that was essential and could not be left out. But, eventually, they managed to reduce it all to one large, weighty tome and this was presented to the king just as before. Again the king was scandalized. 'Do you think that a king has nothing to do?' he intoned menacingly. 'I would never finish that book in three lifetimes, with all my royal duties. Make it shorter!'

(to be continued)

Techniques for focusing attention inwards

As already mentioned, there are many comparisons between the techniques of storytelling and those used in therapy. Anyone interested in using stories in therapeutic contexts would do well to study the basic language patterns used by modern Ericksonian therapists.[15] Here, in brief, are some useful notions from hypnotherapy.

Representational styles and multisensory imagery

People generally have a preferred representational style – that is to say, they represent things mentally through different sensory modes. Very many people visualize, imagining through pictures, but there are also those who use sound, smell, taste and particularly feeling, as well as others who combine some or all of those modes. As a general rule, it is best to evoke all of the senses in telling a story, using imagery suggesting sight, smell, taste, feel, and so on. That way you hedge your bets, so that people listening can find something to identify with – or, indeed, several different levels to identify with, if they already use several different modes. However, if you already know a person's dominant imagining style, you can play to that particularly strongly in one-to-one telling – though it is still wise not to focus on one sense only.

Embedded and interspersal suggestions

These are terms used to describe suggestions for new behaviour, change, positive thinking, etc., made when talking ostensibly about something else and effectively concealed within what is being said. Embedded suggestions are often created by the emphasis they are given in speech. For instance, a therapist talking to someone who is wary about learning how to relax might say, 'It's a matter of observation and experience, really, noticing when you *relax more* than at other times'. The words are respectful of the individual's own judgement but the italicized words represent an embedded command to relax now.

Interspersal suggestions are repeated suggestions interspersed with other talk to occupy the conscious mind, so that (to follow on from the embedded suggestion mentioned) you might find several ways to weave the instruction to relax into an apparently shapeless ramble – perhaps, for example, on the ways of story heroes and heroines. 'And, you know, those heroes and heroines, going on all those quests and journeys, they always seem to have to *find that level of inner focus.* They may seem stereotypical, no more than ciphers really, but there's something about the challenges they face that, if you think about it, just has to bring out that ability to *go into a place inside yourself where you can be calm and balanced* and really keep your eyes on the goal. Climbing mountains, going through enchanted gardens, passing through trials, it's really important to be able to be *gently poised and ready at the same time, just in the moment, going with the flow...'*

You can also intersperse suggestions while telling a traditional story. For instance, suppose you are describing a heroine's decision to leave a lowly position as a servant to an abusive mistress and seek her greater destiny. You might add something like, 'Sometimes you have to do that, *make a decision now*, do you not? Sometimes you just *know you have to move on.*' And these remarks might be directed towards the individual you are talking to, who perhaps wants to leave behind a habit or change another behaviour, or to particular members of a group whom you know need to find new motivations. You are offering direct advice but, because it is in the middle of a story, listeners unconsciously pick up on it and register it – if it chimes with their intentions. For this way of making suggestions retains respect for personal choice.

There are many other ways, of course, in which skilled therapists structure and deliver suggestions. Some people reject the very notion of suggestion as covert manipulation and therefore somehow dishonest. Yet those very people are often unaware of how much these particular techniques are in use all around us today, in advertising, by politicians, by salespeople and by many others who want us to do something or believe something or accept an attitude. Embedded suggestions occur again and again in the picture language of film; very many people who have identified with heroes and heroines of the silver screen have found themselves sooner or later swaggering around with a momentary feeling of having become that person, doing something as that icon might do it. Much novel writing contains suggestion after suggestion, not only in the overt opinions of the author but in the very manner of description and, indeed, unfolding of plot. And in the traditional storytelling of many cultures it is the convention to include wise sayings, elements of mythology extraneous to the tale and all sorts more. So why not be aware of embedded and interspersal suggestions and use them to the good in ways that do not insult the listener?

Resistance and confusional language

In therapy, clients are sometimes deemed to be resistant. This generally means that their self-aware, self-conscious minds stand in the way and refuse to allow them to relax into a trance state, a difficulty that is, for example, common in tense but intelligent people who use analytic skills constantly. Modern trance therapists tend to reject the label of resistance, defining it instead as a trait to be used and worked with. One way of doing this is by the use of confusional language – a series of apparently logical statements purposely delivered in a confusing and possibly nonsensical way. Confusional language constantly sets up paradoxes, may also be deliberately boring and repetitious and can contain various embedded suggestions. For example, you can apparently wander off track in a story...

> It was the kind of house...you know the kind, with four, maybe six windows at the front and a shabby old door and the paint peeling off. I was walking past a whole row of houses like that only the other day. You look and you wonder what kind of people live in there. Maybe you see the dirty old curtains and the windows not cleaned and maybe a couple of houses in the row have been done up and you think to yourself what is it like for those people. I mean, people do sometimes, don't they? People do wonder and think and go off into fugues about all sorts of...things can be arranged in all sorts of ways, can they not? And people have a range of arrangements arranged in quite different ranges of ways. Because there are ranges of places and situations that are different and have different kinds of demands, of course. Some sorts of places you know as soon as you see them that *you could easily get back into shape, just with a little work here or there...* You go in through the door and into the hall and you see at once it *just needs to allow the light in...*tidying away this, tidying away that...

The theory goes (and the practice generally confirms) that doing this ties up the conscious mind (the busy, questioning, analytical part of our brains) in a vain attempt to make sense of what is being said. Eventually the point is reached where it gives up and switches off, allowing the creative, imaginative, receptive and unconscious element of the mind space to function.

Such a therapeutic practice might appear to be very much at odds with performance/entertainment storytelling ways – you would think that anyone trying to hold an audience would hardly aim to bore and confuse listeners. To anyone familiar with both fields, however, there are striking similarities between hypnotic confusional language and the traditional techniques described earlier, such as preambles, listing and many more. Riddles and conundrums are used by many tellers for quite similar purposes, to say nothing of that 'time before time when monkeys spoke in rhyme and all the birds flew backwards', which is the backdrop to many tales of once and never.

Developing trance

Finally, it is worth just noting that many of the techniques and tips given in this chapter are, in themselves, essentially trance-forming. They take listeners inwards, eliciting inner imagery that makes the outer world recede and become less important.

The Perfect Storyteller (episode 5)

This time the storytellers went away and they cut and they trimmed and they cut and they trimmed and came back with a slim volume. Still the king commanded them to abbreviate it. 'Look,' he said, having by now, in his preoccupation with his royal role and dignity, almost forgotten his once ardent desire to learn the craft. 'I want just seven sentences, no more and no less than that! Have those done by tomorrow and stop wasting my time!' The king glared menacingly at the storytellers, who noticed the royal executioner standing nearby, looking alert.

(to be continued)

Storytelling and consciousness – psychological dynamics

In this section, we'll take a look at some often neglected aspects of storytelling interactions which can be quite crucial to their effectiveness. They concern:

- the consciousness of the teller of the story

- the consciousnesses of the single listener

- In group situations, the consciousness of the group as a whole.

In this, I'll draw on some of my own earlier published speculations on the subject.[16]

Focus

A teller of tales needs to be in a state of focused attention. We are all sorts of things apart from storytellers and we need to find that sharper, clearer awareness that knows the stories, and how to tell them. I know hundreds of stories but sometimes I can't even recall one of them. Many of the techniques described in this chapter could be looked at as ways of tuning the teller into story mode as well as of getting through to the audience.

Pondering the focus metaphor for a moment can be useful – despite the fact that it is, in some respects over-used these days, with all sorts of focus groups and courses and coaches to help you to develop your personal or business focus. But you *focus* a camera or a microscope or telescope to give you a clearer image, better sight, a closer view, to align the lenses, etc. You *focus* rays of the sun's light with a magnifying glass and make a fire. You *focus* thoughts and energies on a task. There is a suggestion of strengthening and concentrating something, in this case the individual storyteller's consciousness.

Flow

The term 'flow' is increasingly widely used to describe states of absorption experienced by different people in different activities, from running to composing to cooking. The psychologist Mihaly Csikszcentmihalyi, who coined this term, and his co-workers in many other countries have found evidence of this state in all kinds of people, from high achievers writing novels or music to factory workers turning production line boredom into life-enhancing work.[17] Sportsmen and their coaches often talk about 'getting into the zone', which is the same state. Daniel Goleman, in his book *Emotional Intelligence*, describes it succinctly:

> Flow is a state of self-forgetfulness, the opposite of rumination and worry: instead of being lost in nervous preoccupation, people in flow are so absorbed in the task at hand that they lose all self-consciousness, dropping the small preoccupations...of daily life. In this sense, moments of flow are egoless. Paradoxically, people in flow exhibit a masterly control of what they are doing...[18]

Goleman's description almost perfectly describes the state of the storyteller who has achieved a good level of personal focus and is in good rapport with the listener and the story. It is almost as if the story seems to happen despite the teller, despite the listener – though, paradoxically, perhaps the best way to achieve such a state is not to be self-consciously preoccupied with a concept such as flow.

Flight

This is a metaphor I have introduced to suggest something that sometimes happens, which is beyond personal absorption, however egoless. With some competence and a little bit of a following wind, you can achieve a measure of personal focus and hope to get into flow. But then sometimes there is a moment of 'lift off' when something extra happens and you suddenly find yourself discovering new things about a story you thought you knew so well – as if the 'chemistry' between you and the audience/listener and the time and the circumstance had produced something unexpected. Flight is part of the real magic and mystery of storytelling that keeps practitioners of storytelling fascinated by the craft, perhaps for the very reason that it happens only sometimes, and you never know when that will be.

Doors and locks and keys

These metaphors are useful when thinking about the consciousness of the individual listener or group. No one would rush up to a house and expect to walk straight into it, if the door had not already been opened or if the occupants were out or were ignoring the door bell. Listeners to stories may sometimes initially have their doors closed – they are self-conscious, distracted, excited, depressed, in their own separate worlds to a greater or lesser extent. You need to find ways to open those doors. Because people, adults and children, are different and circumstances are different and time is different, you need a range of tricks up your sleeve to do that, which is the nature of real storytelling skill, distinguishing it entirely from acting a tale. The various techniques and skills described in this chapter could be thought about as being ways of opening doors, ways that are a little more subtle than the way of the bailiff and more respectful than the way of the thief.

Emotional contagion and the notion of torque

Anyone who works with large or small groups should be aware of group mood and how it can affect communication. In evolutionary terms, it must have been adaptive to be aware of and able to respond to the mood of the group. Our ancestors lived in smallish groups; they needed to sense danger or indeed advantage and reward at more or less the same time, and to be tuned into each other in all sorts of other ways. They would no doubt have been able to do this, before language evolved, by reading small cues and signals. Think of the way flocks of birds flying across the sky arrange themselves into aerodynamically effective formations, bank and turn and wheel together, responding effortlessly and intuitively to each other and to conditions.

Human beings are, of course, more complicated than birds because cultural influences mediate and interact with basic natural responses. But those natural responses are still there in basic form. This means that, at times, moods can move through a group, making audience members less or more able to concentrate and take in what is being presented to them. Crude examples of extreme group mood can be seen in footage of the carefully orchestrated fever pitch reached at the peak of Hitler's orations, but also at many a football match or rock concert. Hysteria is easy to spot, but there are all sorts of shadings of emotional effects along the way. Studies have shown that upbeat emotional moods are more easily spread in groups than negative feelings, possibly because depressed body language tends to be about withdrawal rather than communication.[19]

To describe the level of emotional tension in a group, I introduced the word *torque*. The dictionary defines this as a 'twisting rotational force', an effect engineers have to calculate and take into account. By analogy, the emotional torque of an audience is a force to take into account, though this is intuitive rather than calculated and calibrated. As with so many other aspects of communication, one can understand it best by working with children, whose responses tend to be more primitive (in the best sense of the word) and obvious, since they have not yet learned to conceal them. Skilled performers know how to take them 'up' (which is the easy bit, since most children love to laugh and shout together and submerge themselves in the group mood) but also (more difficult) to take them 'down'. Excitement and maybe even momentary hysteria can be very useful in enlivening an audience – think of the relief a good laugh provides in the midst of an intense lecture or sermon. But laughing and screaming and otherwise indulging infectious and convulsive reactions means that more subtle things disappear, a point missed by many entertainers.

Spirited occasions – some extra dimensions of group mood

It is interesting to note that in many traditions associated with performance arts, including the telling of stories, group mood and the 'spirit' of an occasion is important in the development of many useful practical concepts. In Ireland, for example, the term often used to describe social events where people become absorbed in the group mood and the talk flows and everything seems to gel is *craic*. Because of the association with excessive alcohol consumption in Irish culture, this is easy to dismiss as people simply getting drunk together. However, many traditional musicians and *seanachies* (the traditional Irish name for the community storyteller[20]) evidently used the term to describe a mood created among people, which alcohol may have oiled but was not absolutely essential to, and that distinction is helpful to keep in mind.

In Java, where alcohol has traditionally had much less importance, there is a concept possibly comparable to *craic*. Kathy Foley writes in a study of Sundanese *wayang golek* (rod puppetry):

> The primary criterion that villagers use for judging a performance is whether or not it is *ramai*. When a performance is not *ramai*, people soon drift home to sleep. The word will pass that the *dalang* (puppeteer) was mediocre. The family that hired him will gain little status and he will probably not be invited to play in the area again. A *wayang* [drama] must first be entertaining.[21]

For the *dalang*, *ramai* is something he needs to be aware of; it is, for him, almost a technical term. According to R.A. Sutton, it translates as 'busy, noisy, congested, tangled – but in a positive sense'.[22] For Indonesian taste, there has to be a lot going on – as in the designs of batik, for example. The *wayang* typically goes on all night, with the telling of stories from the Mahabharata or Ramayana mixed with local legend. People have the opportunity to be absorbed in the performance but also to drift, talk, buy satay and other spicy snacks, smoke clove-scented kretek cigarettes, chat, all sorts of things. So the performance must vary as it goes along and the accompanying gamelan[23] ensemble and singers have to take their cues from the puppeteer, helping to maintain the drama itself and the whole quality of group mood. Which all makes the event *ramai*.

These two words, *craic* and *ramai*, are just two traditional concepts used to describe and judge qualities of what you could call group consciousness, both, as it happens, describing a mood of easy social flow. Other expressions from around the world attempt to delineate apparently more intense moods. The Spanish concept of *duende*, these days most commonly associated with flamenco performance but also traditionally ascribed to performances such as bull fighting, refers to a moment when people are stirred deeply in some indescribable but recognisable way.[24] In neighbouring Portugal, *fadoists*[25] appear to use a very similar concept when they speak of moments of real *fado*. In the Scottish traveller tradition there is *conyach*, a quality individual storytellers might bring to their stories and their interactions with listeners, as described by storyteller Sheila Stewart, the last of the Stewarts of Blairgowrie.[26] Or, contrastingly, there is the Middle Eastern notion of *kayif*, which appears to be a quality of essential virtue sometimes present in things and people and processes from meals to meetings, a quality that makes everything somehow whole and complete.[27] There are many other comparable ideas from cultures around the world, some, such as Polynesian *mana* and Native American *wakan* and a host of apparently kindred terms, relating to larger concepts of an underlying 'life force' and sacred power.[28]

It is easy to dismiss any or all of these traditional notions as simply superstitious or as only superficially related and quite different social constructions – or as, perhaps, improperly understood group hypnosis or forms of mass hysteria or dependent on certain chemical balances in brains. But such labels do not entirely explain anything and tend not to allow for the subtle and practically useful shadings each idea contains. Perhaps it is best to keep an open, respectful and receptive mind.

The attention bargain

A useful way of looking at and summarizing the art of learning and telling stories is through the lens of 'attention'. Storytelling is a kind of attention bargain. The first stage is the attention the teller gives to learning the story thoroughly. Give the story attention and it will grow in your memory and imagination. The better you attend to the tale, the more you'll get from it.

Second, you give the tale attention as you stretch it and explore it still further in the telling. Yet someone telling tales is not only attending to the story but to their own body language and all the dynamics of the situation in which they are speaking, and especially to the people or person listening and their levels of attention. There is absolutely no point in telling a story perfectly to someone who is not listening. Indeed, that is a contradiction in terms, since what makes the telling of the tale perfect is engaging the listener(s) perfectly.

Attention applies at a different level here too. We seek attention. It is a basic human need. Some people manipulate attention by telling stories in social settings; they are usually the people who don't listen to tales others tell, since they are too busy rehearsing the one with which they are about to blind you. This attitude is the opposite of that of the good storyteller, simply because it is counter-productive: show-offs may grab attention but are rarely really listened to, in the sense of the taking in and remembering of what they say. Show-offs may also not learn much, being preoccupied with their own performances. A storyteller needs also to be a good listener to time, circumstance and people, 'paying attention' to his or her own attention need to make sure that it doesn't get in the way. Attention from large groups can be quite delightfully intoxicating (one reason some professional storytellers, along with many other kinds of performer, become addicted to performing), but anyone who really wants to stay sensitive to the dynamics of the situation and the real potentials of group mood needs to stay sober inside, focused on and in the story.

There is also the need to adjust the story to the situation, to make it smaller or larger, scaling it to the place and the person or people. One-to-one telling involves sensitivity to attention levels and increases the possibilities for a story to be interactive. Telling to a group involves a larger, sometimes exhilarating, dynamic and may require all kinds of on-the-hoof adjustments.

Through these various levels of attention, there is that possibility of what I have called flight, which happens when all of the attention elements are in the right place at the right time. If one is not paying attention in the right way, this never happens.

At heart, however, storytelling is simple. Anyone can do it at an effective level. What matters far more than developing sophisticated techniques is being straightforward, knowing your story well and trusting it to do its work – and using your common sense. Some ways of developing and delivering a story that are appropriate when you are working with a large group are entirely inappropriate in a one-to-one situation.

The marvellously eccentric English folklore collector Doc Rowe once said to me:

> What really gets up my nose about these revival storytellers is the way they suddenly have to wind up into storyteller mode. They sort of puff themselves up and wag a finger at you and they're suddenly a storyteller – and I'm out the door. The old guys I've recorded, the real old storytellers and singers and all, they didn't ever do that. They just tell you the story. It's part of what they are.

Being straightforward and unpretentious, respecting the person or people you are talking to and knowing a story to the point where it is part of you is by far the most likely way to communicate it well.

The Perfect Storyteller (episode 6)

Well, the storytellers' minds were wonderfully concentrated now and they worked quickly that night, suddenly seeing and agreeing exactly what they should do. The next day they went back to the king with a suitably grand scroll. With the usual pomp and ceremony, it was presented to his royal majesty, who beheld at last the seven sentences which summarized the great art of the absolutely perfect storyteller.

The king blinked, and looked again and blinked again, not quite believing the evidence of his eyes, but slowly, slowly beginning to understand what he saw and even (fortunately for the storytellers) to smile. For the seven sentences he read were just one sentence, written out seven times over. The sentence was this:

> 'The perfect storyteller is the one whose story you remember long after you have forgotten his face.'[29]

Chapter 4

Traditional Ways of Storytelling

The value of information does not survive the moment
in which it was new... A story is different. It does
not expend itself. It preserves and concentrates its
strength and is capable of releasing it even after a
long time... It resembles the seeds of grain, which
have lain for centuries in the chambers of the
pyramids shut up airtight and have retained their
germinative power to this day.
– Walter Benjamin[1]

Two things make a big difference to the meaning and the effect
of stories: the context in which they are told and the intention
with which they are told. In this chapter, I look at some traditional
contexts for storytelling as well as at two specific types of teaching
story, the fable and the dilemma tale, and at ways in which these
can be focused and used. I'll also touch on the metaphorical
complexity of other kinds of story too – how indeed some may have
multiple levels of meaning.

Traditional stories and storytellers

If storytelling is basic and essential to being human, you would
expect it to occur in some form in virtually all cultures, and this is
exactly the case. You would also expect ways of storytelling to be

as varied as is human culture across the world. Indeed, in many cultures, storytelling may appear not to be a discrete activity at all, with rules and conventions. It may be a part of life that is taken for granted or is entwined with religion or history keeping and much more. But if we look at oral traditions around the world and in times past, expecting to find rules and conventions similar to those we are familiar with through our literature and performance arts, we may ignore what doesn't 'fit'. We can find ourselves simply looking in a mirror.

Mirror gazing is a problem that has arisen over the last two or three decades, during which time there has been a considerable revival of interest in oral storytelling and traditional stories. People bring along their baggage, as it were, from their backgrounds as actors or teachers or folk music enthusiasts or therapists or political thinkers or religious activists or whatever else and make a storytelling in their own image. After all, you can very much make of those two words 'traditional' and 'storytelling' what you choose. Even anthropologists and folklorists, whose job it is to define such things, can be found disagreeing about what constitutes tradition. So here are some brief sketches of storytelling people from different ages and different traditions, to give at least an idea of the extensive and kaleidoscopic backgrounds from which oral stories emerge. (Apologies in advance for the inevitable simplification and generalization.)

Pundits, pilgrims and plebs

Oral traditions are created by the thousands and millions of ordinary people, who passed on the tales and the lore, adding their own insights and experiences here and there as they entertained each other whilst working at the loom or with axe or adze, or in the market or the inn or caravanserai or by the campfire. Long before modern transport, stories travelled the length of the known world as the invisible luggage of travellers, or grew and blossomed here and there, with roots apparently deep in one soil.

One excellent model for how all this existed in developing societies, before universal literacy and industrialization, is Chaucer's *Canterbury Tales*, the first great work of a recognizably English literature. If you recall, Chaucer's pilgrims are on their way to Canterbury and, to 'shorten the road', as the saying goes, they agree to tell each other stories as they ride. Whatever their actual source (and scholars have traced many of the tales to all kinds of earlier written and oral versions), the pilgrims tell their stories each in their own way, adding their own stamp of character and experience. That is how oral traditions have always worked. Chaucer observes this and uses it to make great literature with the reflexive quality of being a story about stories, a teller telling about tellers. Characters such as the knight and the clerk, who may be assumed to be literate, tell tales freely adapted from Boccaccio and Petrarch and from other literary sources; others draw on what would have been 'in the air' from minstrels and tellers of tales encountered here and there, or expand on what today would more or less fit the description of dirty jokes and risqué anecdotes.

Chaucer's work also demonstrates that close, symbiotic relationship between the oral and the written, seen in many comparable earlier works of world literature. For centuries, in cultures where writing had been developed and was in widespread use, literature and oral traditions coexisted. Books could be seen as repositories of stories, many and most of which began as oral tales rather than being created for the page. Stories could very well be taken from the page and altered and changed in further oral tellng. Thus the *Panchatantra*, the *Alif Layla wa Layla*, (familiar to us as the *Tales of the Arabian Nights*), the *Ocean of Story*, the *Decameron* and many more works revered as classic literature were in a sense pattern books for telling, storehouses where precious tales could be kept proof against the vagaries of oral memory. Literacy was not so common and books were relatively rare, but people were not illiterate in the sense of being cut off from the world of shared stories. Indeed, you could argue that people involved in oral storytelling in earlier times, and in some parts of the world today, were and are far more connected and involved with a living literature than are consumers of books and films, who are dependent on authors and film-makers.

Of course, noteworthy among Chaucer's pilgrims (and some other storytelling models I sketch out below) was the predominance of men, because typically it was men who took the official, public roles. The pilgrims, therefore, cannot be taken as a metaphor for oral storytelling in general because women have always been just as involved in creating oral traditions, albeit that much of such transmission was 'unofficial'. But, if we are all storytellers, then we are also, like the pilgrims, all very individual storytellers, shaping individual stories from tradition. In that primary sense, the metaphor works.

The seanachie

'Specialists' in stories clearly existed, before there were writers. As a piece of evidence, we can take a figure from quite recent history: the *seanachie*. This is the traditional name for a specialist traditional storyteller in Ireland, a name with its roots in ancient traditions in Celtic culture. Because Ireland was, until recently, relatively undeveloped in the industrial and economic sense, people in large areas of it continued the old traditions uninterrupted. There are still many people alive today who recall the visits of the *seanachies* to the village, and the name is still applied to people who have large repertoires of anecdotes and tales. However, the old tradition of the *seanachie* has long been considered to be dying out. Mara Freeman painted this poignant little picture in an article in the magazine *Parabola*:

> In the tiny mountain hamlet of Cíllrialaig in County Kerry around 1920, a strange figure might have been seen among the farmers returning from market. An old man toiled slowly up the hills behind his grey mare, reciting stories to the back of the cart!
>
> He was none other than Seán Ó Conaill, a farmer-fisherman of seventy years, master-storyteller or *seanachie* of those parts. Once the center of cultural life, be it at holiday gatherings, weddings or wakes, he was now no longer needed in a rapidly-changing modern world, and was forced to practice his art without an audience, lest he should lose his skills altogether.[2]

Whilst many ordinary people would tell stories, the *seanachie* would have a particular role as keeper of legends and lore, as well as being an entertainer. In the winter months, the *seanachie* might be expected to keep people under the spell of tales and legends, night after night, so that repertoires of these tellers were often very large. The *seanachie* was not, however, a professional in the modern sense, since he might also be a farmer or a fisherman to make his living.

The figure of the *seanachie* in traditional Ireland is mirrored in many other figures in world traditions – the history and myth keepers, the individuals who develop a particular memory and are given a particular status within the community. The role could be conceived of as developing naturally enough in human groupings, since there will always be people especially good at memorizing and then telling in an arresting way. Many such exponents across the world have been expected to offer not only food for imagination, not simply legends and history, but also practical advice and analogy in the form of metaphor, insight and illumination: practical wisdom of a kind different from the interpretations of priests and orthodox thinkers.

Bards, ashiks, griots and all

Another specialist teller of tales in ancient times was the bard. Nowadays, the popular image of an ancient bard might be a strange, harp-toting figure, maybe rather wild-eyed and definitely inspired by weird pagan muses. Or maybe one thinks of the 'immortal bard' epithet, as applied to Shakespeare. In fact, the *filidh*, the bards of the ancient Celtic culture in Ireland, for example, were first and foremost trained craftsmen. (Some people trace the *seanachies* back to the *filidh*.) They were the guardians of a revered tradition handed on orally and, according to legend, underwent a training that lasted at least 12 years, which honed their powers of concentration and memory. In the process, they learned hundreds of stories and verses, as well as genealogies and histories, and they learned to master intricate metrical forms in which they might compose more or less spontaneously, whilst playing on a small (by modern standards) though versatile harp, its front pillar carved in the shape of the salmon of knowledge. A trained *fili* carried a golden rod, wore a cloak of crimson and yellow feathers and held a high status within the community.

The *fili* was literally considered to be inspired, since his breath was supposedly the gift of Brigit, the great goddess who was patron of poetry and divination. His title meant both 'poet' and 'storyteller' but can also be translated as 'weaver of spells'.

There are comparable bardic figures in many other societies. The West African *griot*, for example, is another keeper of legends and histories; the *ashiks* of Turkey and elsewhere also underwent an extensive training that contained strong elements of mysticism. Poet–storyteller–musicians from many other cultures traditionally studied their craft through instruction from a master or grew up in families in which this role had been fulfilled for generations, absorbing legends and histories and whole mythical sagas at the knee or as a form of initiation. Great classical works like the Homeric epics were preserved and recited by bards with trained memories and skilled performance techniques, who very likely honed and even contributed in their own ways to what we conventionally think of (using our own cultural mirrors, of course) as the individual genius of Homer.[3]

The storyteller in the market place – from *rawis* to wandering minstrels

The story of Lakshmi and Vishnu related in Chapter 1 gives a vivid snapshot of a tradition that has been very much a reality in Eastern countries like India: the storyteller quite literally in the market place. Much further west, in Morocco, you can to this day witness the public storyteller, the *rawi qissas* (narrator of legends) at work at tourist destinations like Marrakesh. Few visitors can follow their Moroccan Arabic, of course, but they evidently remain amongst the most popular entertainers with locals at the Djem el Fnaa, the main market place. And then there's the so-called 'wandering minstrel' of medieval European tradition.

Actually, the wandering minstrel is another of those stereotypes of popular imagination, usually thought of as a musician in parti-coloured jester-like clothing, clutching a lute. Minstrels didn't in fact wander unless they had to, preferring patronage at castle and palace, whilst a far more typical instrument might be a small harp or something like a gittern. French minstrels, called *jongleurs*, were advised to learn at least seven instruments and tended to be highly versatile all-round entertainers. *Jongleur* literally means juggler – another minstrel skill, along with storytelling. According to legend, the Battle of Hastings was begun by the Norman minstrel, Talleifer. The two armies were standing off when the minstrel put himself between them, juggling with two swords on horseback. As he did this, he recited an inspiring legend, perhaps some lay of Roland and Oliver and Charlemagne. Then, at its end, he hurled a sword at the Saxons, who promptly killed him, and the fighting began.[4] Not every story has a happy ending.

'Minstrel' came to be used as a general term for entertainers; some appear to have had specialisms in tumbling or conjuring and magic tricks – and indeed in storytelling. Minstrels replaced the earlier bards in medieval castle halls and the minstrel is reckoned to be a prototype of the modern secular entertainer. All kinds of fables and tales of wonder and imaginative fantasy appear to have been part of minstrel repertoire, along with heroic tales. Some were reckoned to be able to create 'apparitions', as mentioned in Chaucer's 'Franklin's Tale' and rather in the style of modern stage hypnotists. The best minstrels appear to have been able to get their audience to enter into and be held in trance-like states of absorption through their tales and tricks. (Interestingly, the English word entertainer come from the old French *entretenir*, in turn derived from the Latin *inter*, which means 'among', and *tenere*, 'to hold'.)

But it is too simplistic to categorize minstrels as being a bit like variety entertainers: their world was entirely different. The Moroccan *rawi qissas* also comes out of another very different world, not founded simply on material values. He may, in our terms, be an entertainer, not unlike a busker in market place and coffee house, but his role has affinities with both the *seanachie* and the *filidh*, as well as with something unique and special and rooted in a culture where dervish mystical fraternities have been common. I was once lucky enough to speak to one through a translator in Taroudant, south of the Atlas Mountains in Morocco. He was sharing the 'pitch' at a market with a colleague, who was telling the tales at the time, so it was his turn to listen, jingle the 'voluntary contributions' pouch from time to time and perhaps subtly entice people into the *halqa* (circle of listeners) and away from the competing snake charmers and hawkers. He told me that, when he was 12, he had begun to learn from his uncle to be a teller of tales. He had to learn all of the stories in *The Arabian Nights* plus all kinds of tales from Moroccan and Arab mythology. He had a big repertoire and also made up some of his own stories. He supported a wife and family on his telling of tales, though was clearly not at all rich on the proceeds. I duly gave to the collection and, as we walked away, the lad who had translated for me told me I had done the right thing. 'It is good to give to this man,' he explained. 'He can do things for you, things you do not know – with his stories.'[5]

Shamans and healers

The term 'shaman' is a rather catch-all term applied to individuals in many different cultures who say and do and believe a lot of different things. There is probably no such thing as a typical shaman but in many traditional tribal societies, the shaman had

– and still has – a vital role. In the anthropologists' primer, the archetypal shaman would undergo demanding inner discipline, either self-generated or at the command of an experienced master or mistress of the shamanic path. This might involve fasting or the ingestion of hallucinogenic substances or various kinds of imagery or chanting and breathing. As a result, she or he would experience intense visions, thought to represent contact with the spirit world, and, by learning to control these to a degree, would develop the power to intervene in the lives of people, healing illnesses and solving difficulties.

Shamans told stories considered to have power and held to be 'secret', only to be revealed at the right time. (The tribal teller of tales may also have been the shaman.) And, indeed, one can say that stories are potentially just as powerful as claimed, because imagination is powerful and potentially healing, especially in a context of heightened suggestibility and expectation.

Preachers, priests and politicians

Stories play a part in all religions, though religious folk do not often call themselves storytellers nor do they regard such stories as fiction. It is often a case of 'He/she/you/they have mythologies and stories; I/we have the truth'. This can be a difficulty, certainly when more narrow and fanatical religious people attempt to communicate: to adapt an old saying, they can't see the stories for THE WORD.

But priests and preachers are indeed storytellers and, for many people, have been the source of the stories that shape and underpin their lives. This doubtless has had positive benefits at different times in history and some inspired preachers have drawn in all kinds of fabulous material and wisdom teachings from outside the strict confines of their own sacred texts. But there is a definite downside. Unlike some of the founders of the religions they promote, and certainly unlike most other kinds of storytellers, priests very frequently interpret and pin down and define the stories they tell. Priestly castes have often also been associated with social power structures rigidly bound by orthodoxies. The more fundamentalist the religion and/or the more dominant, the less scope there is for individual reinterpretation.

Something similar occurs in simple tribal societies. Stories are told to young people and then, at a certain stage, the 'meaning' of the story may be revealed. In many instances, the knowledge may be genuine and useful, if couched in mythology; in other cases, the interpretation may be narrowing or limiting, based on a superstition or on an ossified or partial knowledge.

Politicians and leaders are often storytellers in their way. In the past, some quite literally used fables and jokes and even quite long narratives as part of their oratory. These days, in the age of the soundbite, the storytelling is more usually of the future fantasy variety – how we will all go forward together in strength and security and positive hope towards a world of democracy, freedom and universal prosperity, etc., etc. Politicians, like preachers, are more likely to interpret in ways that are limiting and lacking in real insight, since encouraging flexibility of thought is not generally in their interest.

Scoundrels and saints

Many years ago, when I was briefly involved in the antiques trade, a lady asked me for an opinion of her most treasured piece of furniture. It was a largish oak china cabinet, mass-produced in the 1920s and not worth very much at the time. I was beginning to say so when she jumped in with, 'Of course, I know it's probably out of your league.' I asked her why she thought so and she explained: 'A few years ago, a man called round to give me a valuation. He'd been in the trade for years and he really knew his stuff. Anyway, he told me he really couldn't afford to buy it.' At this point it began to dawn on me that she might have been the victim of a 'knocker'. In the days before television antiques shows wised everyone up, knockers used to make a good living going round to unsuspecting people, knocking on the door and offering to value their antiques with no obligation. A classic ploy was (and, for all I know, may still be) to admire one piece of very ordinary furniture, but to say that it was far too valuable for them to make an offer. They would, however, be interested in such and such another much less valuable piece – which would be the real gem. The really unscrupulous ones would carry a dart or something similarly sharp, with which they would surreptitiously make a few holes to simulate woodworm damage in the coveted piece, whilst apparently admiring the decoy. They would then 'spot' the worm damage with well-feigned horror and suggest that the offending piece be removed immediately from the vicinity of the 'treasure' and offer to carry out the service themselves. Something very like this, I'm afraid, is what had very probably happened to this lady – that is to say, he had taken away a 'damaged' desk leaving behind this very ordinary furnishing item. 'I never really liked it,' she said, wrinkling her nose. 'Far too fussy, with all that silly marquetry and stuff...' It was a piece of furniture which, as she described it, would probably have been worth at least ten of her cabinets. 'He was such a nice man. He gave me this beeswax polish to use on my cabinet, to feed the wood. I polish it every day.'

There is currently a growing interest in storytelling for commercial purposes and as a means of developing corporate identity. Some of this may well have integrity and validity; some may be yet another form of handy manipulation, and hardly a new one. Amongst Chaucer's travellers to Canterbury, the pilgrim most frequently condemned as truly evil and manipulative is the pardoner, a charlatan who sells cheap absolution to the gullible, carrying fake holy relics and spinning a nice line in guilt-inducing rhetoric. This includes a classic story, which he tells to the pilgrims. In un-Chauceresque style and with a bit of licence, here are the bones of it.

The Pardoner's Story

In Flanders long ago, there were once three revellers who had given themselves up, day after day, entirely to drunken indulgence and all available vices. These three fellows, hearing at the tavern that Death had been carrying off their toping companions all around, decided to find the grim reaper himself and sort him out once and for all.

As they hastened across the fields, they met an old man and, treating him with little respect and much rudeness, demanded to know where they could find Death. He indicated a twisted tree not far away, where they might, if they were lucky, find what they were looking for, and they at once rushed towards it. But, as soon as they reached it, all thoughts of revenge left them instantly, because what confronted them there was an enormous pot of gold.

It was theirs, of course; they understood that at once. The main problem, however, would be carrying it to safety without spies and far-too-nosey tongue-waggers noticing and spoiling it all. They soon decided to guard it until nightfall, when they would be able to take it home under cover of darkness. The youngest of the three agreed to go at once to town to fetch bread and wine to sustain them through their vigil. But as soon as he was gone, the two remaining rascals quickly agreed on their plan – it would be far better to share the gold between two people than three.

In town, the youngest villain bought the bread and wine and then visited the apothecary, where he claimed (with a certain amount of honesty perhaps) that he needed poison to kill some rats. This he used to spice the wine and flavour the bread, having done some mathematical calculations of his own and come to the conclusion that not dividing the gold at all would be the best solution. Smiling broadly, he arrived back at the camp to proffer the excellent fare he'd prepared only to find that, on the excuse of a little high-spirited wrestling, the other two had set on him and used their daggers in very deadly earnest. As he gasped his last breath, his former companions celebrated by eating the wonderful fresh bread and drinking the excellent, if slightly bitter tasting wine...

The story is widely known and there are versions from India, Arabia, Italy, Spain and various other countries, each presenting a different emphasis. In the work of the Persian mystic Attar (c.1145–1221), the story is evidently used with a gnostic spiritual meaning – the equivalents of the revellers representing the greed and deceit of the false self, which is transcended on the spiritual quest.

More or less honest salesmen and completely dishonest tricksters of one kind and another have been telling stories to their customers for centuries and might well be major unrecognized propagators of oral traditions of all kinds. At the heart of their use of the stories is the accurate enough perception that, if you get someone to see what you are seeing, they will begin to trust you; that if they begin to trust you, you can then get them to imagine a future in which they have and use and benefit from what you are selling; and that imagination of this kind is strong, stronger than rationality.

Like the preacher, priest and politician, whose use of tales may be similar, there are distinct limitations here, because many metaphors used in this manner are being used superficially for the way in which they can bypass conscious resistance – not for their deeper resonances. Sales people are not essentially concerned with whether your understanding grows and your wellbeing increases as a result of hearing their story, only that you should sign on the dotted line so that they can meet their quotas.

The visiting or wandering holy man has been an established traditional figure in many Eastern cultures and was invariably a storyteller. Kedar Nath Dwivedi writes:

> The precursor or prototype of the Western style of psychotherapy is said to be the confessional, a clear and honest confession to the priest in a private and confidential setting. In the East, the counterpart is the holy person's visit to the village. All conversations are open, in public, and therefore metaphorical and indirect. Each member of the audience can make use of it in his or her own way. Unlike direct and clear communications which aim at transmitting precise meanings, metaphorical communications in the form of stories aim to create space for reconstructing one's own meanings and provide play-space, so that people can get the meanings ('penny-dropping') as and when they are ready and change at their own pace.[6]

Wandering dervishes and genuine gurus, dedicated monks and other figures from authentic mystical/philosophical traditions that cultivate insights and understanding often used stories to communicate those insights and understandings. Unlike orthodox preachers, they do not generally explain their stories, since the process of understanding them has generally been held to be part of their effect, a process sometimes likened to digestion and nutrition. As one Sufi analogy has it, the teacher does not explain the story for the same reason that the man who sells you fruit does not also peel it and eat it for you.[7] Stories from those insight traditions are often absorbed into general oral traditions – and incidentally into many mythical cycles regarded as works of literature. Stories are a means of understanding, and the understanding that such unconventional and unorthodox teachers offer is often so sharp and revealing that anyone who hears such stories and understands them feels they simply have to pass them on.

The Sweet Merchant and the Peasant

A peasant from a remote country village went to the big city for the first time one day. He was wandering through the bazaar when he saw a man selling honey cakes and sweetmeats, squatting impassively behind his stall, like many another trader in an eastern market place.

The peasant went up to him and waved his hand in front of the man's face and said, 'Ha!'

'Why did you do that?' said the man.

'Because I thought you were blind.'

'Well, I'm not.'

The peasant looked very puzzled and said, 'So why don't you eat your sweets?'[8]

Some people are more interested in trade than taste, of course – and buying and selling is important; people need to buy into ideas as well as things. We value what we pay for. Many of the ideas the 'saint' sells you look a lot like sweets, though perhaps they feed you a little differently.

By the way, I think the woman with the china cabinet kept on polishing it until she died.

Travellers and chosen peoples

Travelling people in Scotland, Romanies in many other countries and various other nomadic peoples have been regarded as illiterate outcasts, but have yet been found to be highly literate in oral lore, the possessors of rich cultures of their own. In this respect, they have much in common with other minorities often oppressed and despised in the past, such as the Jews or First Nation Americans. There are thousands of marvellous Jewish stories and strong storytelling traditions amongst a lot of Jewish peoples. First Nation American peoples have complex and highly intelligent mythologies and all kinds of tales. When outsiders and the powerful treat you with contempt, your own culture becomes all the more valuable in defining who you are and, through its wisdoms, proving to you that you are probably more humane and educated in real values than your persecutors.

Since storytelling has become popular again in Western societies, representatives of ethnic minorities have been able, as public storytellers, to represent the much stronger living storytelling traditions of their own cultures. In England, there are many fine tellers from, for example, African, Caribbean and Asian backgrounds; in Canada and America, there are similarly some excellent First Nation tellers. There can, however, be a downside to this development. Storytelling is basic to being human and is a fundamental way of communicating. Only after that should it be seen as a badge of cultural identity. Many of the stories told by minority groups are versions of universal tales, not exclusive to those minorities. When stories have to be presented with a cultural costume by people with a particular skin colour or exotic clothes, something is being lost or ignored.

Storytelling is all around us and goes on all the time. Just as it is very easy to misunderstand the storytelling of exotic, remote or ancient cultures because it doesn't look the way we expect, it is easy to miss and devalue storytelling that is happening in the pub or the community centre or the youth club for the same reason. People always have something to narrate from their own lives and times. Reminiscence work with old people has recently been shown to have enormous value for the individuals involved, quite apart from the fact that many have fascinating stories to tell, if encouraged to do so in ways that suit them. All kinds of jokes and anecdotes and urban legends still circulate amongst all sorts of people. Yet it is less easy to pretend that nothing is lost, if we look at the majesty and scope of what has been.

Once upon a time, storytellers/bards/minstrels of one kind and another developed extraordinary powers of memory, imagination and invention, and cultivated marvellous and compelling arts of which only fleeting shadows remain. Once upon a time, people sat and listened and imagined and concentrated for hour after hour as tellers of tales spun incredible yarns. Once upon a time, it was considered normal for just anyone to at least be able to tell a tale or two to while away the hours by the campfire. Once upon a time, people were not awkward and self-conscious in the presence of told stories, nor did they doubt that there was value in the experience. Once upon a time, some people could tell stories in such a way that they could affect people's minds and bodies for the good, just through the way they shaped their words and images... All these fairy tales and mythical idealizations have at least some truth, some actuality in some past time and place. When we draw on traditions of storytelling today, it is good to be aware of those dazzling potentials.

Fables and short teaching tales

Choosing to look at fables and teaching stories might suggest that there are boundaries between forms that are always recognizable. That isn't necessarily the case. Whether one type of story is distinguished from another depends upon the view of the receiver and the context in which it is received. Here is a joke that circulated on the internet relatively recently:

The Wooden Bayonet

A young soldier has lost his bayonet, so he carves a replica from wood and keeps it in his scabbard. This gets him out of trouble for weeks, but eventually the sergeant-major gives the order to fix bayonets. Everyone obeys except the soldier, so the sergeant-major repeats the order and, when he still doesn't move, marches along the line and stares him in the eye and barks fiercely: 'You'd better have a good reason, soldier!'

'Yes, sir! Certainly, sir!' says the soldier. 'It's a solemn promise I made to my poor departed mother on her deathbed, you see, sir! Today is the third anniversary of her death and I promised by Almighty God and the King's honour I'd not bear arms on that anniversary.'

'Poppycock, soldier! Fix your bayonet!' snarls the sergeant major.

'Yes, sir!' says the soldier, just before pulling out the weapon. 'Certainly, sir! But, since I must disobey my promise to God, if he is displeased with those who ordered me, may he turn my bayonet to wood!'

Quite funny and certainly cunning, but, because it's a joke and I also mentioned the internet, which we tend to surf in a half awake state, you'll probably not think about it much, unless it appeals to you enough to pass it on. As it happens, this story also exists in several much longer versions. One of these, from *Elijah's Violin and Other Stories*, a collection of Jewish folktales edited by Howard Schwartz,[9] concerns a Jewish cobbler in Afghanistan outsmarting the king, who tests his faith in his God by continually setting him challenges. Eventually, since he shows himself to be clever and wise using the wooden sword trick, he becomes the king's adviser. As I said at the outset, what a story conveys depends a lot on the context in which it is told and the intention with which it is told.

The story of the wooden sword/bayonet can certainly be a teaching tale, but is only likely to be received and understood as such if it is presented within a frame that suggests it might be meaningful.

Everyone knows that fables are supposed to teach us things. We know this because of the way in which we learn about fables and indeed refer to them. Films and plays and books we consider to have some moral to them are talked about as fables. The name of Aesop will come up for many educated people in the West, not necessarily with the fond feelings associated with some other tellers of tales, because of the rather chilly and pompous morals with which his fables end. But the originals didn't have those. Whilst they may look like Victorian additions (and some are), apparently they were first added in classical times, albeit hundreds of years after Aesop lived – if, indeed, he did live and if the fables were the work of one man, which can't be clearly established. Collections were popular products of the scribe–publishers of the day and were drawn on by orators. To save such busy and important professionals time, these collections were put out with the morals conveniently displayed at the end, so that an orator could thumb through and find something to make his point.[10] The morals often don't even match the stories, evidence that the compilers either didn't understand them or were too slap-dash to bother.

Let's take a fable of Aesop that most people are likely to know. Its subject matter, 'crying wolf', is so well known that the expression has passed into the language. We know, or think we know, what it means. Here is the fable as it appears in most Aesop collections:

The Boy Who Cried Wolf

There was once a shepherd boy who used to look after his flocks away from the village. To relieve his boredom, he played a trick on the villagers one day. He shouted out, 'Wolf! Wolf!' When they all came running to help, he laughed at them. This happened several times. But then one day, wolves did come and attack his flock. When he shouted 'Wolf!' people thought he was playing his old tricks again and ignored him. So the wolves ravaged his flock unchecked.

Moral: Even when he is telling the truth, a liar is not believed.

The moral, in this case, is all right as far as it goes. But, because it seems to summarize the meaning of the tale, it closes it off. You can now neatly file it away as understood and go on to the next story snack, thinking no more about it. Unless, of course, something about the interpretation has jarred a little. Unless it seems to be rather like cramming a quart into a pint pot – or, indeed, 50 litres into a thimble. 'Crying wolf' happens over and over again in the 'inner economy' of the mind and, indeed, at a physiological level, in social events from family to business to national, in all kinds of day-to-day, week-to-week or minute-to-minute situations. The 'devastating revelation' that was nothing of the sort, the nervous jolt you felt when you thought a piece of rope was a snake, the hypochondriac who convinced you he was dying, the hurricane warning for what turned out to be a bracing breeze, the hype for the 'life-changing' book you rushed to read only to find it trite and empty – all of these and a host more enervating if commonplace experiences are pre-figured in the story. Again and again we don't spot the 'wolf' when it really does come because the 'boy' has been at it again.

Something else to notice: the telling is too short. It provides the bare bones, a pattern to flesh out in telling; it is not a fully told story. The techniques of elaborating the story described in the last chapter or simply the Embroidery game set out in Chapter 3 could make it grow and breathe and live in the mind for long enough to be taken seriously. In the days before copyright and property rights and big bucks deals for film rights, this was what authors used to do – elaborate and extend and magnify basic patterns in ancient, received stories. That includes great writers like Shakespeare, some of whose plots (such as that of *King Lear* for example) have clear analogues in folk literature. It is what oral tellers of tales have always done too. Faced with a live audience and the exigencies of getting them listening and involved, the story naturally starts to grow as it spills from the teller's tongue.

To make 'The Boy Who Cried Wolf' work, you might talk about the shepherd boy (or man or girl or woman, if it suits your purpose) and what he does and why it is boring and why he needs to entertain himself by playing the trick. If you were shaping the tale for some immediate purpose, you might imply a few subtle comparisons between the state of mind of the individual or group you were working with – habits, say, of using attention for immediate satisfaction or of playing tricks which trigger and waste responses one may urgently need at some other time. Or, if you just wanted to get some children interested in taking in the pattern and relating to and remembering it, you might explain a bit about the village setting and how sheep are looked after and how dangerous packs of wolves can be in some parts of the world, all of which would be very unfamiliar to the average urban and suburban child. Of course, the story ends abruptly, which is fine for adults and older children, because it works like a warning, but some younger children may prefer something to soften the savagery – the point can still be made if not all the sheep are eaten up and the boy does a bit of quick thinking and later some slower rueful learning and changing. By spinning the story out, the central meaning-carrying motif is held up for attention for long enough for the imaginative mind to be engaged. Then it can be left to simmer and cook: to resurface from time to time as experiences match up to and confirm its pattern. It will thus be shaping and moulding learning.

This way of learning has tended to be overlooked in our own culture and goes on being shunted to one side as educators focus on the 'central' tasks of encouraging literacy, numeracy and factual knowledge – which is rather like learning about methods of cooking and cooks and about food and where it comes from and how much it costs, etc., but never having time to eat more than snacks. Perhaps it is no wonder that nutrition is poor, despite the abundance of food. We desperately need ways to develop wisdom as well as cleverness; we desperately need children to develop all kinds of practical everyday understandings and take responsibility for themselves and their own complexities as they grow up. Yet we ignore or simply devalue the wonderful resource of fables and short teaching tales.

Another prejudice against Aesop concerns his use of animals, an ancient ploy in fables from many other traditions too. But the animals are used as metaphors, as in this animal fable from Aesop.

The Fox in the Well

A fox jumped into a well to drink some water and then found that he couldn't climb out. A billy goat saw the fox there and asked him what he was doing. The fox, being cunning, told him that the well was a marvellous and magical place, that the water was very special and powerful and that there was grass to eat and all sorts of other tasty vegetation. Tempted by his stories, the goat jumped in. Whilst he was looking around in disappointment, the fox jumped onto his back and used it as a platform to make his escape, leaving the goat stuck in the hole.

As with many metaphors, you have to bring to it a little imagination to arrive consciously at some real insights into deeper patterns. It is a story of a fox, but it isn't really about a fox. It is about human types and traits. We know what being foxy means; we know, indeed, that the word has become a verb, and that you can fox someone. Our ancestors lived in close contact with animals and, as language developed, they naturally used what they saw as the characteristics of animals as a shorthand for human foibles and capacities. You can wolf down your food or be a real rat or a bitch, though there might be something fishy about the idea. You might be eagle-eyed or a bit of a rabbit, eat like a horse whilst ignoring someone who is a cow. Perceptions of and indeed misconceptions about animals are enshrined in many phrases. Beast fables are an extension of this activity. Real foxes may be cunning but they are not actually devious in the manner of human beings; they are honed to survive. So the story is about a human type or a part of the human mind – a person or a part of the person that is clever but not wise. It jumps into the well to satisfy an appetite without considering consequences. It then uses unscrupulous cunning to manipulate and use the goat, which also is associated with particular traits and habits of mind, social behaviours, and so on. In this way, one can see the fable as a psychological snapshot, a parable about people and the knots they get each other into, a story about addiction or indoctrination and all sorts more.

The fable is also a wonderfully creative form and one thing the English national curriculum has absolutely right, at the moment, is the introduction and study of the fable form in Year 3, at the age of seven to eight. Children can go on to create their own fables and some can make profound enough points, of which their creators are not necessarily aware. Here's an example from a bright eight-year-old.

The Spotted Snake

There was once a snake, which came out in brilliant purple spots that just wouldn't go away. The snake learned to live with them but one day some hunters saw it in the jungle and chased it and caught it and took it back to be shown off in a zoo as a rare specimen. A lot of people were very interested in it. However, the snake was so upset at this change in its life and so unhappy with it that all the spots fell off and it just looked like an ordinary snake after that.[11]

The timing of the fable teaching might be right but, regrettably, modern education rarely attempts to reap a harvest of understanding by revisiting ideas studied and artefacts created when they have had time to brew a bit. Fables are studied as literary forms that need to be known about and because they seem a simple place to start on studying structure for fiction, not as instruments of thought to be developed and refined through a combination of reflection and experience. Two years on, the boy who wrote the fable very probably regarded it as kid's stuff.

Some more fables will crop up in further chapters, but here are some examples with content that deserves to be heard and marked as much today as when they were created in their original forms centuries ago.[12]

The Four Wise Men[13]

There were once four men who were considered wise and learned. They had studied all the arts and sciences of the day and had learned many strange and wonderful things in their journeys around the known world. These four wise men met up on the road one day and decided to compare notes on the most important things they had discovered.

'You know,' says the first of them, 'I've come to realize that the most essential thing is common sense.'

'Common sense!' says the second. 'That's ridiculous! Why travel the world to discover something any householder will tell you? Why, I've learned something much more important.' He picked up an old bone lying beside the road.

'Now,' he continued, 'by my art, I can show you the form of this long dead, ancient creature.' So saying, he placed the bone on the ground, arranged around it some twigs and stones and, muttering a strange, esoteric word, he opened a small bottle and poured a little of a potion onto the assemblage. At once, there was a puff of red and green and purple smoke and, as it cleared, the bone became many bones – jaw bones, thigh bones, breast bones, tail bones, rib bones and vertebrae, all marching around and taking their places and becoming an enormous skeleton that lay before them, the bones bright white in the sunlight. 'There! Is that not better than common sense!' he proclaimed triumphantly.

'Better indeed,' said the third. 'But what I have learned is even better. For what use are bones without flesh?' And he set to work, arranging dust and dried leaves here and there over the skeleton, then muttering his own outlandish mantra as he sprinkled a pink and yellow powder here and there over the frame. Suddenly, there was another puff of smoke and veins and arteries and organs and sinews began to appear and a scaly skin began to weave itself over them all until there it was, the long dead ancient beast lying prostrate before them just as it had been the day it died thousands of years ago. He bowed and asked rhetorically, 'What is mere common sense beside such arts?'

'Very little,' said the fourth. 'But what use is a body without life? The secret of inspiration is the most sacred and marvellous of all!' With a certain amount of ceremony and a large amount of self-importance and indeed dramatic style, he leaned down beside the nose of the long dead creature and breathed into its long dead nostrils. At once, the great lungs heaved and the great heart pounded and the long dead eyes flickered open and the creature jumped up and roared. Then it chased and ate all three of those fools for its first snack in centuries.

Three, but not four. The first, you see, had learned common sense. As soon as he saw what the others were doing, he went and climbed a tall tree.

Words[14]

A man was walking by the sea one day when he saw something washed up right in front of him. It was a skull, and the sight of it shocked him for a moment, but what happened next soon shocked him even more, because he heard himself saying, 'Whatever brought you here?' and then, quite distinctly, he heard an answer: 'Words!'

'What! You spoke to me!' said the man. 'That is amazing. Do it again!'

'Words brought me here,' said the skull. 'Words, only heedless words!'

'This is incredible. I must go and tell the chief at once!' the man said to himself. Off he went immediately and found the chief, lying on a leopard skin covered couch, being fanned by a lackey under the shade of a tree and dealing out justice to his people with the help of armed warriors. The man rushed up and began to babble about the amazing thing he had seen, this talking skull, this miracle. The chief looked more than a little displeased at the interruption and he said, 'If you are lying, then you will pay with your head!' And he gave the command to his servants to carry him down to the beach to witness the wonder.

When they arrived, the skull was still there. The man went up to it and he said, 'You see, here is the skull itself. Listen...' He stooped over the skull and asked, 'How did you get here?'

Silence.

The man looked a little desperate. 'Tell me please!' he said loudly and distinctly. 'How did you get here!'

Still silence – apart from the breaking waves and the seagulls. There was silence, too, when he screamed and implored and beseeched that skull to speak, again and again.

The chief looked angry. 'You have wasted my time with your lies,' he said. 'Now you must pay the price.' He commanded his warriors to behead the man and throw his body to the fishes of the sea for food. This they did and the chief was carried back to his court.

Time went by and then, on a bleak morning, a wave threw up a skull...and then another skull, so that the two of them were side by side on the wet sand. One of those skulls asked the other, 'How did you get here?'

And the second skull said, 'Words!'

The Ploughman and the Snake[15]

There was once a ploughman who found a frozen snake in a field. As he was admiring the delicate patterns on its stiffened skin, he was amazed to realize that he could actually hear it speaking. 'Help me!' it hissed faintly and desperately. 'Pick me up and warm me...please!'

The ploughman was fascinated, but naturally wary. 'You are a snake,' he answered. 'Snakes bite!'

'You have my promise,' said the snake. 'I won't harm you. Just warm me please! Otherwise I shall die.'

The ploughman felt sorry for the snake and privileged because he had been able to hear it speaking, so he gently picked it up. It was as hard and solid as a stick and he carried it with him as he went home, marvelling at the beauty of the thing and holding it against his chest so that it might revive. As he passed his master's house, the farmer himself came out and shouted at him: 'Put that down, you idiot! Don't you see what it is?'

'I do,' the ploughman insisted. 'But it has promised me not to bite and I feel sorry for the poor thing. We should after all do good to lesser creatures, should we not?' He strode off towards his own house purposefully.

But just then, stirred by the sheer heat of the exchange and the vigour of the ploughman, the snake began to squirm and a moment later it bit its benefactor in the neck, wriggled out of his arms and slithered away. 'Vicious creature! Why did you do that?' screamed the ploughman. A moment later, he sank to his knees, already affected by the deadly poison. As he did so, he heard the snake's voice again: 'Because that is my nature. I had no choice and no voices to tell me to do otherwise – unlike you!'

The Man, the Snake and the Fox[16]

In the days long and long ago, when a man was Man and a fox was Fox and a snake was Snake, this one man was riding along a track when he saw a large snake trapped under a tree that had fallen onto it. As he rode, he realized that he could hear the snake actually speaking to him and begging him to help. Astonished at being able to understand the creature's language, he leapt from his horse and, with a lot of effort, managed to move the tree trunk (which fortunately was not too large) and release the serpent. But when he had done that, the snake immediately coiled itself around him and said, 'Now I shall kill you!'

'Why?' said the man. 'Did I not help you? Have you not heard of gratitude?'

'No,' said the snake. 'That is not in my nature. But killing is what I do and you are Man and deserve to die. Let us ask your horse whether he agrees.'

The horse was consulted and he said, 'This man rides upon my back all day long and thinks he has paid me well when he gives me hay and oats and water. But what will he do when I am old and infirm? Sell me to the knacker's yard, that's what. He should die!'

Just then a cow wandered by and the man (who was getting used to talking to animals and thought the cow looked kind) said, 'Get a second opinion. The horse is tired and has forgotten all that I have done for him.'

But when the cow was asked whether the man should die, she said, 'Indeed he should. Men have kept me many the long year, killing my calves and stealing my milk and now they would be eating my flesh, had I not heard their plan and escaped from them.'

Much the same answer came from a donkey and a camel and a sheep that also happened to pass by. Each had suffered at the hands of men and believed this one should die. The snake was about to get on with the execution with the support of the other animals when a fox happened by and the man said, 'Fox! Fox! Please explain to these creatures that they are punishing me for deeds done by others. Help me and I shall never forget you!'

Now, when the fox heard what the case was, she looked puzzled. 'I am not sure how this can have happened,' she said. 'Was a creature as strong and quick as you, snake, really trapped under a tree? I don't believe it.'

'Yes, yesssss!' said the snake. 'Let me show you how it happened.'

'Very well,' said the fox. 'Man, you must help by lifting the tree again since we cannot stand it up alone...' And she watched as the man, with yet more enormous effort, levered the tree up and the snake slithered under it and then she commanded that the tree be lowered again so that the snake was trapped, just as before. 'You sssssee!'

'Yes,' said the fox, 'and that is where you should stay! Don't forget your promise to me, man.'

That really is just about the end of the fable. The man went off and the other animals did too and the snake was left trapped. Whether it found another creature to release it, I don't know. Have men remembered their debt to foxes since that time? Well, ask yourself this. The last time you saw a fox, what was it doing?

The Two Otters and the Jackal[17]

An otter caught and killed a large fish of such a size that he couldn't land it himself. Another otter was hunting nearby and, with grunts and squeals as he struggled not to let go of his catch in the rushing water, the first otter attracted her attention and, between the two of them, they got the fish onto the bank. But then they began to argue about how they should divide the spoils. The second otter wanted an equal share for her work, whilst the first wanted more because he had caught it in the first place.

As they were arguing, a jackal happened by. 'Are you having some difficulties?' he enquired politely, and the two otters at once began angrily to protest their cases.

The jackal held up his paw. 'If you will trust me to judge between you, I shall divide the fish in a just and fair way.' The otters agreed, so he at once bit off the head and gave it to the first otter and then he removed the tail for the second. 'What about the body?' the two otters cried indignantly.

'Oh,' said the jackal. 'That is for me. Haven't you heard that when you employ a lawyer, you have to pay the fee?'

The Frogs and the Snake[18]

In the kingdom of the frogs, the royal couple did not swim or jump, as did other frogs. That was considered unseemly. They squatted regally upon the royal lily pad, giving their commands and growing fatter by the day. When they wanted to move on the water, the lily pad was pushed by 30 strong bullfrogs. When they travelled on land, the bullfrogs bore the lily pad on their heads, hopping in strict time together, which gave a bumpy if majestic ride.

A snake came to this kingdom. It was a very old snake and had lost most of its teeth. Unable to catch prey as it had done when it was younger, it had developed guile and cunning. When it reached the edge of the pond, it attacked no frogs but began placidly to eat the grass and leaves.

The king and queen at once gave orders to the general of the frog armies to attack the monster and banish it, but when they surrounded it pointing their reed swords and threatening, the snake merely said, 'I have come in peace to serve your royal master and mistress. Please inform them that I am a vegetarian and there is no need to fear.'

This surprised all of the frogs. When the general reported this response, the king and queen frogs had themselves taken by the royal bullfrogs to a place a safe distance from the snake, where they asked how it planned to be of service. The snake smiled a snake smile and said, 'Your royal majesties, just think how uncomfortable that lily pad is. Why not ride upon my back? You would be the envy of other frog monarchs.'

The king and queen hesitated. The idea certainly appealed. 'How do we know we can trust you?' said the king.

'Test me,' the snake insisted. Humbly and meekly, he allowed himself to be ridden by several soldier frogs and eventually by the large general frog. No harm came to any of them, so at last the king and queen mounted their royal steed.

Nothing unpleasant happened to them either. They sat astride the snake and the frogs cheered as they were carried around the pond and through the water and then on beyond to visit their royal neighbours at other ponds, who of course were all even more green than ever with envy.

This went on all day until the king and queen were thoroughly used to their marvellous bearer. Then the snake began to slow down and eventually he stopped. When asked what the matter was, he said he needed food. The vegetarian diet wasn't giving him the strength he needed. 'What I really need to eat,' said the snake apologetically, 'is a frog.'

'Is that all?' said the queen. 'General, bring a prisoner frog for the royal snake.'

That is how the snake got the food it wanted. Day after day, it ate frogs – prisoners, criminals and then poor volunteers who sacrificed themselves for the good of the frog kingdom. So it went on. So it still goes on, though as time goes by, the snake is looking healthy but there are somehow far fewer frogs. The king and the queen are looking juicy and tempting too. But what happens in mythical kingdoms of frogs has no relation to our world, of course.

Dilemma tales

The dilemma tale may initially seem less familiar than the fable but is a closely related form that has been firmly established in the traditions of many parts of the world for centuries. Modern dilemma tales occasionally circulate on the internet, though they are perhaps not passed on as avidly as are jokes. They are also sometimes presented, in various trainings, as philosophical problems or as thinking exercises. The more than two-thousand-year-old Indian collection known as *King Vikram and the Vampire* or *The Vetala Tales*[19] contains 25 such stories, each of them ending in a question as to what the characters should do next. Dilemma tales have been popular in many African oral traditions too. Here, in brief, is one story from West Africa, part of which was already trailed in Chapter 1 and which is, interestingly, a transposition of a plot that occurs in those Indian *Vetala Tales*.

The Man Who Died[20]

There was once a man who had three wives, all of whom he loved dearly. He would never say which one of the three women was the most important to him, though they often tried to persuade him to do so. The man would hunt in the forest and bring them back good meat for the pot.

One day the man went off hunting and did not come back. When three days had gone by, the first wife became very concerned. She had a great skill and this was to dream and to see through her dreams that which she needed to see. She dreamed and, in the mirror of her dreams, she saw her husband lying in a pool of blood and understood that he had been speared by the tusk of a huge wild boar he had been hunting and then trampled under its feet. She awoke and told her co-wives.

Now, the second wife had the skill of following tracks. She could read all kinds of signs and use all of her senses in just the right way. She led the way through the forest, following what tracks there were and the little almost invisible signs and they found the husband, who seemed to be dead.

The third wife, however, had the skill of healing. She gathered herbs in the forest, mixed them together in a little pot over a fire and made a potion. This she gave to her husband, who soon revived. The three wives escorted him back to the village and all of them rejoiced.

But, once back in the village, the three wives went off. They each took a separate pot and made a separate dish. The first, who had dreamed the dream, made a stew of chicken; the second, who had tracked, made a stew of groundnuts; and the third. who had healed, made a stew of pig.

Now the question is, since he had only one mouth and one stomach, which dish should he eat, as this would reveal which wife had proved herself the most important? Or what else might he do?

Dilemma tales vary. There may be several options or apparently just two, as the strict meaning of dilemma might suggest, but the essence of the dilemma presentation is the same. The story is not finished and you are left to decide how it should. There may be wise solutions which make the dilemma melt away quite quickly, allowing you to argue for one of the alternatives presented, so that the dilemma is really only rhetorical. Or the dilemma may really be solvable in several different ways, equally valid. Or the way forward may be to challenge the terms in which the dilemma is presented. There are all kinds of options.

In the case of the story of the man who died, in place of the last paragraph and the dilemma, you could add an ending like this:

> The man at once picked up the chicken stew and gobbled it up, because he knew that, without imagination and vision, life is as nothing.

This would turn the story into a fable of a kind. But so would this ending:

> The man thought for a moment, and then chose the pot of ground-nuts. When he was asked why, he said, 'What good is dreaming and what good is healing if the patient cannot be found?'

And this one:

> The man picked up the chicken stew and shook his head. He picked up the groundnuts and, again, he shook his head. Finally, he picked up the stew of pig meat. 'This is for me,' he said smiling broadly. 'For its maker gave me back the gift of life and, without that, I could neither track nor dream!'

Each of these endings would be valid in its way, but might leave a nagging sense of injustice. Without the dreamer, how would they have known what had happened to him? Without the tracker, how would they have found him? Without the healer, would he not have been dead and buried? Each, then, was as important as the other, so perhaps this is how the tale should end:

> The man looked at each of the dishes and marvelled at the wonderful skills his wives had shown. He pondered a long time and the dishes began to cool. Then he leapt up and rushed away and came back with a large pot. Into this he tipped all three dishes and mixed them up.

> For life needs dreams and dreams need to follow signs and signs are
> nothing without life and consciousness to perceive and order them.

Maybe this is a satisfying end, but you can very easily go on
arguing and considering other possibilities. Perhaps you will come
up with a better ending. The tale is widely distributed in world
oral literatures because there is a metaphor there that is central
to being human and the dilemma presentation brings that up for
consideration.

In some of its other forms, this story is not a dilemma tale at
all and the decision is made for you through the telling – which
you could say is true of many stories you hear and read. It is
possible, conversely, to make many teaching stories into dilemma
tales simply by leaving them unfinished and discussing possible
outcomes and choices with your hearers. In certain contexts, that
can be a useful thing to do.

A good few years ago, before I knew very much about therapy
and particularly little about psychosis, I had an early morning visit
from a friend, who complained that the sky was coming in through
his head and raved incomprehensibly about all kinds of things,
like someone in the midst of a nightmare from which he cannot
escape. I allowed him to ramble, settled him down and made a cup
of tea, but somewhere along the way began to intuit the need to
get him to simply wake up. I knew that he liked stories and had a
lot of ideas about them, so I began to tell and to discuss the well-
known *Arabian Nights* tale of the fisherman and the genie in the
bottle. In this story, the fisherman finds a bottle in his nets and
opens it. In a flash, a huge genie is towering over him, which had
been imprisoned in the bottle by King Solomon many years before.
Now released, it vows vengeance upon mankind. This dreadful
apparition announces that it will kill the fisherman who, thinking
very quickly, refuses to believe that the genie has actually come
out of the bottle at all, since it is so big. The genie, put on its
mettle, demonstrates how it can shrink down and fit into the bottle
and the fisherman promptly replaces the stopper. From inside the
bottle, the genie now promises wishes and wealth and all sorts if
the fisherman will only let it out. At this point, not really knowing
why, I stopped the story and asked my visitor, who had quietened
down considerably now, what the fisherman should do. The effect
was extraordinary, as we discussed possibilities and he gave me a
series of answers that indicated at once that he had picked up on

the relevance of the story to his state then and there. In a sense, we had managed to put the genie back in the bottle through the activity of telling and listening. In a sense, he became aware that the fisherman's dilemma mirrored his own predicament.

This is only an anecdote. Stories are not a cure-all prescription for psychosis, or for anything else, and there are plenty of cases where their use would be ineffectual. It would be impossible to separate out the effect of the attention I was giving my friend and the calming suggestions my body language and general concern were conveying. Nor can I say that the story actually healed him on the spot, which would make the story even better! What it did do was bring him back to his more normal functioning for long enough to consider his options more clearly: to break the dream.

Many people could benefit from working through the possibilities contained in a dilemma tale, especially when a metaphorical relevance is likely to register. If a person is indecisive, or cannot see the wood for the trees or tends towards inflexibility or is locked in black-and-white mode, a dilemma tale (or a dilemma presentation of a suitable story metaphor) may be the very means to break the circle – even when the relevance is not obvious. As a general teaching tool for use with children and adolescents, it has several possibilities and really should take its place alongside the resurrected fable. (It doesn't need its own space in an already congested curriculum because looking at dilemmas can and should be part of literature and social education and other disciplines too.)

Here are two more traditional dilemma tales of proven usefulness.

The Two Thieves and the King[21]

Two thieves presented themselves before a king. 'Your majesty,' they said, 'we are the most excellent thieves in all this land. You should employ us, for there are many ways that thieves could benefit a king.'

'Indeed,' said the king. 'I would have thought it better to have you locked away at once, as the danger to the realm you no doubt are.'

'But, your majesty, think of it. With our guile, we could steal secrets from your enemies.'

'That is true,' said the king. 'But, if I do have need of a thief, it should be only one. A king should not be seen to support too many scoundrels. I shall choose between you. So now, show me what you can do.'

'Watch me,' whispered the first thief as he crept out through the palace window and along a ledge, away up to a high tower, where a crow was nesting. Without that crow even suspecting, he put his hand in under it and stole away an egg. Then he crept silent as a shadow back through the window and stood before the king.

'Very good,' said the king. 'Most excellent! But what can *you* do?'

'This!' said the second thief. He held out the egg of the crow, which he had stolen from his companion.

Now, what should the king decide?

The Three Wizards and the Tree[22]

There were once three wizards who knew many secrets and they went together to the chief of many tribes and they said to him, 'Oh great chief, we are the three finest wizards in all the land. You should employ us as your own magicians.'

The chief looked doubtful. 'Three wizards? I am not sure that I have places for all three of you, but one wizard could be useful. Show me what you can do.'

The first wizard reached into his robe and drew out a small leather bag. This he opened and then shook from it a seed, which he placed in the ground. He took a little pot of water, poured it out over the buried seed and said some strange words. At once a little shoot appeared which grew and grew and got bigger and bigger until, before the astonished chief, there was a great tree shading the ground all around. The wizard bowed and the chief looked impressed.

'But wait,' said the second. 'See what it is that I can do.' He took a small twist of parchment and spread it out to show a fine dust with grains of many colours. He began to mutter a weird incantation, which he concluded by blowing the dust towards the tree. Suddenly the tree was covered in fruits every colour of the rainbow, some large as globes, some small as pebbles, but each of them juicy and ripe and ready for eating. 'Such is my skill,' said the second wizard.

'But mine is different again,' said the third, brandishing a small axe and then hurling it up into the air. As it fell, it split the tree into pieces and stacked those pieces in piles ready for burning. The fruit too was arranged in neat piles. The wizard bowed low.

Which of those three magicians should the chief choose?

Three modern dilemma tales

These three dilemma tales mirror some of the traditional patterns. The last of them is similar to an Aesop fable. They are presented here to give an idea of how the dilemma form can be updated.[23]

The Scientists

Three groups of scientists were working together on human intelligence. They discovered, through a programme of experiments, that it was possible to increase dramatically the intellectual capacities of children of average intelligence by a combination of drugs and diet and various mental exercises. Many of the children in the experiments became startlingly gifted prodigies.

However, a side-effect appeared to be that the marvellous children were severely retarded in their emotional and social development. As the findings became clearly established and their funders pressed for clear marketable results, the scientists met to discuss their options.

A scientist from the first group said, 'We should suspend this programme. It is damaging these children and it may well damage others.'

'Quite the reverse,' said the spokesman for the second group. 'We have to press on and find ways to solve the problems before we go public. These children may benefit the nation in all sorts of ways. We suggest bringing in some educational experts.'

'That would be a waste of money because there is no problem anyway,' said a scientist on behalf of the third group. 'These children are so clever that they will be able to survive very well, regardless of their lack of these skills, since the world loves winners. We should think about marketing strategies.'

Which group was right?

The Three Artists

The town hall was completely gutted and refurbished and a large, central civic space was created. A big mural was to be commissioned and the field was eventually narrowed to three artists. The choice of the three artists was to be made by an open ballot in which all of the townspeople could vote.

The reputation of the first artist was for style and contemporary statement. If he won, there would undoubtedly be national and perhaps international press attention, since his name was well known. The town's image would be boosted.

The reputation of the second was built on her popular touch. Her work was much enjoyed by people who bought reproductions to keep in their houses. They felt they could understand what she did, though serious critics dismissed her work as sentimental ephemera.

The third had a reputation for giving satisfaction, though what he did was often unusual and followed no regular pattern. Sometimes it appeared modern, sometimes traditional, but its main quality was appropriateness: it was right for the people and the place, so it was said (with good evidence) by his supporters – though again these did not include the critical experts. And many ordinary people had been puzzled by his work.

Which artist should the townspeople choose?

The Tree

A couple bought a house. In the front garden was a tree, a very old tree that had stood for more than a century. The tree was a local landmark: it was on the perimeter of the property and overhung part of the pavement. In the summer, when it was hot, people would often linger in its shade to enjoy the view across the way. In the winter, its gnarled shapes were often sketched by local amateur artists and, of course, in autumn, the colours of its leaves were a wonder.

There were problems with the tree. Because of its position, the safety of its branches had to be monitored constantly, since passers-by might be injured if one of them came down. The insurance position with respect to this was a little unclear. Clearing up the autumn leaves was hard work. And the couple realized that the tree definitely restricted their own view, especially in the summer, when it was in full leaf and made one side of the house dark. They were also advised that, since it was an unusual tree, its timber would have considerable value.

How should this story continue?

Puzzling tales

Two legs was eating one leg and sitting on three legs.
Along came four legs and grabbed one leg from two
legs' hand and began to run away. But two legs threw
three legs at four legs and four legs dropped one leg
and ran away. So who or what were one, two, three
and four legs?

Perhaps you know this riddling story, for which I'm grateful to
Pete Castle, editor of the excellent small circulation UK storytelling
magazine *Facts & Fiction*.[24] It may be baffling if someone introduces
it to you out of nowhere; it may sound like complete nonsense.
However, it is easy enough to work out, even if you don't have
anyone on hand to drop hints about men and dogs and stools and
chicken bones.

You could call this story puzzling only to the degree that it
sounds mysterious and strange before the penny drops. It provides
a good analogy, however, with sides of the traditional story that
need to be clearly flagged up in any discussion of their use for the
meanings and sense they may contain.

If you read through a few good collections of traditional stories
from around the world, you will soon get a sense of the huge range
of story forms available, including fairy tales and wonder tales,
myths, legends, trickster stories, jokes, ghost stories, heroic tales
and many more that fall into other categories identified by folklorists
and others. Along the way, you might discover some tales that are
like fables and dilemma tales, some that are highly imaginative
with all sorts of strangely allusive fantasy, some that are gripping
and absorbing, some that might just seem a little esoteric, some
that are funny, some that are very appealing and, one would have
to say, a fair number that will seem opaque and dull. Not by any
means every stone in the mine is a diamond, after all.

Amongst all kinds of tales, whether short or long, famous or
obscure, exotic or mundane, there are some that stand out and
may even stick in the mind because of a certain quality they seem
to have. As with the best fables, they contain analogies on far more
than one level. They can be deceptively simple at first sight and yet,
as you consider them, they can seem teasing and even confusing,
because you can look at them in quite different and even apparently
conflicting ways. A short example would be the tale of the sweet

merchant and the peasant quoted earlier in this chapter, a story also known as a tale of the Mulla or Hoja Nasrudin – a series of what are often thought of as jokes, which nevertheless are traditionally said to contain seven different meanings.[25] You can certainly look at this story from two quite contradictory angles. From the point of view of the peasant, it is crazy to be more interested in trade than taste, to ignore the possibility of eating, nourishing yourself. From the point of view of the merchant, the peasant is ignorant of the 'higher' world of trade. which requires restraint of appetite. By teasing out these and other possible interpretations and linking them together, a series of interesting complementary perspectives may begin to emerge.

The great Sufi writer, Idries Shah, who published many hundreds of stories, amongst them the three best and most coherent collections of Nasrudin stories, pointed out that there are, in the many traditions of the world, a lot of stories which are, in their fuller reality, complex teaching tales, containing all kinds of psychological and spiritual maps.[26] These seem to form the essence of the stories that crop up around the world in hundreds of different forms, always shaped around the same essential plots. Amongst them are many of the stories with which we may have become familiar in childhood, since they have been thought of as 'nursery tales' because of their outward simplicity – stories like Cinderella, Rumpelstiltskin, Sleeping Beauty, and so on. The characters and events in the stories – animals, strange people, mythical beings, etc. – may represent parts of the mind and being and can simultaneously make many other kinds of metaphor. They could be described as multiple-meaning allegories.

Whilst I will return to this theme in Chapter 7, it's not the aim of a primer in story use such as this one to travel very far in explaining what is really the province of a specialized understanding, and those interested in investigating this further are referred to Shah's richly rewarding books. But at a time when many stories from traditions are being pressed into service in business, in training, in therapy and in many other arenas, it is, perhaps, worth observing that a jewel is indeed a wonderful and beautiful thing in itself, but that it may have a different and more majestic function in the crown from which it has been stolen. To end this chapter, here is a jewel of a tale from Chinese folklore.[27]

The Wonderful Tapestry

There was once an old woman who made beautiful small embroideries and brocades for sale in the local markets. She had three sons and, since her husband had died, she supported them as they were growing up by doing this work. They lived in a poor little cottage on the edge of the woods.

One day, as this old woman was walking in the market after making her sales, she saw a painting that caught her eye. It seemed to her to contain everything she had always wanted to put into a picture and much more too. There was a fine house, a garden with flowers every colour of the rainbow, fields and forests and streams and mountains. You could almost hear the birds singing and smell the rich scents of blossom and leaf. She asked the price and it turned out she had just enough to buy it. She took it home and told her three sons that this was a picture of the place she wished to live in. The two eldest sons shook their heads and told her it was impossible, but the youngest said, 'Mother, you could live in that painting in a way, because you could make a copy of it using your own fine skills. You could weave it into a tapestry.'

The old woman agreed to this with some excitement and, with the help of the third son, set up a frame and a canvas and pricked out the basics of the design and got out her very best thread and needles and scissors. She laid out the red thread and the blue, the green and the yellow and the purple and the pink and even a little silver and gold she had been saving. Then she set to work.

After a while, the eldest two sons began to complain that she was making no money any longer and the food was running out. The old woman told them they would have to work. The youngest son volunteered to gather wood in the forest for sale in the market – people always needed wood for fires. He invited his brothers to help him, but they never did.

The old woman went on working and working. After a year, she had completed only a third of her tapestry and, before she could prevent it, a tear had rolled down her old cheeks onto the tapestry, at the thought of how much more there was still to do. Where the tear had fallen, she decided to weave in a pool of water. It wasn't in the painting, but it made the picture better. She soon forgot her sadness as she busied herself.

She went on working and working and another year passed. Then one day, as she again thought wearily of how long it would take her to finish the work, she pricked her finger and blood fell onto the tapestry and made a red stain. Suddenly, she had another idea. This would make the beginnings of the sun rising, something that was certainly not in the painting but now she could introduce light and radiance and stitch all around that stain and make it fully part of that picture. That is just what she did with all kinds of 'little accidents' that occurred after that: she worked them into the composition, so that, when it was finished, it was the most incredible combination of design and experience.

She had worked in the gloom of her house with whatever light came through the window by day and with lamplight by evening. Now she wanted to see her work in the full light of the sun, so she cut it from the frame and she took it outside. She looked at it proudly, with tears in her eyes again, but suddenly there was a gust of wind and the tapestry was whisked into the air and carried up and over the trees. She heard a kind of strange laughter in the wind. Desperately she called her eldest son and told him to run after it and find it and bring it back.

The first son followed the tapestry as best he could, running through the woods and along the valleys until he came at last to a mountain. There he saw the tapestry disappear beyond the highest crags and he was about to turn away and go home empty-handed when he saw an old, old woman, shrivelled up like a dry old leaf and squatting outside a cave. 'I know where your mother's tapestry has gone,' she croaked through puckered, wrinkled lips. 'It was the Dragon King of the Eastern Heavens. He saw your mother's tapestry in his magic mirror and envied it and commanded the Fairies of the Western Winds to bring it to him. If you want it back, you must climb onto this horse.'

The first son then noticed a horse, but it was made from stone and had been there many a long year, since it was streaked green from the rain and covered with moss. It stood under a tree, looking up at branches on which there were berries red as blood, as if it wanted to eat them. 'This is a magic horse,' continued the old woman. 'You must knock out your own front teeth and put them in the mouth of the horse and then it will come to life and eat those berries. When it has done that, it will be able to carry you through the air, over that mountain, across a sea of boiling oil and then a sea of ice and, finally, through a fiery mountain. If you can hold on, then you will reach the Dragon King's kingdom and find his jade palace. You must demand your mother's tapestry and he will not be able to refuse.'

All this talk of knocking out teeth and danger didn't appeal to the first son, who said, 'Isn't there another way?' The old woman reached into the cave and said, 'Well, there is this.' And she handed him a pot of gold. 'Take this back to your mother and tell her she has been well paid.'

The first son was amazed and stammered his gratitude – the pot contained wealth beyond his wildest dreams. He promised to take it back to his mother and brothers but, somehow on the way, the thought occurred to him that it really belonged to him and that he should at least go to town and spend a little on himself first. Once in town, he somehow forgot all about taking the money home, as he enjoyed the company of the many new friends who flocked to help him spend the money.

When he didn't return, the second son set out to find him and the tapestry. He followed the trail and arrived in time at the cave where he met the old woman. She told him the same things, but he too preferred to take the pot of gold, he too somehow came to the same conclusions as his brother. Soon he too was in town, enjoying the parties and the fun.

The third son had to go, though his mother begged him to stay, since she was so filled with remorse and sorrow at the loss of her two sons and the tapestry. He promised that he would return and, when he finally found the old woman at the cave, he promptly jumped up into the stone saddle, knocked out his two front teeth and put them in the horse's mouth. The horse suddenly sprang up and ate the berries. Soon the third son was hurtling through the air on its back at great speed, way over the mountain and then across the bubbling, boiling black sea of oil and the bright white sea of ice. He clung on as the horse that had been stone leapt straight into the midst of the fiery mountain and was surprised when the flames did not burn him. And he found himself approaching the great jade palace of the Dragon King, who was coiled around a huge jade throne, his red scales glistening. But the third son, after his ordeal, showed no fear at all and he stood before the Dragon King and he said, 'Give me back my mother's tapestry, which you stole.'

'Wait!' said the Dragon King. 'We only borrowed it. I saw it in the magic mirror and saw that it was the most beautiful thing in all the world. My maidens are copying it. Let them finish and I will give you a magic you will not regret.'

The third son agreed to that and watched as four and twenty beautiful girls worked at a great loom in the palace gardens, copying the tapestry. He could hardly take his eyes off one of the girls, the most beautiful of them all. She was working with great skill and artistry, more quickly than the others, and she finished her part first. But she shook her head. 'No,' she said to herself, 'my work is good, but not as good as the original. That is where I should like to live.' To fill her time, she embroidered a picture of herself into the original tapestry.

Once the others had finished, the Dragon King commanded that the tapestry should be rolled and bound with golden cords so that the third son could carry it back, and soon he was again racing through the air, through the cold and the heat and back over the first mountain to the cave, where the horse came to rest beneath the same tree. The same old, old woman was there. She reached into the horse's mouth, removed the teeth and put them back into the third son's mouth. It was just as if they had never been removed. 'Now,' she said, 'take the tapestry back to your mother.'

The third son thanked the old, old woman and hurried back to find his mother. She was almost dead with grief at all her losses – she had thought he too would never return. But she revived when she saw him and the tapestry. The two of them spread it out in the sunlight to admire it all over again. Then suddenly the wind was blowing again and the laughter was there again. But this time, the tapestry was not carried away anywhere at all; it simply spread out and spread out until it covered the whole land. And it became a real place and the third son took his old mother to live in the fine house that had been in the midst of the picture. There, beside a pool, feeding the fishes and wearing a flame red dress, he saw a girl with long hair black as night and with almond eyes that sparkled like the dew in the morning. And if he didn't marry her and live happily, this isn't a fairy tale you've been reading.

But happy endings are not for all. Two old beggars came by one day and they looked in at the gates and saw the beautiful house and the marvellous lands beyond. They shook their heads in shame and went on their way. They were, of course, the two elder brothers, who had soon spent all their gold and now had nothing. That is their story and I hope it isn't yours.

Chapter 5

Marvellous Miniatures: Making Short Metaphors

If your face is ugly, learn to sing.
— *African proverb*

All communicators know, at least intuitively, that the right saying, the pithy maxim, the apposite joke, the brilliantly allusive simile or the cunning and resonant analogy are all worth ten or maybe a hundred times their weight in more linear forms of explanation. This chapter is about this very accessible miniaturist's art, a habit of thought and expression that can become second nature. A lot of people find that they can simply catch that habit and begin straightaway to use it creatively – maybe abandoning one or two common prejudices along the way.

In the subtle world of story and metaphor, forms tend to flow into each other – to expand and proliferate in one context and to distil down to essences in another. These 'miniatures' provide an opportunity for instant 'reframing' – a metaphor in itself, which is now used and understood quite widely. As psychotherapist and writer Rubin Battino puts it:

> A reframe creates a new story, a new metaphor, about the client's life. In effect, to do a reframe, you ask the client to step outside the picture of her life and to put it into a new frame or context... In fact, it is the author's contention (even conviction) that the central

factor of almost all effective change work is reframing. It is also his contention that effective reframing is metaphoric in nature.[1]

A reframing technique of any kind puts the concern or the situation or the thought or the feeling in a different frame, showing that it can be viewed in a different way, that there are more facets to the diamond than might appear – or that a stone might indeed be a diamond or an emerald, looked at in the right way. Reframing is an essential tool in counselling and psychotherapy, but reframing of all sorts has applications way beyond therapy, because changing perceptions is important in very many fields – education, science, business, negotiation, healing, design and problem solving, for a start. It is no accident that very many of the founders of religions were storytellers, since stories can operate in so many different situations at so many levels. In the current era, where religion is so often used as a tribal identity or has become fixed around sets of inflexible dogmas, it is often difficult to appreciate that the founders of many religions were in their day quite radical. The parables of Jesus, the teaching stories of Muhammad, Zoroaster and Gurū Nanak, and the Jataka Tales of Gautama the Buddha challenged people to think in different ways, to reframe the ways in which lives were lived.

Whilst there are plenty of people whose hardships would have tested the patience of the proverbial saint, there are plenty more whose difficulties come very much from the way in which they are viewed. Change the perspective, get them to see that the bottle might be half full rather than half empty or that the bait could look different when hunger is satisfied in other ways, and you are well on the way to changing the concern itself. Indeed, even an extremely severe problem such as a significant physical impairment or the aftermath of a devastating experience can be changed in its effect and diminished in its power when it is viewed differently. And this change in perspective can often be achieved extremely quickly, when employing one of the many manifestations of metaphor described below.

Jokes and anecdotes

Jokes usually rely on causing a sudden shift of perception in the listener through a punch line. A major part of the art of telling a good joke is to make the listener think one thing and then be 'caught' by the ending. Comedians are commonly expert at this and there is a lot any storyteller can learn about timing, non-verbal language and so on from watching a good one.

Enoch and the Cockerel

Ely says to Enoch: ''ow's your new 'ouse?'

Enoch says: 'Well I like it now, but it was bloody awful to begin with. The neighbour 'ad this cockerel, see. Every morning the damn thing was crowing. Four o'clock it'd start and you couldn't sleep a wink after that.'

'What did you do about that, then?'

'Oh, I bought it off 'im.'

''ow did that help?'

'Well, now I keep the cockerel in my garden and it wakes 'im up!'

If you're not familiar with Ely and Enoch, that could be because you are not from the English West Midlands. Ely and Enoch are two Black Country characters – the Black Country is an area to the west and north of Birmingham and up towards Wolverhampton. People from that general direction are inclined to do exaggerated imitations of the local sing-song accent when telling Ely and Enoch stories, of which there are very many. I well remember my two uncles, both of whom lived and worked in the area, swapping dozens of them at my grandfather's funeral many years ago.

But the story above doesn't need its local setting to work. In fact, it doesn't 'belong' exclusively to the Black Country at all, since it is known in a lot of other versions, including a Middle-Eastern Nasrudin version and an American Mid-Western tale. (I'll be taking a look at how stories migrate and change in the next chapter.) The interesting thing about this tale is the way it illustrates reframing from another perspective. Indeed, it might turn out to be a story that 'faces more than one way', as explored briefly at the end of the last chapter. In other words, it has a lot more content than 'just' a joke. It also summarizes a possibility for change through reframing.

To begin with, Ely is disturbed by the cockerel. It is not his – not part of his familiar world. So he notices it. Then he buys it and it becomes his own and, now he owns it, he doesn't need to notice it any more. Anyone who has ever lived by a busy road or a railway line will know the cycle very well, more or less literally. Metaphorically, on all sorts of levels, this kind of thing is happening to us all the time.

It brings to my mind a conversation my mother used to quote on Sunday mornings, when the village church was drumming up business in the traditional way. 'Isn't it lovely?' says the visitor. 'Eh?' says the villager.

'Isn't it simply charming, that wonderful peal?' says the visitor. 'How many are there?...one, two, three, four...'

'I'm sorry, you'll have to speak up. I can't hear anything for these damn bells!'

A quick reframing story doesn't have to be at all complex. Of course, it is great if it has depths the recipient can come to gradually but, at the level of first aid, as it were, it has to hit the spot. There is no point in offering a tale you know to be profound and meaningful and many-sided if it doesn't have the initial zip to thwack through the usual hedge of prejudice and habit. In fact, a trivial joke or a little personal anecdote might be much better for the purpose than a story of real depth – which you could always add later anyway. If you want to hit a nail, you use a hammer, not an engraved brass pot...and certainly not a flower.

There's a curious affinity between the work of the founders of major religions mentioned earlier and the medieval jesters, many of whom were also storytellers and who, by tradition, were allowed, through their humour, to say things to monarchs that would have led to imprisonment or instant death, if said by others.

The Jester and the King

A certain king was, according to legend, returning from a battle, blood-stained and sweaty – and very thirsty. He loudly called for water and the jester rushed out with some. 'Your majesty,' he said, as the monarch grabbed at the cup, 'at this moment, if such a drink could not be found, how much would you give for it?'

'Oh!' said the king loudly and carelessly. 'Half my kingdom!' And he gulped the water down.

'And now,' says the jester, 'now that you have that water inside your body, if it refused by some enchantment to leave your body, how much would you give for its removal?'

'Why, half my kingdom,' came the reply.

'I suppose, your majesty,' mused the jester, with a show of perplexity, 'that a kingdom you'd exchange for a mouthful or two of common water and a jet of piss is worth all these bloody wars and battles...?'[2]

When someone makes you laugh, you are more likely to trust them – and more likely also to hear what it is they are saying.

Sayings, maxims, et al.

'Look before you leap!' 'Too many cooks spoil the broth.' 'Decide in haste, repent at leisure.' What kind of reaction do you have to these widely known, admittedly shrewd but maybe rather dog-eared old sayings?

Those who are familiar with them may feel an element of irk – if of a certain age, they may recall these as the kind of sayings with which an older generation tried to cut them down to size. Some people might even feel confrontational: 'Decide in haste...? Yes, I will, if I want to, thank you very much, and you can forget all your guilt trips and repentance! Who are you to come telling me what to think and do? Where would Bill Gates be if he hadn't done his bit of leaping?' Others might challenge the wisdom of the saying. 'Too many cooks...? Well, no doubt there comes a point but, on the other hand, there is such a thing as intelligent teamwork. And who's to say that the broth that combines ideas about seasonings won't be better? Two heads are better than one, after all.'

Some may find themselves nodding sagely and a little ruefully: 'Yes, of course we should look before leaping and if only we had known that back whenever when we did this or that rash thing. Oh yes, there's a lot of truth in these things when you come to think of it. If only such and such a person we know would listen...' The overall conclusion, however, is quite likely to be that sayings are redundant and idiotic things surviving from a conservative and unthinking past, possibly something to snigger about and mock. (That certainly seems to be the thrust of a little book I was given recently; it is named *The Languid Goat is Always Thin*,[3] after one of the strange sayings it contains.) At best, they might be useful for summarizing, after the event, what we ought to have learned, though not much use as preparation for it.

The reality may well be different. Perhaps, culturally, we have simply lost contact with the ways in which such aphorisms can operate. It could be that familiarity with and thought about a number of sayings produces an acute and flexible understanding of everyday realities. Indeed, as a starting point for working with sayings, I'd recommend taking a common saying and turning it over in your mind, noticing all that it might mean, what different kinds of reaction you and others might have to it, how you might justly challenge what it appears to assert (in the way I've done above) and how that could dovetail with other understandings, and so on. Used in this way, many hoary old saws can become great ways of holding up, freezing and beginning to see more clearly what you and others may think, feel, believe, see, experience, etc., instead of something to which you have a knee-jerk reaction. In other words, they can provide a powerful reframe.

Seven perspectives on sayings and maxims

1. The saying is right in these ways... (Think of several instances)

2. The saying is wrong in these ways... (Again, think of instances)

3. By combining these two sides of it, these insights arise and might lead to these practical principles...

4. Some less than obvious interpretations of the saying might be...

5. Some metaphorical applications might be...

6. People who quote this might be saying...

7. I could imagine using this saying (or a version of it) in these contexts...

But whilst it is a great exercise to look at such sayings with a fresh eye, I am not suggesting that you go around using them just anywhere and everywhere. These days you might not get many brownie points for informing an audience that 'the journey of a thousand miles begins with a single step'. This powerful and resonant Chinese metaphor, a relative newcomer in Western culture, is one of those which caught on, got taken up, found their way into speech writers' palettes and that Universal Book of Instant Clichés on which we all draw. Once that happens, all sorts of associations begin to obscure the original sense, whether or not the saying enshrines a marvellous truth. Alfred Korzybski's much quoted maxim 'The map is not the territory' is a wonderful summary of the kind of understanding we need perpetually to develop and renew if we are not to fall victim to the limitations of our own personal maps. Most depressed people could learn a lot from it, along with many scientists, politicians, philosophers and others. But, again, it is almost too widely quoted to retain its full meaning.

Sayings, aphorisms, apothegms, etc. tend to wear out with repeated use. We can become so habituated to hearing them that some highly resonant multi-level metaphors become mere verbal wallpaper. So a second very valuable exercise is to experiment with recasting a saying.

Look before you leap – example re-workings

Just because you can jump, it doesn't mean that the far bank is close.

Good pilots check the length of the runway before taking off.

High jumps are great – but there are such things as low ceilings.

Before you use the ejector seat, make sure you aren't in a helicopter.

It's great diving into the water – if the crocodiles really are asleep.

The good thing about doing this kind of exercise with a saying is that you can take the essence of it and put it into a form that can work especially well for the audience you have in mind. After all, although we might object to the bullying, nannyish quality of the original, most of us would accept that there are circumstances where it is indeed wise to look before we leap and that there are many of us who need to absorb that kind of advice. With constant practice, it even becomes habit to recast in a modern, meaningful way. Here are some suggestions for practising on. (Those that aren't attributed are all anonymous.)

Sayings familiar to most

Pride goes before a fall (Old Testament – Book of Proverbs)

You can lead a horse to water but you can't make it drink

Least said, soonest mended

A stitch in time saves nine

Decide in haste, repent at leisure

Don't throw out the baby with the bathwater

Look after the pennies and the pounds will look after themselves

What a tangled web we weave when first we practise to deceive (Sir Walter Scott)

You can have any colour you like as long as it's black (Henry Ford)

To have friends you first have to be a friend

If at first you don't succeed... (attributed in folklore to Robert the Bruce)

Not so familiar perhaps

One lie in the sultan's head will drive out a thousand truths (Arab saying)

When the teacher is asleep at the desk, the children may well misbehave

If there is no rain in the mountains, the bed of the Tigris will be dry in a year (Persian saying)

If you've not made a mistake, you've not made anything

If you want to know what God thinks of money, look who he gives it to

The richer your friends, the more they will cost you

Habits might start out as cobwebs but they turn into cables

A fool is a person who believes his/her own publicity

Aphorisms punch above their weight

A chef sought therapy because of concerns about what he described as inappropriate sexual feelings – becoming aroused unexpectedly in various everyday situations, sometimes even when dealing with his own children. As a loving and concerned father, he was deeply worried that he was a potential abuser, though very clearly he had no inclinations in this direction. The therapist, reaching for a reframe, pointed out that 'when you've been peeling onions, you don't have to take your tears too seriously'. The man found that this one saying hit him like a revelation, provoking all sorts of reassessments and insights.

A girl whose challenging and sometimes aggressive behaviour was proving extremely disruptive for other pupils hero-worshipped the members of a certain girl band. 'If you want to be in the band, you have to dance the same steps and sing the same song,' said her teacher. This evidently struck her with such immediacy that she began to change of her own accord.

A good metaphor, used at the right time with the right person or people, can bundle up what needs to be recognized and make it stick. It can punch much more than its apparent weight.

Aphorisms to analogies to parables

Aphorisms and analogies often have similar starting points. Sexual arousal can be triggered in the same way that any other mechanical and automatic reaction can be triggered – like onion tears, for example. Dancing and singing are forms of controlled social behaviour. Comparisons are selected intuitively, stressing the elements of pre-existing experience and understanding that need to be transferred.

Everyone makes analogies sooner or later, in explaining how they feel, what they have done, how to do this, that or the other. Analogies can be rather everyday, quite prosaic and limited. Or they can be profound and resonant. Plato's 'shadow watchers in the cave' extended analogy from *The Republic* remains charged with meaning many centuries after it was invented. Christ's parables have been enormously influential.

On the face of it, and as the word suggests, an analogy is logical and linear. Two situations are set up in parallel and a direct comparison implied – with the further implication that, if it works in that context, why not in this one? If the feeling there works in that way, can the feeling over here work similarly? But, in making at least some analogies, one is possibly making a leap to another level where a pattern underlying a whole series of different, apparently disparate outward realities is being exposed. It is likely that, in choosing an analogy to suit an individual or a target audience, and choosing well, we are working as a poet works, with a part of the mind that can grasp whole patterns and unconscious subtleties. 'When you pick up one end of the stick, you also pick up the other', as one saying/analogy has it. But you also pick up the piece of elm or willow, the broom handle or the club or the baseball bat. You also pick up the straightness or the curve, the brownness or the redness or the whiteness, not to mention the flexibility or brittleness, the dampness or dryness and many things more. There are all sorts of dimensions to an analogy, many of which may be irrelevant of course. Some, however, will have impact, maybe a searing and important one at the right time and place – just as the meaning of onion tears can be registered and understood by a chef or dance steps by a wannabe dancer.

Analogies can be brief, as are most of the ones I've mentioned so far. They can also be extended until they become stories. The following example picks up on an earlier theme.

The Lachrymose Peeler

There was once a man who spent a lot of time peeling and cutting up onions. Now most people know that onions can make your eyes smart and that, when this happens, tears automatically come into your eyes. Most people also know that such tears have nothing to do with sadness or depression or life circumstances that need to be examined. They are just onion tears, no more and no less than that. But this man...well, he had somehow or other forgotten about this and, finding the tears streaming down his cheeks, he began to wonder what had made him so sad. Perhaps it was something traumatic and dreadful in his past he had unwittingly been reminded of, though he couldn't think what...or perhaps it was a premonition, from a part of his mind that knew and appreciated such things, of a terrible event that was to come. Or perhaps he was ill... The more he thought about the tears, the more concerned and worried and, indeed, lachrymose he became.

Now, the question is did he need sympathetic understanding and antidepressants or did he need to stop peeling onions and start thinking?

This has now become a fable, or maybe even a satire, instead of a short aphorism. In this form, it allows the analogy to be held up for inspection for longer. It could even be extended further, perhaps taking the unfortunate onion peeler on a voyage of satirical and humorous self-discovery.

Sayings, parables, analogies and the other forms of short metaphor we'll deal with in this chapter are all part of what you could call the metaphor/story continuum – and this is, I believe, an extremely useful and potentially creative perspective. You can take some (not all) aphorisms and extend them to make longer analogies or short stories. You can take some (not all) stories and reduce them until they become very focused maxims or sayings.

You can, in other words, get to know an image or a story or a plot flexibly, spinning them out or condensing them down to suit time and circumstance and people and need.

Anyway, here are some sayings and brief analogies I've made up in the ways we've been discussing and that I have put to all sorts of uses myself, so I can vouch for their effectiveness. You might like to experiment with making them into longer analogies, fables, dilemma tales or even extensive stories.

Aphorisms that could be stories

There are weeds in some gardens you can only banish if you dig up the roots

You can cut your opponents down to size, but you don't have to go on to bully them

That dirty old coin could turn out to be gold when you clean it up

Thirst somehow becomes controllable when you know that the well is poisoned

When enchantment has ruined your castle, better flush out the witch before you start repairing the walls

You don't punish fish by drowning them, nor moles by burying them alive

There may be a lot of thorns, but when it blooms the rose is still beautiful

You don't find the diamonds by digging just anywhere

Similes and smiles

If a man tells a woman that she is as pretty as a picture, how might she respond? Maybe she would blush and smile in a pleased sort of way. Or maybe she would snort and say sarcastically that it depends which picture he is thinking of, a Picasso or a Francis Bacon. Or perhaps she should climb right up on the high horse and accuse him of rank sexism and manipulation? Pretty as a picture is a conventional simile. Like the analogy, it attempts to compare like with like. Like an old saw, it has become fixed and static and also contains assumptions many would want to challenge. It is maybe not the kind of image to offer to anyone you want to really impress, challenge or change.

But at the right moment with the right person and (as orators know) with the right crowd, a conventional image can still be very powerful. When you are in love and your lover says you are as beautiful as the moon or as strong as the sea, you might hear the words in a different way from that in which, say, a literary critic would. For the simile, like many other metaphors, can change its effect from circumstance to circumstance, from person to person.

Now at this point, it might be worth clearing up some confusion that lingers in many people's minds. Teachers of English are inclined to describe the simile simply as a form of language comparison involving the words like or as. A deflated tyre is as flat as a pancake or a shaved head is as smooth as a baby's bum. The same teachers will further explain that this is in contrast to a metaphor in which the comparison word drops out and the tyre is a pancake or that head is...well, not all images work both ways round. But the scope of the term metaphor is much greater than that limited schoolbook definition. The simile is just one kind of linguistic metaphor. It carries meaning over from one sphere into another and can hint at underlying patterns, just as other types of metaphor do. And it is potentially emotive and very effective.

The simile is yet another form of storytelling because simile is clearly close to analogy, which is close to maxim, and aphorism, which, in turn can, with elaboration, become story. Each and all of them can influence people and produce change. Indeed, the good and original simile can effect an immediate change – your perception is suddenly altered and you see a comparison between things that previously seemed quite different, which subtly changes your map of the world.

Something else is happening too. The simile shifts you into more imaginative mode for an instant. In order to think of a simile or to really hear one, you have to stop thinking in linear fashion. There is no reason at all why there should be the slightest comparison between, say, the new moon and the rim of a silver cup – unless you can see the likeness.

Similes can suggest action. If I challenged my daughter Asha to 'act like a lion' when she was a little younger, she would start to roar and stride around boldly, pretending her hands were claws. It could be useful to ask her to do this when there was a dark corner to pass, because she would be so much taken up with being a bold lion that she forgot to be afraid of the bogeyman she imagined was there the previous evening – or perhaps she remembered it and used her new lion persona to banish him. A simile like this can teach children a lot about being brave.

This is one of the first uses of simile to create change – using it to suggest an imaginative behaviour or strategy to overcome a concern. Therapists, for example, know ways to duck around adult resistance and get to that childish response: *'You can recall, can you not, what it was like to be a child and, you know, you really could be anything you wanted in imagination. Maybe an adult would tell you to be like a lion or something like that and you would do it, not even thinking about it, just do it and be a bold lion, a fearless creature, striding around and roaring. And sometimes, remembering something like that, you can really begin to feel what it was like to be that lion, back then, bold and fearless and roaring and growling. And that adult might say, "Come on now, let's go and sort out that bogeyman in the corner!" Soon enough you'd be that lion and you'd be chasing that bogeyman out and attacking that dark corner and really just being the lion...'* In this way, the resource of being fearless through acting is brought to mind for use with more adult fears and difficulties.

Or similes embedded in conversation can be a means of dropping in an image that implies possible actions. *'Sometimes the mind can be as clear as clear water, as all the sediment settles down... Sometimes one can begin to see things better, just like the sun coming up and burning away the morning mist... People find sometimes that there are times when all the possibilities seem clearly laid out, like dishes on a table or like countries on a map...'*

Chaining mixed metaphors

Chaining images – stringing together a series of quick, bright and fairly arresting comparisons, which flash for a moment in front of the mind with a dazzling and even hypnotic effect – can be highly effective in a variety of settings. You can see it done with huge panache and dramatic style in these famous lines from Lord Byron:

> The Assyrian came down like the wolf on the fold,
> And his cohorts were gleaming in purple and gold
> And the sheen on their spears was like stars on the sea
> When the blue wave rolls nightly on deep Galilee.
> *– from The Destruction of Senacherib*[4]

Delivering a series of similes and metaphors (in the strict literary sense I described earlier) can be a powerful ploy, at certain times, in presentations, and in teaching and counselling. In the same way that oral poets and storytellers had their stock of images to drop into different tales, it is handy and practical to have up your sleeve a few you prepared earlier, to use almost verbatim or as templates for new images. Here are a few that I keep to use or vary.

As refreshing as cool water on a hot day
As relaxing as a warm scented bath
Sometimes it feels as though you've shifted into top gear
You know that sense of just flowing along, as if the tap had been opened right up
Like a magnet, drawing all those separate fragments together
Like a tree, branching out here and there and everywhere
Like a spotlight in the darkness
As sharp as a cat's eye when a mouse is moving
As pointed as a pen
Just like hitting that ball right down the middle, the perfect stroke

Vignettes

A vignette is a word sketch, or a story without a plot. It can be a slice of life or a brief character study or just something glimpsed or sensed at a certain time, hinting at significance and thus potentially metaphorical. It comes from a French word which literally means 'little vine' but refers to the vine motif traditionally used to decorate texts – which, of course, provides a metaphor in itself.

Horses in Alexandria

Once, way back when I was a young traveller exploring bits of the Middle East, I was wandering around Alexandria in Egypt. Now it was a hot afternoon and you get plenty of those in that part of the world. People know a bit about coping with them. I'm from a much colder, damper climate, but I'd learned all that from wanderings through heat and dust and very dry lands and I was sitting outside a café, taking alternate sips from a little glass of sugared black tea and a glass of water. Somewhere nearby, in the shade of some palm trees, the driver of a carriage was asleep underneath it, just sprawled out in the dust. There were these two horses harnessed to the carriage, standing there in that shade. They were enjoying it, you could tell that, they were enjoying it a lot. They had their nosebags on and they were enjoying the oats and the shade and the rest and the relaxation. Sleepy time, siesta time, in the shade. Life was hard for them, pulling that carriage all around the streets, heaving the tourists around, the leisured people. But, right now, with the sun filtering down in shafts through the palm leaves and making dappled patterns all around, they were happy and contented, just in the moment and enjoying it. It can be just so welcome, so lovely, that moment in the day when you can simply take a break...

It can be useful to build up a stock of vignettes to draw on. Everyone has had experiences that can be made interesting. Here are some suggestions to gather ideas around:

1. a journey somewhere

2. an unusual occurrence in an ordinary street

3. a haunting image which comes back again and again

4. suddenly noticing something

5. suddenly 'coming to your senses' after being caught up in a crisis

6. a glimpse of extraordinary and unexpected beauty

7. mastering a skill.

The koan principle

The koan, as anyone with some knowledge of Zen may know, is an apparently nonsensical maxim, question or short tale, which the Zen disciple turns over in mind, allowing it to appear in one way and then another and to contradict itself endlessly until the moment of Zen illumination occurs. The example most commonly quoted (at least by outsiders) is *What is the sound of one hand clapping?*, though serious students of Zen may well refer you to less well-known examples, such as those commented on in the Zen classic *Wumenguan.*[5]

Real koans I respectfully leave to Zen specialists. Rather, I want to suggest how it is possible to use what I'll call the koan principle in effective communication and storytelling. Saying something apparently nonsensical, whether or not there is some actual metaphorical depth, can momentarily arrest habitual patterns of emotions and thoughts.

At a lecture or a talk, sooner or later someone will ask a question not to hear the answer but because of a personal need to ask a question. Or there is the individual who has apparently heard it all before and caps everything a teacher says with some wiseacre witticism or superior idea or experience or anecdote of his or her own. Maybe you have had the experience, as I have, of giving a performance or a lesson to a group who all seem fast asleep with eyes wide open. For all of these situations and others, the fake koan is the perfect tool. It should sound meaningful but be more or less impenetrable. It might be delivered with firm assurance or a comforting smile. And it can be improvised, entirely off the wall. You could call it a shock tactic. Used skilfully, with a feel for the time, for the individual or group and for the occasion, it makes listeners go inwards on a search for meaning, jolts them out of the rut of habitual listening, and fixes attention in a different way.

Here are some good ways to find the inspiration for a fake koan or two.

1. Instant improvisations: Look around you. Select some object in the room/hall/general environment (for example a chair). Think of what it can't do (fly? talk? walk?). Think of a phrase suggesting that it might: *And what will happen when the chairs begin to fly?*

2. Bizarre colours: *How often do you see a pink rifle, after all?*

3. Sound: *What would the curtains say if they knew?*

4. Scent: *What is the smell of the perfect symphony?*

5. Physical: *How does a fortune feel in your toes?*

6. Atmosphere: *How does the air feel on your skin when you get that idea?*

7. Baffling anecdotes: *I knew someone once who always had the perfect answer; she could always come up with the goods. A lot of us only think of the right thing ten minutes*

or ten hours later, but she could just do it. And do you know what she used to say? Eggs have shells and shells can break, that's what she used to say. She put the whole knack of it down to that. Eggs have shells and shells can break.

Curiously pondering what may only be nonsense may yield unexpected insights – in the same way that going for a walk sometimes allows an answer to pop into mind that you couldn't find when you were sitting at your desk.

Allegories and satires

According to the Oxford English Dictionary, an allegory is a 'narrative description of a subject under the guise of another suggestively similar', whilst a satire is (amongst other things) 'a composition in verse or prose holding up vice or folly to ridicule or lampooning individual(s)'. If the terms allegory and satire mainly make you think of works such as Swift's *Gulliver's Travels*, Orwell's *Animal Farm* or a religious allegory such as Bunyan's *Pilgrim's Progress*, it could be difficult to see allegories and satires as short metaphors at all. But both forms can also be brief and succinct, and both link smoothly to some of the shorter forms discussed earlier in this chapter.

Allegory and satire can find their starting point on the aphorism/analogy/story continuum I described. For example, one of the trials Bunyan's pilgrim has to face is The Slough of Despond, which draws a parallel between a depressed psychological state and having to travel through boggy ground. This would have been a resonant image for his contemporaries, used to the muddy tracks and undrained fields of the day – and also familiar with the fact that marshes don't go on for ever and that there are ways of navigating through them.

A satire can also be allegorical and an allegory can be satirical. If you want to lampoon certain people, you might say to yourself, 'These people are greedy and self-seeking. That is like the behaviour of pigs at the trough, so let's tell a story about pigs...' And you work on from there, making knowing comparisons along the line. Your aim is to make direct parallels at all stages. You tell a story about pigs but everyone knows you are really talking about such and such a person or political group and can share the joke. It is possible to be far more critical and damning under the veil of this form than one might, in some political climates, otherwise dare to be.

Pure allegory, however, has more possibilities than satire. Playing with comparisons in a way that does not demand that the parallels be exact can hold out the possibility of reaching the multi-level metaphor. An allegory can also be specifically shaped with specific effects in mind, and it is at this level that it may be of most interest to people using stories to aid the finding of solutions.

Take the example of the man who was stuck with a lot of pain – we'll call him David. He informed the therapist that he was 'between a rock and a hard place'. He had other equally emotive metaphors too. He felt 'weighted down', 'as though he were running in mud', yet 'keeping his nose to the grindstone' was essential with all his commitments, financial and other. Now 'those bastards' were 'getting at him again' – by which he meant the asthma and eczema that had blighted his childhood, but particularly the arthritis. 'You never know when the bastard's going to get you,' he explained ruefully. 'Happens when I'm driving sometimes. You just have to cling on and keep going. There's just nothing you can do about it – except turn the car radio up.'

David agreed, however, to learn a short relaxation exercise or two with some simple guided imagery, just as 'first aid' and, as a result, he quite soon slipped into a quiet, inwardly focused state. The therapist suggested to him that he could spend some time there and then, studying and memorizing this relaxed state and learning the feeling of it, but that meanwhile he'd go on talking. David would be able to treat this rather like that car radio babbling whilst he was coping with the traffic. After a few non-sequiturs, the therapist improvised a story. Here is a summary with some literary artifice used in the reconstruction – in the actual telling, it was spun out with all sorts of interspersal suggestions and confusional language that would be tedious on the page.[6]

The Robinson Crusoe Island

There was once a man who was marooned on a lonely island. Being very practical and being forced by circumstance to get on with things in order to survive, he soon managed to find fresh water, berries to eat, branches and leaves with which to build a shelter ('against a rock where the earth was hard'), saplings and vines to make himself a bow and arrow so that he could hunt and, in all sorts of ways, to establish for himself a self-sufficient Robinson Crusoe existence. He was even able to make fire by twizzling a stick around ('just as fast as any grindstone') using the bow, dried leaf fragments, moss and tiny twigs.

He explored the more accessible parts of the island, though there were dense forests and rocky regions. There seemed to be no other human inhabitants, but plenty of evidence of wild animals. Some of the paw prints he saw in the soft earth around the edges of the forest suggested that they would be dangerous so, very naturally, he was always on the lookout for danger and, in his imagination, the creatures loomed very large and threatening. You just never knew when they might strike. Several times, returning to his base in the shadows of evening, he narrowly escaped a confrontation with such a creature, moving around in the bushes nearby and bringing his flesh up in goose bumps in the moment before he sprinted for safety, arriving back at the camp panting and gasping for breath. Once he almost got stuck in the muddy ground as he was running away and, for days after, suffered from a mysterious yet somehow familiar rash. Several times, one or more of the wild beasts had raided his supplies whilst he was weighted down with an improvised water carrier, struggling back up from the stream. At night, he kept the fire stoked up, but one time, when he'd dozed off before feeding it, the flames had almost died down completely. Something sharp and painful gripping his leg awakened him – it could have been teeth or claws and he only saved himself by grabbing the end of a still smouldering branch from the fire, at the same time shouting something like, 'Get back, you bastard!' The branch had luckily sprouted flames at that precise moment and scared whatever it was away. But his existence seemed very precarious whenever he recalled that dark shape in the gloom and the glowing eyes reflecting the fire.

Then one day, when he was out hunting, he happened to climb a tree that rose above some of the rocks and, whilst he was listening and looking intently, he actually saw what he felt sure was one of these creatures, softly padding along the forest path. From the safety of the tree, he watched, making himself very quiet and still. He noticed that the animal was not nearly as big as he had thought it was initially, a strange looking creature that looked half cat and half wolf. Its paws were indeed large, but the body beneath the thickish, tousled fur probably had little more weight than a greyhound might have. And he realized, from the way it was cautiously sniffing the air, that it might be just as afraid as he had been. For an instant, he felt almost sorry for it.

From that moment on, something changed. He began to study this creature and others like it in his spare moments, spying on them, working out the patterns they followed, the habits they had, the little circuits they followed automatically, the territories they defended, the kinds of things they fed on, the kinds of things they left alone, the conditions on the island that made them come out or stay in their caves. He began to sense when they were around – just a feeling he learned to trust, a feeling on the skin perhaps, or just knowing it in your bones somewhere. Slowly, slowly he began to understand these creatures and to relax more and more as he made his way through the forest, trusting the understanding that was growing in him day by day, even learning from the ways of these strange creatures so that he became a more efficient hunter himself. Eventually, he even managed to tame one of them, feeding it little scraps from his store and enticing it into the firelight. He gave it a name and even petted it. By the time he was rescued from that island, several years later, he was living happily alongside a whole family of them. Every now and then, one of them might growl or even give him a nip, but he had learned how to tame and subdue them, so he scarcely noticed. And by watching them and learning to observe all the other creatures of the island in the same way, he had found ways to explore and map all of the terrain, so that he was able to show his rescuers where they could safely traverse the boggier ground and where there were seams of gold amongst the rocks...

The story and the relaxation took 25 minutes, though David was convinced it had been much shorter. He had little recollection of the story, which he said was not really his kind of thing. Nevertheless he began to be much less restricted by the arthritis, taking up both swimming and cycling. A year later, he completed the London to Brighton bike race. There was no sign of the eczema.

You might want to think up similar kinds of story for yourself, to suit contexts and conditions you are likely to work with. Here are some exercises in creating allegories and satires.

1. Use the traditional ruler and realm scheme (eg king or queen of a kingdom or far-off land) to allegorize a condition, such as an individual physical or psychological difficulty

or need, family concerns, group and corporate needs and so on. The structure is very flexible and can be applied to all kinds of activities and situations.[7]

2. Look for other typical allegorical structures that can be 'filled out' in different ways. Examples might include garden/plant imagery, quests and searches, lover–beloved relationships, master–disciple relationships, rider–horse/machine, etc.

3. Analogy and aphorism to allegory: look back through shorter images presented in this chapter and see how many can be extended to become full-blown allegories or satires (as in 'The Lachrymose Peeler' on p.194 above).

4. Think of allegories and satires with which you are familiar and see whether you are able to reduce their content to a short maxim, saying or analogy.

5. In a brief allegorical satire, Edward de Bono, inventor of the term 'lateral thinking', describes a plant he calls fogweed 'which grows very abundantly in intellectual circles but serves only to obscure and never to reveal. It is [he says] often impossible to fight your way through the fogweed to get to the basic issue.'[8] You could think of a plant which grows as abundantly with similarly negative effects in your own area of specialism – and, maybe, of some good pest control methods!

6. How about beasts and monsters you or your pupils, colleagues, clients or friends could challenge and defeat?

7. How about allegorizing some of your own personal challenges and concerns, picturing and sensing your way through a whole story? A highly self-indulgent idea, of course, but why not? You would (very naturally) make sure it ended positively.

Working with brief reframing stories

There are a lot of situations in which having a stock of brief reframing stories – particularly humorous ones – can be very useful. Here are some examples from real-life counselling situations. With imagination and thought, they can be applied in other contexts too.

Tim breathes too fast

You have introduced Tim to a practice you reckon he'll find helpful – learning to breathe in a calmer way that will effectively lower his stress and anxiety levels, which are interfering with his performance as a musician, his relationships and his study skills (he is also doing a degree). However, Tim is used to a 'disciplined programme' and obtusely insists on doing his breathing at certain set times only and then getting on with a hectic pattern of frantic activity. He complains that your much-vaunted 'technique' doesn't work very well.

Linear response (inclined to encourage the mbala effect, mentioned in Chapter 1): 'I did tell you that you really need to do it often, whenever you start to notice the stress. It's no good expecting instant results if you don't make the effort, is it now?'

Reframing story: Breaking the Diet

I was talking to a doctor the other day and he was telling me about a patient he had who really needed to lose weight – I mean, seriously, not just for vanity. So he gives her this diet sheet and it spells it all out clearly – exactly what she has to eat, quantities, weights, calorie counts and everything. She goes off promising to take it all with due gravity. But the very next day, the doctor is walking down the high street and who does he see sitting in the window of McDonald's but that very patient, tucking into a Big Mac and fries. He goes in and glares down at her accusingly. 'What's this?' he says fiercely. And she looks back and says reassuringly, 'Oh, it's all right, doctor. I had my diet for my breakfast.'

The example of the woman might be sufficiently removed from Tim's own circumstances to let him laugh at her behaviour, but in the telling one might want to point up one or two similarities, perhaps in the aphoristic style discussed earlier in this chapter: 'You know, there are some people who only want to have the diet for breakfast, others who only want to practise on a Sunday.'

Amanda can't stay awake

This time you have a workaholic on your hands. Amanda informs you that she needs your help to make it easier for her to stay awake when she finally comes home to her family late each night – and also when she is on aeroplanes, because it is great to get ahead on the laptop. She wants you to stop her bingeing on chocolate, as well.

Linear response (mind the mbala!): 'Oh, come on now, Amanda, surely you realize why you're falling asleep. You work all day and you don't take breaks and you eat your lunch at the computer or whilst talking to a customer on the phone. You're suffering from stress and exhaustion. Just remember, for goodness sake, that your body has needs and that you have to take care of that. You'll be much more efficient when you do that. Take these sleeping pills and get a good night's rest.'

Reframing story 1: Self-Diagnosis

Well, there's a man and he goes to the doctor and says he needs to see a physiotherapist to help him to strengthen some of his muscles because he has been experiencing one or two problems. He evidently doesn't want to say what these are straight away, so the doctor asks him to describe his normal day and the man says that he gets up in the morning and has a quick snort from the brandy flask to get himself started. Then, with breakfast, he likes a glass of stout, which sets him up nicely for the train to town. He usually takes along the hip flask for a snort or two more along the way. At work, he has a strong coffee with a dash of rum and then he gets through some work until mid-morning, when he likes a small sherry. Lunch is at the pub, washed down by several beers. During the afternoon, a little vodka and then off to the pub in the evening for a few more beers and a whisky chaser...

'I see,' says the doctor. 'We're really talking about an alcohol problem.'

'No, I can handle that,' says the man. 'It's just that I keep falling over.'

Reframing story 2: The Donkey and the Diet

A very religious farmer was telling some of the other farmers at the market about a plan he had for his donkey. Even animals, he insisted, were sensitive to the power of the Word of the Lord. And his donkey was fat, too fat. So he proposed to introduce a new regime. Each day, he would reduce the donkey's rations, substituting readings from the Holy Bible, prayers and choruses of hallelujah. He had also made some large glasses for the donkey to wear during the readings, so that it could learn to read the text itself in due course.

Well, when he was next at market, he was full of enthusiasm for the plan. The donkey was clearly responding to the influence of the sacred text and had become more nimble and frisky by the day. Same the following market day and the one after that. The farmer was happy to explain to all the other livestock men how they could work out a similar plan.

But another market day came around and the farmer arrived with a long face. Everyone asked him how the plan was working. 'Terrible!' he said. 'Indeed, the wiles of Satan are never to be underestimated. That donkey has suddenly become deaf to the Most Sacred Word, just when he had become slim and even thin, just when he was able to survive on nothing more than the Word itself. I had high hopes that I'd have him reading and even reciting very soon. But this morning, he let us all down – by dying!'[9]

Both of these stories can work very well wherever the common factor is an ignoring of some basic need and an almost wilful misinterpretation of symptoms and effects. However, since there is plenty of scope for firm grasping of the wrong end of the stick, it can be helpful to back up the 'statement' of the story with something intended to hint at the first sense you would like to be taken. In some of the earliest therapy work I did, I once offended a slim and very attractive, rather overworked lady, who wanted to temper a mild snacking habit, by telling the second story without any comment – at the time, it had simply leapt into my mind and seemed appropriate. 'I do not have a weight problem, as you can see,' she hissed through clenched teeth – though, fortunately for my self-esteem as a storyteller and a budding therapist, the unintentional offence the story caused anchored the metaphor long enough for a more insightful interpretation to 'arrive'.

Sally and Simon's divorce

Sally and Simon are in the midst of an acrimonious divorce. Their relationship had been based on a deep mutual respect and loving, or so they'd always insisted at the New Age workshops they had frequently attended. Unfortunately, Simon had strayed into another quite possibly mutually respectful, loving encounter with a different lady during Sally's prolonged absence on a retreat, which had led to her becoming involved in a series of not-so-deep and not particularly respectful liaisons, loving and otherwise. Now they apparently can't stand each other. The successful small crafts business they have built together is in jeopardy. Their two children are confused.

Linear responses (mbala perhaps): 1. 'For God's sake grow up and face your responsibilities. You have the children to consider and they deserve better, so you had best handle things in an adult way. All right, if you don't want to live together any more, organize things differently. Do you really need to trash everything? After all, some things obviously worked pretty well between you, unless you were lying and unless that business is just a mirage. Forget all that jealousy stuff and get it sorted.'
2. 'Let's explore your issues around jealousy...'

Reframing story 1: Baklava

A friend of mine really used to love eating Turkish honey cakes – you know, those syrupy pastry things, baklavas, stuff like that. You know what it's like when you really like a taste and you can't get enough of it. Honey cakes and, if he could get it, strong Turkish coffee in one of those little cups, with a glass of clear water to balance the tastes. He got into the habit on an extended visit to Istanbul, but there were plenty of good Turkish bakers and stores near where he lived in London. Then, one day, so he says, he bit into one he had bought from a dodgier place along the backstreets of a town he was visiting and it didn't taste right. He soon discovered why because there was a cockroach in it. He told me that baklavas never tasted quite the same after that; he was always just waiting for another cockroach. Which is silly, he knows that. As he puts it, the chances of his getting another one from his trusted Turkish bakers are probably a lot less than the chance that he'll get run over by a Centurion tank crossing the Edgware Road. But he says he's just gone off them now, completely. Funny how the mind generalizes from one particular experience, isn't it?

Reframing story 2: Two Disciples and One Guru

Two disciples would sit at the feet of a guru during the *darshan* (audience). The first would wash and anoint the right foot and the second would do the same to the left. Each thought that he did the better job. But one day the first disciple was ill and so the second did both feet. Unfortunately, he had to rush the job and, in his haste, broke the guru's right big toe. When the second one discovered what had been done, he broke the guru's left big toe by way of revenge.[10]

James won't go to school

James is nine and should be in his second term at a large junior school, but refuses to attend. He had been excited at the prospect of going on to the big school from the small village primary he attended prior to his parents' move to the area, but then felt daunted by the sheer size of the place and was fearful that he might be bullied by older children or even classmates – although that didn't, in fact, happen. However, he became ill at that time and had to spend a month in bed. He is now too embarrassed to go back and again fears he will be picked on. James is evidently nervous and fretful and alternately giggles and sulks as you talk to him. You want to establish a rapport with James, opening up ways of discussing the problem areas indirectly.

Linear responses: 1. 'Look, James, I'm basically on your side, you have to realize that. You know you can't go on forever dodging school. We've checked out the ground and there are a lot of kids who would be on your side too. School's an okay place. Lots of kids get nervous to begin with in new schools.'
2. 'Let's explore those feelings you have, James. It's really important to acknowledge them and get them out there...'

Reframing story 1: The Gorilla

A man goes to the zoo and he is excited about seeing the animals. He has never been to the zoo before and he is imagining big fierce lions growling and snarling, huge pythons writhing around wildly, elephants lifting up tree trunks and all sorts. You know what it's like when you're expecting a lot.

Well, it's one of those hot, dusty afternoons and the lions are lying in the dry grass asleep and scarcely even twitching. The pythons look like decorated bits of leather hanging up behind the glass and the elephants are placidly munching twigs. The man is disappointed. He wants action. He goes in to see the gorillas. And there leaning up against the bars is a giant silver-backed male, sitting and scratching himself, just like a fat old man. A big sign says: 'These animals are dangerous. DO NOT TOUCH!' The same message is repeated in several places. 'NEVER TOUCH THE GORILLAS.'

You know what it's like. Don't do this, don't do that. What does it make you want to do? To do it, of course. This man felt cheated, as I say, and he wanted action. So he hops over the safety barrier and he pokes that gorilla with his finger through the bars. Well, the gorilla whirls around and spits some leaves at him and the man smiles and thumbs his nose. The gorilla thumps his chest and the man copies him. The gorilla is infuriated. He grabs the bars and bends them back as if they were rubber and squeezes out.

The man runs for it but the gorilla runs after him. He runs out of the zoo and jumps onto a passing bus. But the gorilla runs behind the bus growling furiously. The bus stops and the man manages to lose himself in the crowd getting off the bus and leaps into a taxi. 'Quick!' he says. 'Take me to the airport!'

The taxi sets off for the airport, accelerates along the motorway and the man looks out of the back and sees the gorilla sprinting along and about to leap onto the vehicle. 'Faster!' he says and the taxi breaks the land speed record and leaves the gorilla in the dust and finally screeches to a halt at the airport. The man runs across the tarmac and jumps onto a plane, before anyone can stop him, and the plane takes off. Up in the air, he feels safe as he looks out of the window at the matchbox houses and thin little ribbons of road.

But suddenly, he feels a warm, heavy presence, hears loud breathing and he looks around and sees the gorilla towering over his seat. And the gorilla reaches out with its thick, hairy finger pointing straight at him and pokes him in the chest, hard. Then it actually speaks! It says: 'Right! You're it now. Catch me!'

Reframing story 2: Tom and Yesterday

Tom was a lad who had no sense at all but his mother reckoned he would learn some in good time. She sent him off to work for a farmer because at least the lad could do a day's work, if it was explained to him. The farmer did that and Tom worked hard in the fields and, at the end of the day, the farmer paid him a penny, which was a day's wage back then. But by the time he got home, he had lost it. It had dropped out of his hand as he crossed a little bridge over a brook. 'Idiot!' says his mum. 'You should have put it in your pocket.'

Tom memorized that lesson and went to work for the farmer again the next day. This time it was work in the dairy and the farmer paid him with a jar of milk, which he carefully poured into his pocket. 'Fool!' his mother screamed. 'Why didn't you carry the jar on your head?'

Next day Tom helped the farmer's wife selling cheeses in the market and she gave him a big cream cheese as a reward, but it melted all over his head as he carried it home. 'You should have carried that carefully in your hands!' his mother screamed.

When Tom helped the farmer in the barn next day, he was given one of the farm's fiercest cats to catch the mice in his mother's house but, when he tried to carry it, it scratched him and ran away. 'You should have tied some string around its neck and pulled it along behind you!' his mother insisted.

So, the next day, Tom ruined a ham the farmer gave him by dragging it along on a string behind him and was told by his poor mother that he should have carried it over his shoulder.

Well, Tom worked particularly hard for the farmer for a whole week and the farmer, who was pleased with the lad and wanted him to come back, gave him one of his donkeys, intending him to ride it to work. Tom, with a lot of struggle and sweating, heaved the poor beast up over his shoulder and staggered off with it. On the way back, he was so taken up with the effort of carrying the donkey that he didn't look which way he was going and ended up walking along a road which led past the royal palace.

Now it so happened that, three years before, the princess had been struck dumb and she was in a terrible state. The king had called all the best doctors and makers of magic, but none had been able to cure her in all that time. The king and the queen, in their desperation, had issued a proclamation. Anyone who could cure her would be given seven sacks of gold, seven of silver and seven of precious stones and would then be married to the princess herself.

The princess looked out of her window just as Tom was passing and she took one look at him stumbling and tripping his way along under the great weight of that donkey and she let out a huge peal of laughter. She rolled around tittering and shrieking. 'Just look at that!' she said through her mirth, when the king and queen came running. 'Isn't that absolutely incredible!'

The king and the queen did look and they saw Tom and they had him called in. When he stood before them, they thanked him for his clever trick and paid him the money. And, since the princess and he liked each other at once, the two of them were married the very next day. A long life they had and a happy one, and I believe that princess taught him good sense, but that's another story.

People sometimes get very complicated or just too literal as they try to think of appropriate metaphors for particular circumstances. The first story here is just a joke, but it is a joke about fear and children understand that very well. Being a child, James will probably accept the idea of a story told just for fun; he won't need to see a point in the tale, and this is an advantage, though there is a good straight point about fear in the final line and, if he gets the joke, that will scarcely need underlining. He'll be able to laugh at the nightmarish scenario suddenly made safe and laughter is very powerful in itself.

The mood of humour created in the first tale can be continued with the second one. However, the second one is particularly relevant to anyone trapped in feelings that relate to the past because it carries to an absurd level the notion of staying with fixed responses appropriate only to yesterday. Dropping in what are effectively interspersal suggestions,[11] it is possible to underline this subtly – 'And there was that cheese melting into his hair and all down his neck and running down inside his shirt. What a mess! All right for a jar of milk on a cool day, putting it on your head, carrying it that way. But days change, temperatures are different, the sun shines differently on different days, everything changes from moment to moment, day to day. Soft cheese on a hot day, on your head! Yesterday is yesterday and today is today and tomorrow is tomorrow and you have to take them one at a time...' This sort of thing could be improvised accordingly.

Both stories serve as examples of how one may not need a story that is obviously connected with the problem with which one is working – they can both be adapted to suit quite different circumstances.

A small cornucopia of quick reframing stories

The 25 short pieces in the following set are unequal in weight. Not all are strictly stories – as well as jokes, fables, anecdotes and vignettes, there's a rhyme, a saying or two and a couple of riddles. Some are ancient and some are modern. Some of them will seem lightweight; others may be irritating; whilst a few are deeper and more satisfying in themselves. Some work alongside others, amplifying a theme, whilst some are not obviously connected at all.

They are presented together as a 'starter pack' of reframing tales and metaphors that can be used in a wide range of situations. For myself, I find that some stories I don't like to begin with turn out to be very useful, whilst others that seem meaningful I don't come back to. One particular tale might seem as if it will be useful for this or that purpose, this other one for something else. But, because of the way metaphor works, it is worth staying flexible, not expecting a story always to come up with the same meaning attached each time. I also find that stories 'pop out' sometimes when I think I've forgotten all about them, very often with a meaning and a relevance. The stories are presented without commentary to leave readers free to make their own connections. (Those seeking further stories for specific use in therapy could not do better than getting and reading and re-reading *My Voice Will Go with You*, the collected teaching stories of Milton Erickson.[12])

1. Roof and Walls[13]

Two theoreticians were building a house. They decided that it would be a good idea to put the roof up first, so that they would be able to keep working if it rained.

2. Crocodiles and Cares

Some young travellers are up in North Queensland and one of them suddenly strips off all his clothes and leaps into the crocodile-infested salt waters. Well, the crocs are after him at once, but luckily there is a boat on hand and his friends drag him out, though not before he has lost a foot. His friends visit him in hospital and ask him why he did it and he says, 'Oh, it seemed kind of a fun thing to do at the time.'

3. The Optimist

The optimist fell ten storeys and, at each window bar,
He called out to the folks inside, 'Doing all right so far!'

4. The Treasure Hunter[14]

In the far off days of hugely powerful kings and sometimes even more powerful politicians, there was a great treasure hunter. He had the treasure finding instinct to a high degree. Buried hoards of long-lost kings he seemed to be able to see far beneath the ground. The king hired him as court treasure finder and gave him free access to the court and the palace gardens and grounds where, it was said, there were many secret treasures. He could come and go as he liked.

This arrangement worked well to begin with and the yield was great. The king's fortune was hugely increased. But the Chief Minister was suspicious and concerned at the freedom the treasure finder had, with the possibility of access to important state secrets. So, as a precaution, he had the treasure finder's eyes put out.

5. Two Existential Riddles

What is it that everyone is waiting for and it never will come?
What is it that everyone has lost and they will not find it again?
The answers, of course, are tomorrow and yesterday.

6. Simple Arithmetic

There are three monkeys sitting under a tree and one of them decides he will climb up and get a banana to eat. So how many monkeys are left sitting under the tree?

The answer is three. Decision is just the first stage. After that, you have to actually do the climbing.

7. The Hoe[15]

The old man was working in the fields in the early morning and his wife called out to him that his breakfast was ready. 'Just a moment!' he shouted back. 'I need to hide my hoe over here by the haystack!'

When he went in, his wife went for him. 'You're a fool!' she shouted. 'What's the point in hiding your hoe and then shouting so that everyone can hear? You should have whispered it softly or mimed it or something.'

The old man took it all in, finished his breakfast and was off to work again. But within five minutes he was back. 'You were right,' he whispered, very, very softly so that no one could hear and miming the act of hoeing a field. 'Somebody did steal my hoe.'

8. Dog Snuff[16]

A couple of centuries ago, in a fashionable part of London, a rogue found a snuff tin lying in the street. It looked almost new but it was quite empty. This rogue knew very well he had something to sell now – the tin was the authentic item and snuff taking was all the rage. All he needed was some content. With some likely-looking gents in his sights already, it was the work of a moment to scoop up some dried bits of leaf and dust (which, as it happened, contained some bleached fragments of dry dog dirt) and put it in the tin. For good measure, he shook in a little twist of pepper he had kept from a meal somewhere. Then, as the gentlemen approached, he cried out, 'Snuff, my good sirs! The very best. Only six pence. My last tin today.'

Now one of these gentlemen, a young dandy with more pretensions than his meagre purse would usually support, was attracted by the cheapness of the deal. After all, he reflected, as he handed over his money to the rogue, the tin was convincing and, if the snuff was no good, he could fake a sneeze as well as any. As it happened, he had a heavy cold so suspected nothing of the trick that had been played on him. Tucking the tin into his waistcoat pocket, he hailed a sedan chair and told the bearer to deliver him at once to a fashionable club.

Once inside, he took his place in a smoking chair and ostentatiously drew out his handkerchief and his snuff. Opening the tin, he distractedly placed a pinch of the mixture he found inside on the patterned silk and lifted it to his nostrils, immediately giving vent to a loud affected sneeze.

Within seconds, he began to smell a bad smell. He looked down at his boots, examining the soles of them carefully. No sign of the source. 'Excuse me, sir,' he said, tapping the occupant of the neighbouring chair on the arm, 'I hate to draw your attention to this but can you smell dog dirt?'

'No old chap, sorry I can't smell a thing,' this gentleman replied apologetically. 'I've got the stinking cold that's been going the rounds.'

'So have I! You should try this new snuff I've just bought. Really seems to do the trick.'

'Thank you very much,' said the neighbour. He duly placed a pinch of the stuff on his own paisley patterned kerchief and soon gave his own version of the almighty sneeze. Then he gave a surprised looking sniff or two, wrinkling up his nose. 'My goodness!' he said. 'You're right. This is splendid stuff. Do you know, I can smell that dog dirt already!'

9. The Fortunate Dog

You've probably seen the sign; last time I saw it, it had been turned into a plastic plaque you could buy and stick up on the wall. It goes something like this: 'Lost, one small dog. Three legs only. Blind in one eye. Very smelly. Answers to the name of Lucky.'

10. To Them that Have…

Then there's the old tale about the new vicar, who was doing the rounds of his parish and he passed a beautiful and well-tended garden. Flowers of every colour bloomed on all sides and then there were fruit trees in full fruit, rows of vegetables ready for harvesting, hedges neatly shaped and cut. The owner/gardener was standing proudly by the gate. 'Isn't it marvellous,' said the vicar piously, 'what man can achieve with the aid of the Almighty?'

'Aye,' says the local. 'But you should 'ave seen it when the bugger 'ad to do it all by 'imself!'

11. The Bean[17]

My daughter Asha, in her first term at primary school, proudly brought a bean back from school. It was in a jam jar and was rooted on damp absorbent paper. In a formal note that accompanied it, parents were asked to look after the bean and bed it in a little soil, so that the children could go on learning about plants and how they grow. As the weather warmed up, we could plant it outside. Very worthwhile, of course, and we did our best – in fact, I put it in an attractive Moroccan pot we had about the place. The bean grew well in the kitchen through the early spring and clambered up some sticks we put into the pot. Asha was very interested and excited.

But the time came when it had to be planted outside, and I have to admit I hadn't thought that one through. In getting the plant out of the attractive but, as it turned out, impractical pot, all of the soil fell away from the roots. I did my best at planting it outside but I can't say I held out much hope. A small, sad, disappointed face witnessed my struggles.

In the next few days, the plant withered and looked about to die. The face got sadder at the thought of it. Other parents comfortingly told us of similar experiences. But Asha refused to give up, and we kept on watering the plant and feeding it, and the thing picked up. It lost a lot of its early growth but optimistically put out more... Well, when I first wrote this anecdote down, Asha had just eaten her first beans from that plant. Through the autumn we picked dozens and dozens more.

12. The Emir's Robe[18]

The robe marked the man out instantly as an emir or some other man of great worth. The cloth was of the finest, the stitching the most intricate, the folds and pleats elaborate. The few tasteful buttons were of gold and silver. The dazzling whiteness was almost too hard to bear in the brightness of the desert sun.

That this lord should arrive at the oasis settlement alone was harder to understand, until he explained the skirmish with the bandits. He and his men had beaten them off once, but they had reckoned there'd be another attack. Since he had an important mission on behalf of the sultan, he'd left the caravan to take the long route and lead the robbers away whilst he himself rode away on the fleetest of camels on the shorter but more difficult track across the desert. It had taken courage and it had been hard, but he had done it. Might he rest at this remote place? In three days, he had agreed to rendezvous with messengers from a certain foreign kingdom at a place some 30 miles away, near the border, but this seemed the safer location to pass the days he'd saved by taking the hazardous shortcut.

The people, were, of course, sympathetic and also admiring since they knew the dangers of the route he'd taken well enough. What is more, they were sure they knew how to welcome such an important visitor. After he had rested and refreshed himself in the guest quarters of the best house in all the town, he was treated to a magnificent banquet with music and dancing and storytelling far into the evening. The emir himself, better dressed than any, cut a fine dash amongst them all and the worthies of the community hung on his every word, their eyes straying every now and then to the delicate yet manly perfection of his attire. Why could not the weavers and seamstresses of their own community produce such work?

When he retired a little earlier than they might have hoped, he was provided, at his request, with some pots of water, a very natural request. He was no doubt tired, the night was warm and travel in the desert dehydrates, not to mention the salt in the pilaf and meat dishes he'd consumed.

The next morning he appeared from his rooms late, no longer wearing the gorgeous white robe of the previous day. This time he was clad in another robe of sky blue. Again its exceptional qualities could not but be noted. The blue was exquisite, the needlework exact yet artistic. He was taken on a tour of the town and shown the best sights and the most treasured possessions of the community. The worthies felt proud that their humble settlement was not without its own wealth and artistic merit. With true breeding, he declined to admire anything excessively lest its owners should feel obliged to give it to him at once under the unwritten laws of generosity. Elegant compliments, however, dripped naturally from his honeyed tongue at just the right moments.

Again he was well feasted that evening whilst he told anecdotes about far-off cities and courtly ways that daunted all with their sophistication and cleverness. Again he retired early asking only for the refreshment of large amounts of water.

The next morning he appeared in a fabulous robe of midnight indigo. Once more he was full of beautifully expressed praise for his hosts, their kindness and their hospitality. Once more he was treated to the best of what the town had to offer.

On the last morning, he appeared in a black robe, a colour unexceptional in those parts perhaps and yet this, too, was no ordinary Bedouin covering. More fine cloth, more fine stitching. The comforts these courtly folk took for granted were amazing. Why, to take such robes with you on a mere desert journey, to change each day into another and another fine robe, each one made in the same faultless style!

It was very natural to shower him with gifts, loaded onto donkeys, to provision him well for the journey. Indeed he was offered guards to go with him, until such time as he would meet the messengers, but he refused. There was no point in risking the lives of yet more brave men. His own retainers would, he felt sure, be waiting for him at the agreed spot with the foreign emissaries. They watched him ride away, cheering him and calling down blessings upon him – and asking to be commended to the sultan.

It wasn't until some time later, when they began to miss some of their best treasures, that they found the pots hidden away in his room, blue and black stains around the rim of each. Indeed it was not for several weeks that the emir who had indeed owned the marvellous white robe they had so much admired on that first day sent his servants to their community, seeking the man who had stolen it and escaped across the desert – a bold bandit who had formerly been a master dyer.

13. The Axe[19]

A countryman was convinced his neighbour had stolen his axe. Guilt was written all over the man – you just couldn't help seeing that. It was obvious in the shifty way he walked, the way he wouldn't look you in the eye, the way he failed even to say hello one morning and pretended to look preoccupied. Sometimes you just know; sometimes people just can't hide what they've done.

A day or two passed and the neighbour behaved in more and more odd and guilty ways and the man was determined to have it out with him. But then, when he was working down in a copse he had not visited for a few days, he found the axe where he had evidently left it. Strangely enough, the neighbour stopped behaving in such peculiar ways after that.

14. The Abyss

Near Ingleborough in the Western Dales of Yorkshire, there is an extensive network of caves open to the public. There are good, concreted walkways and the amazing formation of stalactites and stalagmites are dramatically lit. Underground streams bubble along beside the paths. About halfway round, the water drops six or seven feet through rocks, before proceeding on its way at a lower level. The guide explains that, when the first explorers of the cave reached this place, with the simple and primitive lighting they had and in the predominating dark and shadows, the waters at this point looked particularly deep and dangerous. They hence christened it 'the abyss'.

15. German Saying

Fear makes the wolf look bigger.

16. Torture[20]

In medieval times, the religious authorities of Christendom decided to reform the laws relating to torture. To obtain information from suspects, torture of certain kinds was permissible, but only for as long as it takes to say a full Pater Noster. However, it had been found that torturers could be rather too inventive about the length of time taken between separate syllables of the prayer. It was therefore decided that hourglasses should be installed in torture chambers; an hour of torture was to be allowed. This practice also had to stop because this time the victims were favoured. They were able to withstand the pain because they could see the time that was left, and measure the minutes. Pain is easier to bear when you have even an approximate idea of how long it will last.

17. Social Controls[21]

In India, in the 19th century, members of the ruling British raj knew what was expected of them. At the stifling, crowded churches on Sunday mornings, dressed almost as if attending some cool, stone-built ancient monument at the centre of leafy English country villages, they occupied the front pews in full view of the natives, fanning themselves politely whilst sitting or kneeling or standing to attention.

On one such Sunday morning, the rector stood up and approached the bible to begin a reading. As he opened the large and heavy volume, a deadly cobra that had been hiding amongst the pages slipped out and slithered down the lectern. Almost without blinking, the rector began his reading. Meanwhile, the creature wriggled across the floor towards the ladies and gentlemen of the congregation – who also stood firm, not flinching, if perhaps shifting just a tiny bit with more than a little unease.

Now the snake made its way to the aisle where it could clearly register the light from the door at the back of the church, kept open to allow welcome breezes to enter. As it passed each row of worshippers, all followed the example of those in front of them and remained stock still, trying to focus on the words the priest was intoning. At last, reaching the doorway and the freedom it longed for, the cobra rushed forward across the path outside and into the safety of the undergrowth beyond. In the church, the service continued without the slightest comment.

18. Social Proof[22]

A Brahmin was carrying a young goat back from market for sacrifice when three thieves spied him. They at once hatched a plan and the first thief sidled up to the Brahmin and asked him what he was doing. 'Carrying this goat from the market!' was the reply. 'Oh, master,' says the thief, 'Are you sure this is a goat? I thought it was a dog. That's why I asked.'

'No,' says the Brahmin firmly, 'it's a goat. I'd hardly be touching a dog!' To the Brahmin, the dog is an unclean animal. It would be anathema to him to have such a creature in his arms.

The first thief walked off scratching his head doubtfully. A little further along the track, the second thief appeared. 'Nice dog you have there, Brahmin,' he says. 'I thought dogs were forbidden to you.'

'It isn't a dog! It's a goat.' The Brahmin was blustering, but he sounded just a little doubtful now.

'Have it your own way,' says the second thief. 'I suppose it just looks like a dog. And smells like one.' Off he went, holding his nose.

Now it was the third thief's turn, but he lingered, allowing the Brahmin time to ruminate a little on the doubts already sown in his mind. He watched from behind some rocks and, then, when he could tell that the Brahmin was confused enough, he strode out. 'What are you doing with that dog?' he asks boldly.

'Nothing,' says the Brahman. 'It's obviously bewitched.' He set it down there and then and marched off to purify himself after this contact with an unclean animal. So the thieves took the goat and they sold it for a good price and they spent the money.

19. The Wealth of Kings[23]

The glories of the court of King Croesus were beyond comparison, and his wealth was legendary. Nevertheless, his land was conquered and he was captured by Cyrus the Great of Persia, who treated him well, allowing him to attend his own court as an adviser.

Day after day, Croesus watched in amazement and increasing disbelief as Cyrus dispensed justice humanely and even-handedly, giving to all who asked according to their need. 'Why,' he demanded to know at length, 'do you not hold back your wealth? Your palace and your court are nothing compared to mine. One day all your treasure will be gone if you carry on in this way. Only think what splendours you and yours might enjoy if you ceased to give so freely.'

By way of answer, Cyrus had the court scribe take down from dictation a letter to all of his friends and house-holding subjects, explaining that he needed to raise a large amount of money for the immediate defence of the realm. Soon gifts were pouring in from all quarters until the pile of gold and jewels and precious artefacts at that court was ten times greater than any the captive king had seen in his life.

'Now this is a portion of the true wealth of my kingdom,' said Cyrus, when he had given orders for the return of all the treasure to the donors. 'Do you imagine that I could command such respect and loyalty if I kept everything for myself?'

20. Paving the Streets[24]

The queen was furious. Each day she went from the palace to the temple to worship. She had to walk. This was the established custom and showed her humility before the gods. She walked barefoot, as did everyone in her lands. But the streets were dusty when it was hot and, when the rains came, muddy. Her beautiful royal clothes were filthy in no time. The queen therefore ordered her wise men to solve this problem.

Well, the wise men paved the streets but this was little better. The stones became hot when it was dry and they hurt the royal feet. When it was wet, there were puddles. Covering the street with rush mats didn't solve the problem either, since they soon became dusty and worn. There was the same problem with woven carpets. But eventually the wise men hit on a fabric that would, they considered, be just perfect. Leather! If they could cover the streets with leather, it wouldn't let the mud or the dust through and it would be soft to the touch of the royal feet. What's more, it would even look good. If only they could get enough of it – they would need a lot of hides.

The queen was excited and at once commanded that all of the animals in the land should be butchered and skinned. The people were horrified – as were the keepers of the royal treasury, since the crown would have to pay for each skin used in the street, not to mention the work of all the craftsmen. But, fortunately, a man came forward before all the carnage began. He claimed to have learned a strange art in a distant and foreign land. He claimed he could satisfy the queen's need easily using much less than one hide. Everyone was dubious until they saw what he had made for the ruler. It was a pair of lace-up shoes.

21. Pearls

Even though swine may have trampled it in the mud,
the pearl is still a pearl.

22. Knowing Where the Problem Is[25]

The lorry driver detested know-it-alls. He knew the height of his vehicle with its load because he had measured it before leaving the depot. He knew that the bridge was just an inch or so too low because the height limit was clearly displayed. It was obvious to him that he was going to have to take off the top layer of the load and pile the boxes up beside the road. That would give him the extra space he would need to squeeze the thing through. And what does this idiot say to him? Let the tyres down, then you'll get through and you can pump them up again at the garage down the road. Completely stupid! Anyone could see that the problem was at the top, not at the bottom.

23. Delusions

A man wearing an eye patch and an admiral's hat and coat was shown into the psychiatrist's office and the psychiatrist said: 'I understand that you...er, have certain delusions about who you are.'

'Oh no, it's not me,' said the man, 'I know exactly who I am. Horatio Lord Nelson at your service. It's my girlfriend, Lady Hamilton. She goes round calling herself Wendy Smith.'

24. More Delusions

In America, a psychiatrist was treating a man for a recurring and debilitating delusion. It was very specific and well established. He seemed to believe, unflinchingly and unreasonably, that a distant and unknown relative in the Eastern European country from which his grandparents had originally come would one day die and leave him all his wealth. His imagination of the event was very detailed; he could see the letter and the words that would tell him of his good fortune, recite those words, even give some of the figures. The only thing he didn't know was when the missive would arrive, so of course day after day he had spent in anticipation and this was interfering with his life.

It was just the kind of fantasy that is very hard to shake and the psychiatrist was called upon to use all his knowledge and understanding and ingenuity. But eventually treatment was successful. The man accepted that he had created a story in his mind as a kind of wish fulfilment and was able to laugh at his own former folly. He became practical and realistic about his life again. Then the letter arrived.

25. Wine Lover[26]

Long and long ago in China, there was a man who loved wine. One night, he dreamed he was warming a really fine vintage over a fire with some spices. In the dream, he sniffed at it and rubbed his hands and clapped them together so much in anticipation that he woke himself up. 'Oh no,' he said in sad disappointment, 'I should have drunk it cold!'

Chapter 6

New Lamps for Old: Transposing Stories

> My stories are all true – as true as I can make them
> on the day.
> *– Storytellers' saying*

Oral stories change – inevitably. You tell a story to someone, who likes it and decides to pass it on. But they are not you, so they tell it in their own way, using bits of their own experience and imagination, which makes the tale come out differently. Most of us have started listening to a joke we thought we didn't know and then, halfway through the telling, suddenly realized, probably with disappointment, that we knew what the punch line would be. The setting of the joke has changed but the underlying plot is the same. When this happens with folk tales, however, the effect can be fascinating rather than disappointing. A plot that seems familiar goes off at a new tangent or appears gleaming and shimmering in a strange and marvellous new costume, which makes it sparkle with life.

When you know a story and you know it well, you have the key to making all sorts of new stories. And the beauty of this is that you can still keep the old one – you really can get a new lamp without losing all the old magic.

Repeating patterns

There is an old piece of lore that claims that all the stories in the world can be reduced to just seven basic plots. Many times, during workshops or after public performances, I have had people approach me about this. What, they ask me, are those stories? In the past, I have always said that I don't know. What I do know, I've gone on to say (maybe labouring the point a little), is the Greek myth in which the hero Theseus comes across the giant Procrustes. This giant had two beds for his visitors, one of them short and the other long. You probably already know all about him since his name has passed into popular expression – how he would ghoulishly fit his guests to the beds, the tall ones to the short bed by lopping off head and limbs, the short ones to the long bed by hammering them out and stretching them. It is a tale, I've explained, which leaves me a little wary of simplistic theories that reduce complex living things like stories to 'underlying' patterns and numbers.

However, an important book by journalist, critic, historian and founding editor of the satirical magazine *Private Eye* Christopher Booker has recently been published on this very theme. *The Seven Basic Plots* is subtitled *Why We Tell Stories* and took Booker more than 30 years to write; he evidently regards it as his life's most important work. In its more than 700 pages, he adduces hundreds of examples, ranging from classical literature and mythology to folk tales, children's books, opera, novels, film and other modern media, to illustrate the recurrence of common themes across a very broad spectrum. His seven basic plots are overcoming the monster, rags to riches, the quest, voyage and return, comedy, tragedy and, finally, rebirth. These, he suggests, repeat because they mirror essentials of human development and realization. A story that contains such essentials in proper balance is satisfying and, therefore, successful; stories in which the pattern is incomplete or fragmented or in some way subverted (as he believes is the case with much fiction of the past two centuries) reflect a state of ego disharmony and confusion. It is a very well written and generous book, with a lot of challenges to make, and I can now happily recommend anyone who is interested in the seven stories notion to read it, along with anyone else who is curious about stories in general and theories about their importance in particular.

I do, though, have some personal reservations and a central one is the seven plots notion, which is the first part of Booker's larger thesis. I'm frankly still not convinced. First of all, a lot of the brief but powerful stories told in this book – the fables, jokes, anecdotes and short teaching tales, not to mention personal anecdotes and private fantasies – would disappear completely against Booker's scale. But they are clearly stories and not just fragments of larger, more 'serious' narratives, and the telling of them has to be explained in an account of why people tell stories. Booker talks mainly about long stories, and an emphasis on these suggests a cultural bias, despite the multicultural examples: a kind of tunnel vision, even if the tunnel is wide and vault-like.

Booker acknowledges that not every extended plot fits his scheme; indeed, he draws attention to some that do not, as part of the thesis. The problem is that many that are supposed to fit the scheme involve some Procrustean chopping. You have to keep strongly in mind the supposed pattern in order to keep them from leaping from one category into another – though Booker manages to give good reasons within his scheme as to why plots warp or combine. The categorization is a little too arbitrary to be true.

My third reservation is the strongest of all and this concerns the linking of the underlying plots to Jungian archetypes. This is an absolutely essential part of Booker's take on stories and many pages are devoted to it. Yet, outside Jungian circles, Jung's theory of archetypes is widely considered dubious or simply wrong, and based on false reasoning. It is worth a digression to consider why this is so, since this is such an influential set of ideas.

Jung's archetypes

In building his theory, Carl Jung started with a notion that sounds eminently reasonable, even in terms of contemporary evolutionary science: the psyche is not a tabula rasa on which experience and culture write random patterns, according to arbitrary exigencies. There must be patterns, templates or, as he termed them, archetypes that would broadly govern the ways in which the human psyche unfolds. These instinctual patterns would quite naturally also shape the ways in which mythologies would develop, independently but along lines that are demonstrably similar. *Archetype* is a word that, prior to Jung, had referred to underlying ideas and ideals passed on largely through the medium of culture. It also, however, had an association with Plato's forms, conceived to exist in a fundamental world of ideals transcending the physical world, and Jung was particularly aware of this.

Apart from his theory of archetypes, Jung is, of course, known for his concept of the collective unconscious: he conceived that, at some level, human beings not only have a shared biological inheritance but also a shared under-mind (or perhaps over-mind) – a step too mystically far for orthodox science. From his sometimes rather abstruse writings, it is not entirely clear how we should think of the collective unconscious – as a separate pre-existing, unified consciousness beyond conventional time, a kind of Platonic form in itself, or perhaps as a kind of continuous communication: the sum of consciousnesses, with the whole being more than the sum of its parts. Similarly, there is an apparent inconsistency over whether his archetypes have evolved as part of the architecture of the brain or whether they 'arrived' (and presumably continue to arrive) through the supposed unconscious channels.

Jung made several further leaps, drawing on his extensive, if selective, readings of various Eastern sacred writings, as well as traditional literature and art and his studies of alchemical literature, to support a list of archetypes that included father, mother, anima, animus, child, wise old man, helpful animal, trickster and many more. Each of these mythical figures was supposed to express an aspect of the psyche at a particular stage; integration and maturity would be a state in which all were in balance. The 'proof' of the existence of these patterns appears to be somewhat circular: Jung came to believe in their existence, found evidence for them through his selective readings and set out this evidence as confirmation, alongside the experiences of patients at the Burghölzli mental hospital where he first developed his theories, the experiences of later patients in Jungian analysis, common content of dreams and his 'inward explorations' following his own breakdown and recovery.

Jung had immense flair, intelligence, total conviction and a strong element of personal charisma. Many have regarded him as an almost divinely inspired genius or, at the least, as a man of profound insight. Jung didn't always disabuse people of such assumptions. Yet the theory of archetypes seems, to many modern readers, a strange admixture of guesswork and fancy and strangely dated oddments from a rag-bag of philosophies that has no place in a scientific account of the mind. It certainly did not come out of the kind of controlled experiment and careful testing of hypotheses associated with science. Indeed, whilst Jung often talked of himself as a scientist, he seemed in later life happier with a description of his work as a kind of religion.[1]

For anyone interested in stories and storytelling, some understanding of the Jungian position is very useful, since ideas from this source are widely in circulation and are frequently treated as fact by commentators, as regards the images and symbols that stories contain. The much admired and much quoted (and indeed sometimes very lucid and illuminating) folklorist, Joseph Campbell, for example, was heavily influenced by Jung's ideas. But a story analysed according to Jungian principles, the archetypes it is supposed to represent laid bare, can seem somehow to bellyflop into emptiness. It is a framework that, at least in the hands of less able interpreters than Jung himself, ultimately leaves little to the imagination, turning fiction into a code to be broken and read off according to the archetypal tick list.

The many forms of universal plot

The Milkmaid's Dreams

A milkmaid was carrying a pail of beautiful warm, white, creamy milk back from the dairy to her house. As she walked, she was planning what she was going to do, because this was milk from her own cow she'd not long ago been given by her uncle and she had choices she could make. Maybe she would make butter, maybe she would make cheese...or maybe, just maybe she would put it all into jars and sell it down at the market. That was a thought. It was such good milk, people would just love it. They'd pay good money and she'd have a silver shilling or two to spare, so she could maybe buy a new bonnet and an apron with some really nice frills. She could just imagine herself in the new outfit.

But no, she wouldn't get anything of the sort. She'd save the money, that would be the wise thing. Save it up until she could take on another cow, another good milker. Then she would have twice as much milk, so she could sell twice as much, which would mean she could save twice as much. It wouldn't take so long to get the next cow and of course she'd be bringing up calves to be milkers too. In no time at all, she'd have a herd. A whole herd of cows, all her own. Of course, she'd need to rent an extra field or two, but it could be done, what with all the money she'd make.

Mind you, it would be a lot of work, so she'd not have time to do any milking for her uncle like she did now. In fact she'd need help. Perhaps two or three or maybe even four or five girls like herself to fetch in the cows and milk them. Yes, and to do the selling too because after a while she'd be giving up the work and just telling the others what to do every now and then. There'd probably be 20 or 30 of them by the time she had four or five farms and hundreds of cows. She'd move to a big house and have servants and only go out in the evening in a fine carriage.

Yes, she would go to the ball and the music would play. She would be there in her fine silk gown, looking a proper picture. Then the fine young captain in his scarlet jacket and white pants and shiny black boots would ask her to dance and she would be swept up in his strong arms and dance with him, around and around...

The pictures seemed so real and the music seemed so real and those strong arms seemed so warm and alluring that she started to dance, whirling around and around in a dizzying spin – until she tripped over a stone and dropped the pail and spilt every last drop of that warm, rich, creamy milk.

So she got no money that day, only broken dreams.

This is a well-known tale. This version is loosely based on the famous La Fontaine fable. You may well have come across a very similar one about a girl who carries some eggs to market, sometimes attributed to Aesop and a favourite in such European 'noodle and numbskull' collections as *The Wise Men of Schilda*, where I first encountered it myself. Or maybe you know the tale of the barber's fifth brother from the Arabian Nights, a story about a man with a tray of glasses to sell in the market place, which get smashed when he becomes absorbed in his daydreams. Or even the one about Brahman with a bag of grits from the *Panchatantra*. The famous Scottish traveller storyteller, the late great Duncan Williamson, a man with an astonishing repertoire of some 4000 tales, would tell the story of a traveller who saw a rabbit and began to imagine all the things that would happen if he caught it – and ended up clapping his hands and scaring it away.

A number of plots are widespread in world oral and literary tradition, taking on different forms in different cultures but demonstrably and perceptibly the same, or very similar, 'underneath'. This has been well known in folklore study for a long time. In 1898, Marion Roalf Cox published 398 versions of the Cinderella story in what was hailed as the first scientific study of a folk tale.[2] Since then, the number of known versions of that one tale has risen to well over 500, with variants and analogues from all cultures. Some put the figure at 1000 plus, depending on how broadly the transformation plot is defined. And Cinderella is just one among many so-called universal folk tales.

In the huge scholarly work *The Types of the Folktale* by Antti Aarne, not just seven but hundreds of 'tale types' are listed, skeletal plots that have often moved across culture and time. Aarne's work was enlarged by Stith Thompson, who also published the six-volume *Motif Index of Folk Literature*, which details many hundreds more motifs – those smaller transferable or transposable elements within the plot, such as 'motif no 1 H1023.3. Task: bringing berries (fruit, roses) in winter', which evidently occurs in Irish, Indian, French, Japanese and Eskimo mythologies amongst others. It is perhaps a curious approach to something as living and vital as stories, redolent of dusty old museums with endless displays of butterflies pinstuck under glass. Indeed, in its historical origins, it roughly parallels that approach to nature involving catching, killing and then stuffing or pickling wild nature, in the belief that one had somehow then captured its essence. Both approaches have had their values, however.

In the light of such studies, but more importantly in the light of its living, relevant, practically illuminating content, it really is no surprise that this one small story about the milkmaid's dreams crops up in the literature of widely differing, geographically very separate cultures in so many different guises. No one knows whether a single individual somewhere somehow thought of it first and it got passed around – which sounds plausible. After all, people travelled widely in ancient times and at much slower rates than we do today, so there was plenty of time to swap tales along the road or around the campfire. But then again, the kind of experience this story describes is extremely common – something like that has probably happened to you at some time, if you think about it. So it is quite possible to imagine that different versions of the story could arise in different places as ways of describing the common experience of getting lost in associative fantasy and taking your eye off the ball – or the milk pail. These two commonsense explanations express, in microcosm, the whole debate about how stories come to be so widespread and to 'breed', as it were.

Memes and fundamentals

The theory of archetypes can be a form of fundamentalism, suggesting that stories arise spontaneously out of a combination of biology and a kind of divine plan held in a higher mind. Christopher Booker's book, despite its eloquence and admirable breadth of reference, provides a fundamentalist (if telling and very useful) critique of stories and storytelling, especially Western literature of the last two centuries. A contrasting fundamentalism currently popular in some academic and Darwinian circles is a version of meme theory. Meme, defined in the Oxford English Dictionary as 'an element of culture that may be considered to be passed on by non-genetic means, esp. imitation', is a concept introduced by Richard Dawkins in his influential 1970s book, *The Selfish Gene*. It has since been amplified by such luminaries as Daniel Dennett (*Consciousness Explained* and *Darwin's Dangerous Idea*), Richard Brodie (*Virus of the Mind: The New Science of the Meme*), Aaron Lynch (*Thought Contagion: How Belief Spreads Through Society*) and, perhaps most fundamentalist of all, by Susan Blackmore in *The Meme Machine*.

In fundamentalist meme theory, there would be no question of an 'essential' or underlying pattern in a story. As one amongst many forms of meme, the story is a 'selfish replicator', using the minds and mouths of those who pass it on, endlessly recycling itself without any regard for its temporary hosts. We are creatures who imitate one another and we pass on all sorts of things through mimetic (or, in the theory's jargon, memetic) behaviour. We do this in order that our genes and the memes that are the units of culture may survive. There is survival value in stories being told, since getting together and laughing and crying and empathizing through stories binds the group or tribe and makes that group or tribe stronger and hence more likely to pass on its genes and memes. Common ways of behaving can be inculcated automatically through the story; consciousness doesn't have to be involved. The vital element is the imitation. This means that the flow of memes may include mindless catch phrases, clichés or fashionable voice tone patterns, such as the currently popular teenage habit of intoning every sentence as a question ending with 'right?' To the memes and their larger host, the social organism, all modes of transmission have equal survival value.

Meme theory has developed its own jargon. You don't 'get an idea' or 'have an insight'; you are 'infected by a meme' or by a 'memeplex'. The 'selfplex' (you) is reinforced by this. There are, of course, differences of emphasis amongst meme theorists; some writers on the subject imply that the automatic, mechanical nature of the meme can be transcended by consciousness. For Dennett, consciousness arises from the interplay of memes and genes. For Blackmore, the conscious self does not exist; it is a fiction, a view that throws up some fascinating paradoxes, particularly since Blackmore is determined not to divide her professional and private lives:

> If my understanding of human nature is that there is no conscious self inside, then I must live that way – otherwise this is a vain and lifeless theory of human nature. But how can "I" live as though I do not exist, and who would be choosing to do so?
>
> One trick is to concentrate on the present moment – all the time – letting go of any thoughts that come up. This kind of 'meme-weeding' requires a great concentration but is most interesting in its effect. If you can concentrate for a few minutes at a time, you will begin to see that, in any moment, there is no observing self. Suppose you sit and look out of the window. Ideas will come up but these are all past- and future-oriented; so let them go, come back to the present. Just notice what is happening. The mind leaps to label objects with words, but these words take time and are not really in the present. So let them go too. With a lot of practice the world looks different; the idea of a series of events gives way to nothing but change, and the idea of a self who is viewing the scene seems to fall away.[3]

It is intriguing to find this description of a meditative practice in a scientific book with reductionist/academic pretensions (though perhaps not so strange, since Blackmore is also a Zen practitioner), but even more intriguing is Blackmore's curious logic. It is almost as if she had set out to create a koan-like paradox: her observing faculty is observing that there is no observer.

If you or I or Susan Blackmore go through the procedure she describes, the only way we can be aware of the state she describes is by observing, by being aware. The exercise illustrates the existence of an awareness beyond thought and feeling and beyond the 'interplay of memes': an observer. (It is more or less a description of a technique for enhancing the inner observer.) Whilst it may, as she suggests, indicate that the conventional 'received' self is less coherent and independent than we might wish, it does not for a moment prove that we are non-existent as centres of awareness, intention and potentially autonomous action.

The logic of Blackmore's argument has to be that there is no point in attempting to develop a more conscious self and that we should simply learn to allow things to happen. She gives the example of driving a car and allowing the choice of the scenic or the direct route home to be taken for her.[4] Yet letting go in this way only works if we have already made the effort to learn the necessary skills – knowing how to drive, recognizing a route – something we are obliged to do with consciousness at the outset. I somehow suspect Blackmore's method wouldn't work if she couldn't already drive and didn't know the roads.

Psychoactive stories

All of this is highly relevant to stories and the telling and re-telling of them. People who spend time telling stories arrive at a particular insight sooner or later: stories and storytelling situations are psychoactive. In a process which can be continuous, stories and storytelling draw together experiences, perceptions, and both unconscious and conscious learnings within the mind, and from different minds, and synthesize them in new ways. Receiving and then passing on a story is by no means necessarily an act of imitation. It involves increasing conscious involvement as well as just letting it happen.

I was once asked at short notice to tell 'The Seven Crows', a story from The Collected Tales of the Brothers Grimm. I knew the story well enough but had not told it in public and was a little vague about some of the details. I had no opportunity to check the original but, since the context was not too formal and since I was used to letting stories 'roll out' and develop in their own way, I did it, filling in any gaps in my memory by using a bit of imagination and a stray motif from another tale here and there. The audience responded well and, a while later, the story popped into my mind somewhere else as being right for the time and I gave it another airing. Over a couple of years, I told it several more times and various ideas I had about the tale clarified themselves; it acquired a particularly focused and sharp quality for me, always a good sign for a teller that a story is still 'hot'. Then I happened to look at the crow story in Grimm's and was surprised to find only half of the story I had been telling – somehow or other, my tale had become linked with another, called 'The Twelve Geese', an Irish story that includes a series of tasks the heroine has to perform to rescue her enchanted brothers. I had also drawn on brief elements from several other similar tales, as well as improvising and developing some entirely new images. The story had changed and grown through a combination of conscious thought, developed skill, unconscious elaboration and interaction with circumstance and people.

I tell this to illustrate a process that I suspect has happened many times in the unwritten history of oral stories, when similar tales must easily have been confused one with another. At the same time, certain elements within tales may have been emphasized as a means of bringing the narrative to life in particular contexts, or perhaps as the teller perceives possible metaphorical depths and develops them almost without noticing. I doubt that passing on a story has ever been automatic and mechanical; one can't help but bring to it not only one's experience but also one's need to make sense of the world. This is especially true when a story has the reflexive quality of good teaching tales, which simultaneously illustrate and comment upon consciousness, offering multiple-level metaphors showing multi-level patterns. You have to wake up from Blackmore's 'meme dream' to have any idea of what such stories are about.

The writer Doris Lessing was once asked, in a radio interview, whether she thought writers were somehow cleverer than other people. No, she said, by no means so; they could be equally stupid. But, on the other hand, when they were writing, they might sometimes be a little cleverer, a little wiser. And I suppose that's right. When you are immersed in stories, you have access to the mind in a different way, expressing through images a lot of ideas you don't necessarily understand at an everyday conscious level, but rather with a deeper, developing consciousness that cannot intelligently be called random unconsciousness.

Meme theory may really be no more scientific than archetypal theory; it is, however, more intellectually fashionable. It is possible that, once its day has passed, meme theory too will be described as 'a strange admixture of guesswork and fancy and strangely dated oddments from a rag-bag of philosophies that has no place in a scientific account of the mind'. It is possible that 'meme' and 'archetype' will be listed along with 'phlogiston' and 'the ether' as aberrations in thinking no longer part of the 'real' scientific story.

This might just be a pity. The theory of memes does have real insights to offer. Human beings do imitate one another constantly and culture is very much passed on through processes of imitation. This is too often a mechanical process for which we do not have to assume consciousness or free will. What is missing from a meme explanation of storytelling and story transmission is a notion of qualitative scale: the perception that some stories, some 'memes' and indeed 'memeplexes', may function to increase consciousness and therefore individual and group choice. Stories can become relevant and resonant under the teller's tongue and within the hearer's mind or become distorted, mere reflectors of fashion and social trend. What is missing from meme theory in general is a notion of wisdom that is more than simple survival strategy.

Similarly, archetype theory does have insights to offer. What is missing from the scheme is flexibility and imaginative scope. If there are patterns that repeat in stories, if realizing those patterns gives insights into human maturity and development, we do not need to tangle them up with outmoded and indeed half-baked ideas of what maturity might be, nor to assume that the metaphor is limited and is simply a code to be broken.[5] Ultimately, what seems to be missing from archetypal theory is any realization that we may have a contribution to make to a continuing story. Adventuring with story plots in new and spontaneous ways is a fascinating and exciting enterprise in which surprising, revealing and even incredible things can happen.

Transposing a story

Learning to transpose stories, to make new stories from old ones or to absorb and recast fragments of old tales is highly creative and hugely instructive and should be a central feature of teaching about story making and telling. It is the way many of the great writers learned and practised their craft, from Chaucer and Shakespeare to Goethe and Jorge Luis Borges. Being able to 'transpose' a story at will allows you to adjust a tale to time, place and people, so that it can work all the better. When repeated as an exercise over and over again, it becomes second nature.

Here are some story elements that might effectively be altered, according to context:

1. *Time*: An ancient story can become a modern or even futuristic one. Accordingly, what is a cave or palace in one version may be a house, or even a spaceship, in another.

2. *Place*: Countries, cultures, climates, etc. can be changed. Deserts may become arctic wastes; the east may become the west; inside becomes outside, and so on.

3. *People*: Animals from fables may become car salesmen, prostitutes or politicians. Children may become adults with childish minds (and vice versa).

4. *Gender*: Some stories with strong or clever heroes work well as stories about strong and clever heroines. Some don't. Try it and see.

5. *Wealth and social status*: Sometimes this has a meaning in the plot; sometimes it is not important at all. The essential question to ask is, 'Is there a point to his/her being, for instance, a princess, a priest, a peasant or a prime minister in this tale?' If so, will that point survive transposition?

6. *Symbols and images*: Such as a dead tree outside a needy person's house which bursts into blossom when his/her fortunes change (see 'The Man Who Became Rich Through Dreaming', p.238). Again, there is an essential question to ask: 'What does this symbol contribute on a metaphorical level and what happens when I change it?'

7. *Feel and purpose*: The whole feel of a story and therefore its perceived purpose might change. A fable might seem starchy and over-moralistic, but could lighten up a lot as you change and re-set it. A joke might turn out to be more than just a throwaway line or two.

Nicking the plot – transposition games

These are two games that can be used in groups to practise the skill of transposing stories.

Pinkrinse and the three tigers: The storyteller tells a well-known story (for a very obvious example, Goldilocks and the Three Bears), trying to disguise it as much as possible (changing hair colour, species type, etc.). The group members make a guess at what the original is as soon as they have an idea. The teller aims to keep up the disguise till the end.[6]

All change please: The storyteller re-tells a short story familiar to the group, announcing what it is at the outset. As many 'surface elements' as possible must be changed, whilst keeping the underlying plot. The group may challenge any detail perceived as being too similar to the original. The storyteller has to justify the choice or alter the transposition before continuing. To introduce a competitive element, a time limit can be set for the telling – the teller must get through the plot and past any challenges within, say, five minutes. Rules around trivial, time-wasting challenges can be developed as and if necessary.

Nicking the motif

Motifs, such as getting wishes, talking to animals or getting help from magical beings, also migrate. It can be entertaining and instructive to build new tales around them. For instance, in 'The Enchanting Bird', on p.253, a climb up a mountain must be undertaken, while ignoring all kinds of magical (and illusory) distractions. This is a motif or subplot which crops up again and again in traditional tales and can be a very powerful image.[7] You could create an entirely new story, with a new challenge featuring a different sort of climb and different motivation for taking it on. (Some specific ideas about transposing this tale are given in the notes that accompany it.)

Nine adaptable tales

Each of the nine stories that follow can be transposed in the various ways we have been discussing. Most already exist in many different versions and have been travelling the world possibly for centuries. I've included one modern anecdote of my own, which participants in workshops have found fun to re-cast and which, like folktales, seems somehow to invoke a universal pattern.

The telling of each story has been left purposely plain and relatively undeveloped, to allow scope for bringing the tale to life in many different ways. Each is followed by brief notes giving some background to the tale, plus some advice first on telling 'as is' and then on transposing. They're all good tales and you don't, of course, have to change them for the sake of it. On the other hand, I hope any 'new lamps' you find will, as it were, shine away a bit of darkness.

1. The Man Who Became Rich Through Dreaming

A generous man, who had lost all his wealth and had almost nothing left in the world, lived in a small shack beside a crossroads in the country. Beside the house, there was a tree, which was almost dead and had borne no fruit for years.

The poor man had a dream one night. In the dream, he saw a strange figure wearing green and himself all tinged with green, who pointed at the poor man and said in a solemn voice that the poor man's fortune lay in the king's city, upon the king's bridge. Three times the dream recurred and at last the man decided that he would act on it.

With some difficulty, he travelled to the big city and found the bridge. There he walked up and down all day long, but no fortune came his way. Worse, the king's guards noticed him, thought his behaviour suspicious and arrested him for vagrancy. He was interrogated by their captain, who laughed when he heard his story of the dream. 'You're a fool!' he sneered. 'And worse than a fool. Go back where you came from and never let me see you here again, otherwise I'll have you locked away! Take this advice with you: dreams are all nonsense. I myself have had a dream many a time, an idiot's dream in which I walk along a country road and come to a mean little house by a crossroads, with a dead tree beside it. I go to this place and I dig under the tree and right there, under its roots, I find a treasure. Now do you think I'm going to leave a good job here in the city to go on some wild goose chase looking for a place which probably doesn't even exist? Not me!'

Well, the poor man did what the captain of the guard said and went home the very next day. When at last he arrived, he dug under the tree beside his house and found there a large chest filled with gold coins, enough to keep him in happiness and generosity for the rest of his days. When the chest was removed, the fruit tree blossomed and that year it bore a lot of fruit.

Background note: There are very many different versions of this story. One of the oldest is in the *Alif Layla wa Layla* (The Arabian Nights)[8] but, in England, the best known variant is the legend of the pedlar of Swaffham, of whom there is a statue in the Norfolk town. The plot is one which goes on being recycled; the international best selling 'spiritual' novel *The Alchemist,* by Paolo Coelho, is clearly based on it. Psychologist Arthur Deikman in his book *The Observing Self* has some very interesting things to say about the story and uses a Hasidic version.[9]

Telling advice: The motif of the tree is not present in all versions but makes a useful symbol. As its history shows, the story transposes well to various settings and there is no reason why one shouldn't make a modern or even futuristic version. Depending on context, there is a lot of scope for elaboration in the situation of the poor but generous man (or woman) and the initial scene setting, in the journey to the city and its difficulties, in the optimism and then the disappointment of the poor man and in the final 'triumph' of the discovery of the treasure. However, it is easy to sentimentalize the story in telling, so that is something to watch out for and avoid, if possible.

Essential elements: Needy and worthy person in reduced circumstances – dream of 'fortune' in a distant place, usually associated with bridge or similar – journey to the place and disappointment – meeting with local who has had the (second) dream of the treasure's location and thinks nothing of it – return to home territory and discovery of treasure (possibly accompanied by a transformation symbol, e.g. tree blossoming).

2. The Princess Who Died

In India, long ago, there lived a princess whose beauty was such that she shamed both the stars and the sun, so the poets said. Now, though they might have said such things of any princess, had a royal master paid them, of this princess they said it with passion and fervour and with particular eloquence, for she was indeed lovely. But what they did not say was that she had a mind and a will of her own and was not easily pleased.

Fame of this princess spread far and wide and young men came to woo her, but she would always find excuses to send them away. Three princes set out, each from separate kingdoms and each determined to win her. They met on the road and became friends. When they arrived at the palace, each in turn described the beauties of his kingdom, the fine palace in which the princess would live, the luxuries and the treasures and the wonders she would enjoy. The princess listened to them and smiled and then she said, 'I have no doubt that what you say is true, but you must each prove yourselves now by going away and travelling the world and bringing back for me the very best gift you are able to find. The one who brings the best gift may win my hand in marriage, though I make no promises, for the gift must be perfect in itself.'

The three princes rode away together for many miles. Eventually, reaching a crossroads, they promised to meet up in that place when the year was almost up and then one went west and one went east and one went north. Many adventures they had and many sights they saw and, if all those adventures and sights were related here, then they would fill the whole book. But as the year drew to a close, they each arrived back at the crossroads, proud of what they had found and confident of the gifts they brought. They agreed to show each other their gifts.

The first had brought a marvellous mirror by means of which you could see anything in the world you chose. The second had brought a magic carpet on which it was possible to fly through the air at great speed. The third had brought a candle which, when it was lit beside a dead person, would bring him or her back to life at once.

Now, when they had compared the gifts, they decided to take a look at the princess for whom they had each gone through so much. They all peered into the magic mirror and, to their horror, saw that the princess had died. She was even now being lifted onto a bier to be carried to her funeral pyre. As quickly as they could, they jumped onto the magic carpet and commanded it to take them to the palace of the princess, arriving just in time to stop the body being consigned to the flames. The third prince at once lit his candle and the princess jumped up, restored to full health and more beautiful than ever.

As soon as the ensuing celebrations were over, the three princes presented their gifts and each in turn claimed that she should marry him. The first one said that she owed most to his gift since, without it, he and the other princes would not have known she was dead and she would have been burned before they arrived. The second one said that, without his carpet, they could never have arrived in time. The third one insisted that his candle was the essential element, since, without it, the princess would still be dead.

The princess smiled sweetly at the three princes. 'I can never thank you enough for what you have done in giving me back my life,' she said. 'But each of those gifts depended upon the other; none was perfect in itself. So, sadly, I shall have to send you all away.'

That is what happened. The three princes were sent away and they travelled to other lands with their gifts and their stories. In countries where people knew little and wished to know more, they would support the claims of the prince with the mirror. In lands where people wished to travel and could not, they always cheered the prince with the magic carpet most loudly. But in lands where people feared and had no understanding of death, people were sure that the owner of the magic candle that brought back life was the best of all.

Background note: The most ancient version of this tale is one of the Indian *Vetala Tales*.[10] The first version I ever got to know was, however, a Portuguese folk tale. Versions of this tale from many different cultures are often presented as dilemma stories. This version gives the decision of the princess and adds the coda about the three princes.

Telling advice: The very many forms the tale has taken suggest how easily it transposes – and the sex of characters is clearly one change that can be made. Making a modern version is an interesting and rewarding challenge. The gifts of each prince (or wife, as in 'The Man Who Died', the analogous tale in Chapter 4) can be elaborated at length, with questions raised about the nature and quality of each of them, and how much the listener might want to possess such magical gifts (or develop such skills). It is useful to compare in detail this working out of the plot with the one in Chapter 4.

Essential elements: Wives/suitors – beloved/spouse who dies (or is otherwise endangered) – magic powers or gifts used together to bring person back to life – questioning which of these is most important.

3. The Talisman

Long ago and far away, there lived a poor orphaned woodcutter's daughter, who reckoned she had the worst luck in all the world. She was so poor that she could scarcely pay the rent on the little hovel in which she lived. She worked long hours for the local gentry for nothing much at all.

One day, a feeble old beggar came by and the woodcutter's daughter shared what bread she had with him and even let him sleep in the hovel. In the morning, as he left, the beggar, who now looked much stronger, said that he was really a magician. To repay the kindness he had been shown, he gave the girl a shiny ring, explaining that, if she wanted to sell it, it could be worth a lot of money. But, if she kept it and wore it, it might be worth even more, because this ring was nothing more nor less than a talisman of luck.

Well, once the beggar–magician had gone, the girl thought about how she could take the ring to town and sell it and get a bit of spare money for once in her life. Something stopped her, though she wasn't quite sure what. She thought that perhaps she would hold on to the ring until she really needed money. She wasn't sure she believed all that stuff about magic and talismans. Not really.

But somehow her luck did change. It wasn't that she suddenly found a golden fortune or anything of the sort. It all happened slowly and I don't know exactly how. Maybe she found a stray donkey wandering in the woods and used it to carry extra wood to sell at the market. Maybe she bought something at the market and managed to sell it again for more money than she paid for it. Maybe she took on an extra job here or there. However it was, one way or another she tested that talisman ring and soon found that she had a bit more money. So she started buying and selling this or that, just in a small way to begin with. Maybe it was wood and maybe it was donkeys and maybe cloth or fruit or perfume and maybe it was something else entirely. Whatever it was, she did well. She got some money and she used it to make more money. She used her wits and her luck. Slowly, slowly she bought and sold more expensive things. Slowly, slowly she made her fortune.

All the time, she kept that ring the beggar had given her. Over the years, she came to trust it and the luck it had brought her – even when it came to choosing a husband, allowing it to direct her to a man who was kind but not foolishly so, sharp but not hard, loving but not too sentimental, someone like herself in fact – because she remained underneath always kind and generous, just as she had been that day with the beggar. Because of that, people liked and respected her, despite her wealth, and they told the king what a good woman she was.

Well, the king (who, as it happened, was known as a wise ruler) said that he would like to meet this merchant queen who had made no secret of the fact that she was a humble woodcutter's daughter. He called her to his court and asked her how she had made her fortune and if perhaps she might like to become one of his advisers – this king liked to have honest people who had done well to give him their ideas on what he should do.

Now, the woodcutter's daughter was indeed honest. That is why she told the king about the beggar man and the ring, and how she had made her fortune through a kind of magic that came from the talisman she had been given. Of course, the king asked to see that magic ring.

Well, the woodcutter's daughter held out her hand and the king looked at the ring. And then he called the chief adviser, a man who had been a jeweller and knew all about all kinds of rings. 'What do you think of this?' the king asked.

'Worthless!' said the chief adviser. 'Just brass or something of the sort.'

'You see,' the king said. 'The worth isn't really in the ring. It's in you.'

That is when she recognized the king as the beggar she had helped all those years ago.

Background note: This plot recurs in many forms, both oral and written, right up to the present day. For example, I once heard on the BBC World Service a modern Indian author reading a version in which the 'talisman' was her grandmother's gold watch (which was never sold, gave the family confidence but eventually turned out to be worthless tin). In the Disney film, Dumbo the little elephant can fly only when he is given a 'magic feather' by the crows – which is the same trick used as a plot motif. In folk tale versions, the central character is sometimes a woman and all kinds of different episodes may fill the foreground, as the hero or heroine discovers how his or her 'luck' works. A version of this tale is included on my *Powerful Stories* CD set.

Telling advice: This transposes well to all sorts of settings and can expand quite naturally to become a much more substantial story (I've used a version in performance which takes an hour to tell). On the other hand, a quite brief telling in a modern setting can dispense with magicians and courts and could (for example) substitute a belief for the talisman. In therapeutic settings, various suggestions about confidence and decision-making can be woven into the telling.

Essential elements: Obtaining of the 'talisman' (it doesn't have to be something obviously magical) – the working out of the 'luck' and its association with increases in confidence, perception, etc. – the final discovery that the 'talisman' has no power/value (by which time the talisman has had its 'effect' and the heroine or hero has no need of it).

4. The Idol

A young fellow in ancient Greece had spent most of his money fecklessly, secure in the knowledge that he would one day inherit his rich uncle's greatest treasure. However, when at last the old man passed away, he was presented with an idol – an earthenware figure standing a couple of feet high and representing a god he had never even heard of. With this was a note from his uncle, saying that this was indeed his greatest treasure and he hoped his nephew would make the best of it.

The young man rushed out to find people who dealt in such things, in the hope of selling it, but none of them would offer him more than a few copper coins for it. It was quite worthless, they claimed. So he took it home and looked at it and pondered over it for a long time. To begin with, he cursed his uncle roundly for leading him on over the years but then slowly, slowly, he calmed down and laughed at himself and thought perhaps he would keep the idol, maybe even make offerings to it. Perhaps it would change his luck.

Well, it certainly seemed to do that. He settled down and became a hard-working citizen and made good decisions about this and that and began to prosper. Everything went well for him for some time and each day he would go and give thanks to the unknown god, decking the idol with flowers and incense and many kinds of expensive gifts.

But then everything changed and he lost all he had in a sudden stroke of fate and he found himself standing in front of that idol and saying to himself what an idiot he had been to waste so much on it. Somehow or other he ended up picking up that idol and hurling it against the wall where it smashed – and hundreds of gold coins that had been concealed inside it spilled out all over the place.

Background note: This has been developed from one of the lesser-known fables of Aesop. As discussed in Chapter 4, many of the morals at the end of Aesop's tales were added in ancient times but still centuries after he was supposed to have lived, and many of them can seem almost perversely disregarding of the real (and perhaps multiple) points of the story. The story of the idol clearly has something in common with the story of the talisman, not to mention the one about the man who became rich through dreaming.

Telling advice: The story transposes very well into a modern setting and can be received as an ironic joke, if told in that way. It suits an antique and junk dealers setting, though there are many more possibilities. A therapist or teacher might choose to build a bit of a client or pupil's own experience into it. For example: 'Maybe you can imagine just how he felt, getting this lumpish, ugly idol thing that meant nothing at all to him and then trying to imagine just how it could be valuable in any way at all. You know that feeling? Like being told that this or that exercise or practice or action will work for you and it just seems to be yet another chore...' The stages of the young man's perception of the idol and his associated hopes can each be elaborated, culminating in his final frustration with it and the marvellous revelation.

Essential elements: Waster who will inherit – arrival of the idol – initial hope of immediate gain and disappointment – second stage involving reform – frustration and smashing of idol – treasure revealed.

5. The Blue Jackal[11]

There was once a jackal sneaking around a village looking for some food to steal. He saw someone putting something into a big pot and decided that it must be food. As soon as the pot was left alone, he crept up and jumped into it, only to find himself splashing around in a dark, thick liquid.

Now, the pot belonged to a dyer and that day she had filled it with blue dye. So, when the jackal finally got out of the pot, his fur had changed colour. Instead of its normal brown-grey, camouflaged shade, it was now a deep, strong blue. No matter how much he tried to wash it off in the river, he stayed blue.

It all seemed a terrible disaster to him to begin with, because he wouldn't be able to skulk around stealing things. People would see him. But then he found that the other animals didn't recognize him as a jackal any more. In fact, they thought that he looked wonderful. The jackal, being just as crafty as jackals are supposed to be, didn't tell them he had fallen into some dye. Instead, he said that he was a king come to rule over them.

To begin with, only the small animals heard the story, but word quickly spread. Soon every creature, from the mouse to the mongoose to the monkey to the buffalo to the gazelle and even to the tiger, was coming to see the marvellous blue king of animals. The jackal had a marvellous time telling them all what to do.

The only creatures that knew him for what he was were the other jackals, but he had no time for them, now that he was a king. They didn't like that – the way he gave himself airs and looked down on them. So they decided to teach him a lesson. One night, when the moon was big and full, they went up onto a hill overlooking the place where the blue jackal was holding court with animals all around him. They sat around in a ring and they howled.

The animals sitting in a respectful circle around the jackal heard them but took no notice – it was only jackals howling, after all. But then a strange thing happened. Their new king put up his snout and lifted it towards the heavens and howled as well. It is natural for a jackal, pure instinct, that when one howls, the others join in.

From that moment, all the animals knew that their blue king was just a jackal, not royal at all. They left him there and then. And that's the origin of the saying, 'If you want to know which are the jackals, just wait till they howl.'

Background note: This story has been in my repertoire since my earliest work as a professional teller of tales. I think I may have originally learned it as a child from Arthur Mee's *Children's Encyclopaedia*, where a very brief version is listed as a fable of Aesop – although it is not usually included in Aesop collections and the story seems more like a stray fable from the *Panchatantra*: there are plenty of jackals in that collection, none in Aesop. The poet and mystic, Jalaludin Rumi, told a brief tale of a jackal who falls into some dye of many colours and tries to pass himself off as a peacock in his 13th-century masterpiece *The Masnawi*. The *Panchatantra*[12] (meaning 'five chapters'), quoted from in various places in this book, is an ancient and famous collection of fables from India, which includes some other stories attributed to Aesop. It was widely translated into other Eastern languages and is known to the Arabs as *Kalila and Dimna* and to the Persians and others as *The Fables of Bidpai*,[13] and also as the *Anwar-i-Suhaili* (The Lights of Canopus), which is based on the *Panchatantra* stories with associated tales and metaphors woven around them. Many, though not all, of the *Panchatantra* stories are 'beast fables' like this one. The collection is widely believed to have been used in the education of kings, whilst others evidently claim that it contains a hidden teaching system.

Telling advice: You can extend the falling into the dye and the jackal's reactions (initial dismay followed by cunning). You can characterize the animals duped by the jackal into accepting him as king. The jackal can also be characterized using a particular kind of voice (car salesman? posh smoothie?) in a performance situation. With children, you can howl like a jackal too and even get them to howl as a jackal pack. Explaining that the howl is instinctive helps to clarify the tale for children; you could equally point up analogies for adults by emphasizing this feature. Transposition of the tale is interesting. Animals in fables are rarely like real animals and are chosen to stand for (and often satirize) human qualities/attitudes/ faults, etc. Making the characters human again can sometimes make the story more subtle and quite contemporary, in this age of spin and image.

Essential elements: Jackal and situation in which he/she/it will come across dye – the dye and the change in the jackal – animals' (or other beings') reaction and the jackal's cunning manipulation of it – irritation of the other jackals and their trick – jackal's instinctive reaction.

6. The Other Room

I used to know this guy who had a flat in the basement of an old hotel. Well, it had been a hotel, a rather grand one, but now it was converted into apartments and his was at the bottom, with its own separate entrance. You had to go through gardens that had, no doubt, once been spectacular but were now rather overgrown. You would go down these stone steps to find his door. Very bohemian, of course, which suited him, since he was a writer.

Anyway, the flat was quite extensive, with a large main room and three bedrooms. He had more rooms than a lot of people have in a semi-detached house, but he probably needed them, because he was the kind of person who attracts visitors and hangers-on and people were always crowding into his life and distracting him with chatter and booze and fags and problems and all sorts. Also, he was the kind of person who needs space and is always looking for more, which might partly have been why he had recently been divorced, and how he had found himself in his mid-40s living in this place, rather than in the large Victorian house he was used to.

Now, there is a lot I could tell you about the life he led in that place and the women he was involved with and the parties he had and various other bits of scandal and gossip, too, a lot of things we could get distracted by, and they would all be very intriguing, no doubt. Not that any of it seemed to make him any happier or, as people say, fulfilled. But the interesting thing was, and still is, the extra room. I went to visit him one time to find that he suddenly had this large extra room, which he had discovered when he had been doing something to one of the walls. There was something rather dreamlike about it all, but there it was, evidently a part of the basement which had been walled off during the conversion and which no one knew about.

I asked him if it was legally his and he said he wasn't sure he cared. He was going to use it and he did. It became his retreat. He furnished it minimally and he would sit in it and (so he told me) make himself very quiet and still and just do nothing at all for an hour or two at a time. And the change in him after that…well, that was very interesting too because you couldn't help noticing that he was a lot more contented and that the rest of the rooms in the place seemed somehow to become a lot less chaotic – as if having that space apart from them helped him to focus better when he was in them.

Background note: This is a slightly simplified transcription of my telling of this anecdote on my double CD *Powerful Stories*. The anecdote is fundamentally true, though some disguise has been introduced and some simplification, to suggest potentials for use as a therapeutic/motivational tale. Happenings in ordinary life that are just a little unusual (such as the discovery of an extra room in a flat or house) often have a metaphorical quality, which can make the beginnings of a story.

Telling advice: If you don't relate to this one, what about someone you know who added an extension or a loft to their house, how much trouble it was until it was done and then the benefits which followed (unless, of course, the result was a leaky extension and a legal struggle with cowboy builders!)? Another possibility is to take the 'motif' of the extra room and tell it, in a different way, about some fictionalized person who is (perhaps) like someone you know. Writers do this kind of thing constantly, taking bits and pieces from real life and assembling them differently.

Essential elements: Individual (or persons) in need of space – accommodation that allows for discovery of extra space – discovery (or development) of extra space – use and positive benefits of use.

7. The Noisy House

There was once a man who decided that his house was much too noisy. The doors squeaked; the floorboards creaked; the windows rattled when the wind blew and then the cooking pots bubbled and the fire hissed and the wind howled and whistled all around. Everything made some kind of a noise and he could never concentrate on the work he had to do.

Now, there was an old woman in the village who knew a thing or two, and some people even said she was a witch and could do spells. This man with the noisy house, well, he had an ear for those kinds of stories and he went to her and he winked and pulled out a purse of money and asked her to do some magic to make his house quiet, so he could get on with what he had to do.

'Have you got a cat?' asked the old woman.

'Yes,' said the man.

'Well, take my dog to keep it company, and then we'll see about the magic.'

The man took the dog, which of course chased the cat all around the house and made a mess and a din and a pandemonium. He went back to the witch and asked if he could have his spell yet. 'Not yet,' she said. 'I'd like you to take my goat and put it inside your house with the cat and the dog.'

The man took the goat and it butted the dog, which chased the cat and things were worse then ever, so he went back again and this time she said, 'Take my six grandchildren to look after that goat.' So he did, but the grandchildren giggled and shouted and screamed and they teased the goat, which butted the dog, which chased the cat until things were completely impossible.

Well, at last, the witch came to the house and she took the dog and she took the goat and she took the children away. 'Now,' she said, 'I reckon the magic might work.' And, you know, that man went into his house and cleared it up and sat down and, when he did that, you could hear the door squeak and the floorboards creak and the wind howling and whistling all around and all the other things too. But, somehow or other, in some mysterious and extraordinary and completely inexplicable way, that house suddenly seemed to be the most peaceful place on earth. Somehow or other, the magic had worked.

Background note: This also is transcribed from *Powerful Stories*. There are many folk tale versions of this story, as well as several presentations for children that draw on the plot – the best known being about a house that seems to be too small until all sorts of creatures are brought into it. It never fails to intrigue and amuse audiences, as the witch (or other wise figure) sets up what you might call her paradoxical treatment.

Telling advice: This tale is extremely easy to adapt to all sorts of settings. The source of the discontent doesn't have to be noise; not having enough space, being too busy, having vision/view obstructed and many more problems (or challenges) can work just as well. Or staying with the 'ambient decibels' problem, a lot of people relate to annoyances with radios, CD players, DVDs, cars, parties, and drunken yobs.

Essential elements: Individual who is discontented with place/situation – form discontent takes – worsening of it – relief when the extra burden is removed – fresh perception of original concern.

8. The Saddhu's Loincloth

Two saddhus (seekers after truth) were travelling together when they reached a forest. One decided to stay in this secluded spot and absorb himself in meditation and contemplation of inner realities. The other travelled on.

Now, the local people, feeling honoured that the first saddhu had chosen a place near to their village and following traditions long established in India, soon began to bring this holy man the little food that he needed. He had no other needs, as the only clothing he wore was a loincloth, for the sake of decency. After a while, he noticed that, whilst he was deep in his trances, the mice were nibbling at the loincloth and reducing parts of it to a fine lace. He wasn't sure what to do, but the people of the village brought him a small companion. 'You need a cat,' they said. 'The cat will keep the mice away.'

This worked very well for a while and the saddhu could once again devote himself to mystical contemplation. But then he found that the cat was starting to stray and the mice were creeping back. 'You need milk for the cat,' said the local people. 'That will keep her with you.' Very generously they brought him a cow to give milk.

Now there was milk for the cat, but the saddhu found that he had much less time, because, of course, the cow needed milking and driving out to pasture. 'A cowgirl is the answer,' the people said. And they brought a girl to look after the cow.

That was fine, but the girl was lonely living in the forest and the holy man was too busy with his meditations to give her attention. She asked if she might take a husband and the saddhu agreed. The husband came to live in the forest and built a hut for himself and his wife.

The husband invited his friends from time to time and their talk often disturbed the saddhu, so he changed his devotional times to the night and early morning when the men were not around. But one morning, he heard the cry of a newborn baby and that was the first child of the cowgirl. She soon needed a helper to tend the cow and, as the baby grew to be a child, it had to have friends – and then a school with a teacher... Somehow the settlement in the woods seemed to grow day by day.

Some years after he had travelled on, the saddhu's companion returned and saw him, squatting amidst all the hustle and bustle of a town. Forest and solitude had gone. 'However did this happen?' he asked.

'Well,' said the saddhu, 'it is all because of one loincloth.'

Background note: There are all sorts of variations on this story in Indian tradition. It follows a pattern found in other folktales where chains of causation are shown in sometimes absurd and humorous ways, though here the framing centres on the renunciation and attachment which concern mystics. Kirin Narayan, in a fascinating account of the storytelling of an Indian guru, studies a numbers of versions of the plot.[14] A saddhu, in Hindu tradition, generally renounces the world, and some to this day travel as holy beggars in search of illumination, supported by the generosity of devout people.

Telling advice: There are limitations to telling contexts for this tale in its form as above. Many will enjoy it, of course, but there are those for whom anything at all mystical evokes knee-jerk prejudices, whilst others may object to transposing the story from its cultural/religious setting. However, as I've indicated, the pattern in the tale recurs in many folk tales and the story can be transposed to all sorts of different settings, producing a different emphasis each time. For example, how about a woman who had decided to go for a trendy minimalist look in her house and to make her life correspondingly simple? Or a writer who decided to set up a shed at the end of the garden, where he could really finish that novel?

Essential elements: Individual seeking a simple situation to concentrate on 'higher things' – item/affect/attitude, etc. (loincloth) retained for apparently good reasons – threat to item from environment (mice) – need for something to deal with this (cat) – chain of consequent complications (cow – girl – husband – friends – child – school) – punchline ('All because of one...').

9. The Enchanting Bird

Two brothers and a sister want to find out about their origins. They were left in the woods as babies and brought up by kindly charcoal burners, but now they want to know who they really are. They have heard of the Enchanting Bird of Truth and decide that one will go to seek it, while the other two will stay behind.

The elder brother sets out, leaving a knife to be watched over. If it rusts, he is in danger; if blood appears on it, he is dead. He stops in a city, trying to find out where he can find the Enchanting Bird of Truth. A storyteller takes a moment out from the tales he is telling in the market place to inform him that there is a mountain 21 days' march away and that, on this mountain, the Enchanting Bird of Truth perches. To reach it, he must follow the 'heart road' and not leave it, though he may look to the right or the left at wonders he may see as he passes. When he reaches the shadow of the mountain, however, he must look straight ahead and up towards the bird and not be distracted. The huge white bird will look back at him, fixing him with a fierce gaze. At its feet on the mountain peak are two piles of dust, one white and one blue. If he looks away, the bird will fly up into the air and drop the blue dust on him and he will turn to a blue stone on the mountainside, where he will stay for ever, unless someone rescues him. But if he manages to get all the way to the top without being distracted, then the bird will drop white dust on him and he will have the truth and the bird itself will turn into a white sparrow and perch on his shoulder.

This is what the storyteller tells the elder brother and he listens, but he doesn't stay to listen to the story the storyteller is telling that day in the market place. He is too busy preparing and then setting off on the heart road, which he follows, seeing to his amazement to the right and the left of that path enchanted gardens, flying palaces, dragons, giants and all kinds of strange things. He stays on the road and reaches the mountain, but, as soon as he steps into the shadow and begins to climb, voices are calling out to him all around, begging him to turn this way or that. What's more, the bird seems huge and its eyes seem to burn him and, in the end, he is unable to resist turning his head, as a voice offers a short cut. Instantly, the bird flies up and drops the blue dust and he turns into a blue stone.

Back in the woods, rust appears on the knife, so the second brother sets off leaving behind a rosary of pearl. If the pearls stick, then he is in danger; if they form a leaden lump, then he is dead. Of course, he finds the same storyteller, hears about the same Enchanting Bird of

Truth and sets out along the heart road. Like his brother, he doesn't bother to listen to the storyteller's story. Like his brother, he sees wonders of all kinds, reaches the mountain and looks straight ahead as he climbs. Like his brother, he hears all kinds of voices calling him here and there, one of which is his own brother's voice. Like his brother, he can't resist turning, and he too becomes a blue stone.

So then it is up to the girl. Finding that the pearls are sticking, she sets out, finds the same storyteller who tells her about the bird on the mountain. Off she goes, but not before she has listened well and inwardly digested the storyteller's story. She travels the heart road, sees incredible wonders, reaches the mountain and walks up it to the top, where the bird flies into the air and drops white dust on her and perches on her shoulder. So then she has the truth, which is that she is a princess cheated out of her inheritance by wicked aunts who imprisoned their sister (her mother) and had her three children taken out to be killed in the forest. Fortunately, though, the soldiers charged with the duty had taken pity on them and simply left them to wander. Her brothers (whom, since she now commands the bird, she is able to rescue, along with a thousand other young men turned to stone on the mountainside) are princes. The three of them, with the army of young men, set off to set wrongs to rights and what happened to them in achieving that is another story.

What about the story the storyteller told in the market place? It was a story about someone who used a trick to survive a similar ordeal without being tempted to turn to listen to seductive voices that called out all around. The girl had used something just like that – she had stuffed her ears with thick cotton wool and wax so that, when she climbed the mountain and the voices were all around, she didn't hear them.

All of which shows that, if you really do listen when storytellers tell you their marvellous confabulations, you too can climb all the way up to the truth.

Background note: A different but similar, more extended version of this tale is included on the *Powerful Stories* CD. It contains a motif which crops up again and again in folklore and myth, that of the hero/heroine who must somehow resist 'voices' (or temptations of various kinds) to reach some form of treasure or truth. This version is loosely based on one given in outline in the notes to Burton's 19th-century translation of the *Alif Layla wa Layla*.[15] Two analogues for comparison are 'Farizad of the roses smile', also from the *Alif Layla wa Layla* (a version that is easier to read than Burton's is the one by Mardrus and Mathers[16]) and 'The fine greenbird' in Italo Calvino's classic *Italian Folktales*.[17]

Telling advice: This tale lends itself to a lot of elaboration – I've told versions lasting well over an hour, including in them a whole series of episodes. The use of the present tense in this summary actually chimes with oral tradition (think of jokes and anecdotes). With imagination, the story that the storyteller tells can be reconstructed (see, for example, the story of Odysseus and the Sirens in Homer's *Odyssey*, in which, during his sea journey home from war, Odysseus had his crew's ears stopped with wax and himself lashed to the mast, to stop them being lured to shore by the Sirens' haunting song and getting dashed against the rocks). This can be included as a tale within a tale. Conversely, the whole story can be kept short and concise by focusing simply on the climb, the 'distractions' and the success of the third climber (the girl in the version above). The story works particularly well with a fairy/ wonder tale setting as here, but it is possible to create a version that doesn't rely on magic. For example, suppose that someone has to climb a mountain to find an important truth believed to be inscribed in stone near the summit. Suppose that he/she has to cope with loneliness, delusions and even hallucinations... This has long been a plot element in adventure stories and films.

Essential elements: There are three plots here:

1. The three 'orphans' who are in reality special (poverty situation – quest of truth with magical devices left with siblings – finding of truth).

2. Travelling to and climbing the mountain of truth (heart road and wonders – climb and distractions – two failures but third one succeeds).

3. The storyteller's story, which includes the motif of ear stopping imitated by the third climber.

Solution-focused story frames

It is not a big leap from instant story transposing to spontaneous story making. Anyone who invents stories does so on the basis, conscious or not, of a good intuitive understanding of all sorts of plots, many of them like those that we have been considering. (After all, if you had never heard or read a story, you would not have much idea of what a story would be like, how its conventions operate, and so on.) Developing a story frame, which makes use of all this unconscious knowledge, can be a very useful way to prime creativity. It can be more vague and more general than the transposable plot of a particular story, and it can be used flexibly – as a frame for your own telling, as a frame for a client or pupil to use to tell, or as a means of joint exploration through questioning and techniques such as visualization. It is possible, too, to shape your frame with particular results in mind – to make it, as it were, solution-focused.[18,19]

Here is an example of a five-stage frame, which allows for a fair amount of complication without becoming too intricate. Each stage listed describes a part of the tale to be defined and elaborated.

Frame 1. The enchanted castle

1. A place that needs to change (enchanted castle, ruined house, neglected hall, disused station, etc.).

2. Key problem, probably unrecognized (enchantment; need for refurbishment; lack of attention/funding/planning, etc.).

3. Individual(s) who will break the spell. (Why is this person not 'fettered' and hence able to do this, unlike everyone else up till now?)

4. The breaking of the 'spell'. (For dramatic reasons, not too easily done).

5. Marvellous effects of this. (Make it vivid!)

Whilst the title I have given this frame might suggest a traditional fairy-tale setting, it could just as easily have a contemporary or futuristic setting. Programmes about property restoration have been very popular on UK television in recent years, often telling what is essentially a story about miraculous transformations. Another possibility is a science-fiction plot about planets under some kind of evil domination. How you might go about developing your story from this point depends on what you are looking for from it. Here are three possibilities.

TELLING FOR FUN AND SKILL DEVELOPMENT

This is the best way to start – with no end-gaining pressure. Let us suppose we are thinking about a castle and we know it is under some kind of shadow. We might want to linger on stage 1, with a description of the castle, exploring it in imagination, saying (to ourselves or even out loud) a few things about what it looks like, where it is, how old it is, listing details at random before defining the 'spell' or whatever the key problem is going to be.

In stage 2, we define the problem clearly. Let us say that the castle is enchanted. But how is it enchanted? What kind of sights, sounds, smells, feelings, etc. might typify this enchantment? Are there people turned to stone inside the castle, as the convention goes, or does the enchantment work in a quite different way, for example by making people behave like mindless zombies or in bizarre and idiotic ways? How does the enchantment maintain itself? Is it a spell created by a wizard or an enchantress, a curse brought on by unhappy coincidences or something constantly renewing itself by strange and unsuspected means –perhaps the effect of weird vapours rising from murky underground places where cauldrons steam and bubble?

In stage 3, it is a good idea to build a profile of the heroine and hero, before embarking on the main task they are to accomplish. In this way, we can get a sense of whether she, he or they are unconventional, oddly talented, supernatural, magical or simply lucky, when they turn out to be able to defeat the seemingly impregnable enchantment of the castle. Is it a solo effort or some kind of collusion? The answer to these questions may emerge as we explore the characters.

The dramatic peak of the tale is likely to be at stage 4, in which you would need to picture the breaking of the spell and the means by which it is done. C.S. Lewis's children's classic *The Lion, the Witch and the Wardrobe* has the lion Aslan leaping into the White Witch's castle and breathing on the creatures within it to turn them back from stone to life.[20] In some folktales, the hero or heroine has to perform tasks such as finding a princess who is hidden by the enchanter in the shape (say) of a fruit on a tree, a grain of corn in a cornfield or an emerald on a ring in a treasure chest under the sea. In several versions of the plot which most of us think of as 'Sleeping Beauty', the prince has to find his way through the forest and the thorns.

For the transformation at stage 5, what image comes to mind for the immediate and dramatic change that follows the breaking of the spell? Is it people coming to life, or fountains flowing, or birds singing, or flowers blooming, or all of those things, or none of those things? What feelings will you describe and what sights and sounds? And what will happen, as things settle into a new pattern and the castle comes back to life and begins to function as of old or perhaps in some entirely unexpected new ways?

If you spend some time on this exercise and enter into it fully, the images can be quite powerful and engrossing – especially if you begin to identify personally with the transformation processes. Making the story 'mean' is what can make it a powerful instrument for change.

MAKING YOUR STORY MEAN

What happens if, instead of doing it just for fun, you consider telling the story to help with someone's particular problem or concern, or as a motivating metaphor for a group? Let us say that the perceived problem is pessimism, since this can be experienced collectively as well as being very limiting for individuals. You are aiming to tell a tale delivering the optimistic message that pessimism can be conquered, that the 'castle' (representing the mind/emotions/will continuum) can be liberated from the 'spell' of excessive negativity.

In stage 1 and 2, you could elaborate the same castle image, with suggestions about how a certain neglect has allowed the cobwebs and the dust to gather and the weeds to grow, this wall to crumble away here, this staircase to rot and that window to be blocked, so that the light doesn't come in, etc., all because people felt quite powerless in the face of decay or because destruction seemed inevitable. Perhaps this has happened because of the suggestions of some tyrant or wizard. Or maybe, leaving the realms of fantasy for a contemporary realism, the curse might be a dip in the property market and an unduly gloomy prognosis for the value of a house.

Stage 3 can now contrast the attitude of pessimists associated with the castle or house with the can-do approach of the people who will restore it and who see the potential in a dilapidated building. Stage 4 might involve elements of magic or simply the 'magic' of effective cleaning and renovations, recounted at a rapid pace with a feeling of rhythm: 'First it was the walls and the pointing and, of course, the sweeping and the dusting. Then it was opening out this and throwing away that and dusting and cleaning and clearing a little more...'

Stage 5 can emphasize brightness and effectiveness, optimism, looking forward with clarity and maintaining the new state of good repair. In a contemporary setting, of course, there is the increase in value – which makes a good metaphor in itself.

NOT YOURS BUT THEIRS

Another possibility is to use the frame not for your own telling but as a way to encourage a client or a student or a group's own telling. Asking others about the elements of a story, in the way that I have done above, helps prompt their imagination to develop it. Depending upon whom you are working with, you might have a simple outline frame already printed out or you could write it out on paper or on a whiteboard, either all at once or stage by stage, allowing the individual or group to discuss and develop each one before you write down the next. Or you might choose to do the entire process orally. Sometimes it works to ask people to complete the story in their own time, writing it out or imagining it through or even recording it on tape or CD, etc.

In my experience, if the frame is sufficiently appealing, people soon start to identify with the characters and (in the case of this story frame) the transformation. With guidance through subtle questioning (for example, if someone had talked about being imprisoned by a habit or by a condition, it would be relevant to ask details of how the castle is imprisoning), the story can become not just a story but also all that it represents metaphorically to an individual. (A client in therapy who has been discussing a confidence problem is likely to shape the tale in a way quite different from that of a student who needs to find effective thinking and studying methods.) Since the frame is all about positive change, it allows solutions to be experienced imaginatively at the same time. There has to be a hero/heroine or a band of 'liberators'; it has to work in that way because the frame requires it to. In this frame, the individual or group has to have something which will break the spell – some personal quality, some skill, some attitude.

It is at stage 4 that a lot of discoveries can be made. Stuck situations are by definition stuck. But this stage is all about change and movement. You can ask, how does it feel, this breaking of the spell? What kinds of things are happening in the castle? What do you notice first? What kind of changes are occurring? In stage 5, where you confirm the changes and imagine positive futures, you are in effect asking about how the change you have been aiming for is going to work out – and preparing the person for that change.

Here are a few more suggestions for story frames to work with.

Frame 2. Zap Pow

1. Something extraordinary happened to X and this is how.

2. Something about X and his or her situation (to get people to identify).

3. When the extraordinary thing happened, X did A, B and C (this included acting 'out of character' because of the shock).

4. This led to D – an unexpected change, very positive for X.

5. (Optional – the pattern could end at 4) Quickly run back through the chain of consequences: the extraordinary thing happened and seemed a disaster/shock/setback but created effect D.

You could try out several possible openings for this. Such and such a person fell out of an aeroplane and survived. Another person found an ancient treasure. Yet another one had some strange object, which vanished before her very eyes. Each of these examples would set you going in a different direction, attempting to explain how the extraordinary thing happened.

You might want to try different character types. Someone shy and retiring falls out of the aeroplane. How does this differ from a tale in which someone hopelessly brash and loud does the same thing? Could each work equally well? In what ways might the event lead these two contrasting types to behave 'out of character'? How would this out-of-character happening have a bigger effect?

Clearly, this frame is very much about change, but what kind of change are you working with? Maybe you would want to think ahead to the kind of character who will change because, in a practical situation, you would be looking to match this in some way to your pupil or client. Several very different dramatic events could have the desired zapping effect for someone working on issues of confidence and performance, for instance. Suppose, in cartoon style, someone hiding in the shadows on a balcony falls out onto a stage and manages, in a stunned state, to entertain everybody. Suppose someone else is the only other person in an aeroplane and has to fly it when the pilot collapses.

Whilst making a lot of play about 'the moral of the story' or 'what it all means' is generally not a good idea, since it may stop the listener or the story maker making further creative exploration and discovery, the optional stage 5 in this frame calls for a quick replay of the events in the story. This doesn't have to include 'so it was all for the best' sentiments. The purpose is to hold up the chain of consequences for inspection again, to clarify how things appear to have worked and allow some subtle inferences to be drawn. It is a technique that can be used with any of the frames or indeed with other stories when appropriate.

Frame 3. Wishing wells and Crusoe islands

1. Central character in a conflict or held back by his or her own limiting perceptions of what is possible (e.g. someone who believes she is unlucky and impractical, yet wants to prove herself and be successful).

2. Dramatic incident that puts character in a risk situation, which resonates with his or her fears – e.g. someone who already feels isolated or helpless falls into a well or is marooned on a desert island.

3. Process of escape, involving harnessing powers for change.

4. Return to ordinary life, with new perspective on old problem.

5. Dealing with the old obstacles, using the inspiration provided by the escape.

This frame specifies a problem focus at the outset: you or your teller(s) have to define a fictional problem, which, of course, can be made similar to the problem you are working with. Both will then be metaphorically modelled in the well or island or whatever. Escape in some form is also specified. It can be interesting to explore how forgotten earlier experiences or knowledge might provide the key skills for the escape. For example, the heroine in a plot where she is tied up and locked by thieves in the boot of a car could draw on an earlier experience of learning relaxation techniques at antenatal classes to still her panic, slacken resisting muscles and eventually slip out of the knots. The frame also allows for examination of ways in which experience of liberation in one sphere can lead to freedom in others. Incidentally, you may have noticed that the story improvised by the therapist for a man stuck in his attitudes to management of his own pain, set out in the last chapter, uses elements of this pattern.

Frame 4. Amazing Zibbo

1. Problem situation for person or people.

2. Futile attempts to change this (maybe giving some quick examples and/or exploring a typical incident at length).

3. Introduction of Amazing Zibbo (marvellous product, thing, strategy, etc.).

4. Miraculous outcomes.

5a. Amazing Zibbo discovered to be inactive and the effect has another (psychological) source; or

5b. Amazing Zibbo found to work in a different way from the one supposed; or

5c. Amazing Zibbo really is brilliant (the ad men were right, so buy some!).

This is an example of a frame with alternative endings. (It is also possible to leave it unfinished and invite speculation about the ending, as in dilemma tales explored earlier.) Ending 5a is much like 'The Talisman' plot (given earlier in this chapter). Ending 5b could suggest an alternative physical reason for the effect of Zibbo – for example, in order to get it, people have to go a long way to a particular store, which gives them exercise and makes that part of town a new focal point. Ending 5c is the advert style ending (Zibbo really works just the way it says on the bottle) but it's possible to do that with humour and irony and a surprise or two. For example, you might set up the expectation that the 'Zibbo effect' involves some form of deception and then cheat that with the revelation that it really does have 'good, honest, old-fashioned ingredients, put together with good, old-fashioned craftsmanship and tender loving care'. Note that stage 4 (as in the other frames) can allow for a clear imagining of how a solution will feel.

Frame 5. Secret gardens and hidden lands

1. Heroine/hero and her/his needy condition.

2. Blundering into the secret garden/magical land.

3. Magical and wonderful possibilities of the land, including ease of change at personal level. (Maybe through drinking the Water of Life or reading from The Book of All Knowledge for example, or maybe through being called upon to take certain responsibilities or do particular work in that place.)

4. Discovery that she or he can move backwards and forwards between the two lands.

5. Change in both lands.

This is a very familiar theme in myth and legend and in children's fiction, but mirrors a pattern to be found in many life situations, as for example can be seen in 'The Other Room', the true anecdote told earlier in this chapter. C.S. Lewis's Narnia classics are very much in this territory or, for an unusual take, there is Doris Lessing's brilliant and strange novel *The Memoirs of a Survivor*. Fantasy lands are great for liberating the imagination in spontaneous storytelling – you can have bizarre orange skies and weird purple trees and peculiarly compelling sounds and smells and all sorts. Their therapeutic and educational advantages are many, but one (as suggested here) is that it is possible to change things 'over there' which mirrors back to here and now. How well does clearing and re-organizing a marvellous magical garden work as a metaphor for sorting out complex feelings/fears/relationships, etc.? Could a fountain which suddenly jets forth golden water have any connection with boosted immune system functioning or removal of creative blocks? The story told to Rosemary in Chapter 1 (p.57) is an expression of this frame and illustrates how practical change has been achieved through this kind of imaginative work.[21]

There are all sorts of possibilities for further frames. One way to discover some is to think of stories or story types you know and reduce them to outlines. Another, starting from the other end, so to speak, is to think of a series of changes you would like to set in motion, allow a metaphor to come to mind that would express this (repelling an alien invasion, taming an animal, meeting a strange being, etc. – the exploration of symbols in the next chapter may be helpful here) and then to map out a plot in stages. Five stages are convenient but not essential. The minimum is probably three, whilst any more than seven can be awkward to handle from memory but there are no set rules. As always with stories, it is a question of what works – or what at least can be made to work with a little imagination.

Imagination is, of course, as essential with the frames as with transposing and using story patterns in general. Once the stages in a frame become fleshed out vividly as characters and events and scenes, once the pattern in a story takes a firm hold on the mind, it is no longer a theory or a 'nice idea'; it is a form of experience, a place you have visited, a route you have travelled. As the saying goes, when you have been on a journey, you have a story to tell.

Chapter 7

Traps and Treasures: Symbols, Stories within Stories and Metaphorical Literacy

> Some orphaned and very poor children played often
> with the only heirlooms their late parents had left
> them – a few glass balls and baubles. When they grew
> up, however, they discovered what they were: the
> crown jewels of a certain country of which they were
> the rightful rulers.

Where there are stories, there are very frequently symbols too. Symbolic images of all kinds have for centuries been woven seamlessly into stories from countless, diverse cultures. But what do these images mean? Or, to put it another way, how does their meaning arise and where does it come from? These are questions that have sparked not a little debate and controversy. In the perspectives coming out of semiology and semiotics, the modern disciplines concerned with the meaning of signs, and in post-structuralist and post-modernist thought in general, it is more or less taken as a given that the meanings of symbols and signs are primarily socially constructed.[1] Conversely, among the compilers of dream dictionaries and the proponents of some psychoanalytic therapies, as well as in Chinese astrology, medieval European church architecture and Islamic alchemy, to take a few diverse examples, the common starting point is that particular images have fixed and universally recognizable meanings. (At the wackier end of the spectrum is a belief that God/gods/higher consciousness/aliens, etc. are communicating constantly in the form of symbols and that these symbols are a divine language you can read, a bit like messages in tea leaves or tarot cards, and that you should be alert for at all odd times, such as while driving, doing your tax returns or even cleaning your teeth.) Whilst there have also been some cross-fertilizations between psychoanalytic ideas of the 'natural' meaning of symbols and some notions of social construction, particularly when structuralism dominated the field, the middle ground remains muddy and decidedly misty.

Symbols as shared metaphors

It is useful to clarify what could be common sense in this area. Much symbolic meaning has to be unique and personal, whilst a lot more is no doubt culturally specific. There may well be universal elements in many symbols: fire burns and water wets wherever you live, though, if you are a firefighter from London, your ideas about these two elements may differ from those of a desert-dwelling Zoroastrian. Symbols of all kinds may have agreed meanings within a culture at a particular time. At different times and in different cultures, symbolic images and figures that are apparently the same can mean quite different things. Chinese dragons are different in character and meaning from the evil and destructive monsters of Western legend; most of us would be more than a little wary of using a swastika for decoration, even though, prior to its adaptation and reversal in Nazi Germany, it functioned for centuries as a symbol of wellbeing.

So far, so good. It is not hard to see the value of an intelligent study of symbols and signs that tells us quite clearly that shared and agreed meanings are not fixed from on high, that time and fashions change and that people don't carry the memory of all things signed and symbolized etched on their hearts or coded in the chemistry of their brains. These days, only fools fear wizards drawing strange star and circle patterns in the dust as evidence of their powers. Yet a lot of symbols 'mean' because they have meaning – or a virtually intrinsic series of potentials to suggest and represent it for human beings. Symbols are not the things they symbolize; they are, broadly speaking, a metaphor for those things – generally, it is true to say, a metaphor that has been shared and agreed, but generally also after they have first been vividly experienced at a primary level.

'The essence of metaphor is understanding and experiencing one kind of thing in terms of another,' said George Lakoff and Mark Johnson in their 1980 classic guide *Metaphors We Live By*. In their 2003 afterword to a revised edition of the book, Lakoff and Johnson stress the fact that, whilst metaphors can be both highly culturally specific, as extensively illustrated in their original book, recent research has backed up their suggestion of universal elements at the primary level, where they reflect common bodily and environmental experiences as well as basic biology. They wrote:

> You don't have a choice as to whether to think metaphorically. Because metaphorical maps are part of our brains, we will think and speak metaphorically, whether we want to or not. Since the mechanism of metaphor is largely unconscious, we will think and speak metaphorically whether we know it or not. Further, since our brains are embodied, our metaphors will reflect our commonplace experience in the world. Inevitably, many primary metaphors are universal because everybody has the same kinds of bodies and brains and lives in basically the same kinds of environments, so far as the features relevant to metaphor are concerned.
>
> The complex metaphors that are composed of primary metaphors and that make use of culturally based conceptual frames are another matter. Because they make use of cultural information, they may differ significantly from culture to culture.[2]

This is one perspective that usefully balances and moderates the common 'cultural studies' assumption that the only basis for shared meanings in metaphors is social construction, which arbitrarily turns them into conventional symbols. Another balancing and moderating factor emerges from the expectation fulfilment theory of dreaming, originated by Joe Griffin and explained in Chapter 1. Dreaming is metaphorical and dream metaphors have a vital function in helping the brain maintain its integrity. Thus, there is a natural mechanism through which metaphors create themselves at an unconscious level through association of ideas. But, as we are also able to use conscious imagination, we can create metaphors intentionally as well, to try to understand our worlds and to communicate with others. Very importantly, if less commonly appreciated, our metaphors can, on occasions, be intuitive perceptions of whole patterns we do not yet understand sequentially and logically. There are dozens of examples of cases where scientists have experienced metaphorical insights that have led to their discoveries, from the German chemist Kekule's famous dream of snakes biting their tails, which led to his unravelling of the cyclical structure of benzene, to Einstein's image of himself as a teenager riding on a beam of light, which, he afterwards claimed, led him to formulate the theory of relativity. Artists, musicians, poets and writers frequently achieve insights in similarly 'mysterious' ways; the 18th-century Italian composer Giuseppe Tartini famously called one of his sonatas *The Devil's Trill*, after dreaming of a trill played by the devil, which gave him the pattern and the inspiration he needed to complete it.

We may all experience intuitions day to day, if of a lesser order, which we register in the form of metaphors. A shrewd old farmer once told me he had never trusted a certain solicitor because there was something about the way the man looked at people that brought back the memory of stoats he had watched hunting rabbits. Sure enough, the lawyer tried to trick him out of some land, but the farmer anticipated him and wasn't caught out. He might not have known the law as well as the solicitor but, as he said, he did understand stoats.

So, symbols, in the sense in which we'll focus on them here, are generally shared metaphors. Of course, the very word 'symbolic' covers a wide range of things itself, from letters and numbers and geometric forms to more complex pictures and words and experiences, to language both verbal and non-verbal and to representational systems in general. A symbol might be a couple of lines or dots or it might be a work of acknowledged genius, like the *Mona Lisa*. It could be a cathedral or it could be a flower. The central point is that, in a given context, it stands for something other than itself, usually in a form that has meaning to certain people. It may be chosen to stand for something else for reasons that become obscured by time and convention, as is generally the case with letters and numbers. A symbol is more commonly chosen, however, because, in some way at some level, it is analogous to what it symbolizes. The sorts of symbols that crop up in stories are usually arrived at in this way. And a symbol chosen because of its likeness to something else is automatically also metaphorical: you are not just representing something; you are saying and understanding something through the comparison, making a metaphor – and in a sense telling a story through that metaphor, a compact, concise, yet allusive and poetic story about how things are or can be.

Symbols of this kind can be very useful when using stories to bring about change, but only when they have been 'liberated'. Symbols can die, become fixed and static and sometimes even rather bullying – as when myths are interpreted by priests or coteries of scholars. The interpretation is already done for you; you simply receive. A lion is the symbol of courage; a thunderbolt is the symbol of Zeus; and white is the symbol of purity, so now you know. Finished. Done. But a little reflection or exploration, such as a look in a symbol dictionary or other good reference work, will reveal that lions have been used to stand for royalty and command, for justice and even the power of the sun, as well as for courage. Zeus didn't corner the market in mythical thunderbolts. Then the white flag of surrender might come to mind, contradicting the idea of white as an expression of transcendent perfection or simplicity.

This might seem to support the social construction of symbol hypothesis, until we realize that it isn't a case of 'either...or...' but of 'both...and...'. There is a lot of common ground underscoring very many of the apparently different uses of any one image, which becomes clear when we think metaphorically instead of conventionally. Command should (at least, ideally) be based on courage and justice. Thunderbolts are dramatic manifestations of extreme natural forces, so many powerful gods and heroes (metaphors, in themselves, for various kinds of power) would have a quiver full of them. White has multiple associations evoking light and its equally varied associations, such as the multi-level experiences enshrined in verbs like 'to illuminate' or 'to enlighten', experiences where transcendence and simplicity and even surrender might indeed, at some levels, meet up. It is a pity to lose all that entirely to the racialists and biological washing powder promoters.

We are susceptible to metaphor because we are metaphorical creatures. It is always open to a person to take a story symbol and interpret it anew through the associations and ideas it brings to mind or through what can be found out imaginatively. Some symbols that have clear natural qualities and associations at a metaphorical level may very well communicate to us immediately, whether we 'ask them in' or not, especially if we are absorbed in the trance of a story.

Personal symbols

Many people develop their own personal symbols, consciously or unconsciously. People also have their own particular reaction to symbols embedded in culturally familiar myth at the same time as appreciating their conventional sense. For example, a person might appreciate that rivers and streams are often used as metaphors for time passing whilst, at an individual level, a river or stream may carry quite different meanings and associations, reflecting, say, the intense yearnings once experienced on a walk with a lover on a sunny spring afternoon whilst the sunlight sparkled on the water, or the chill of terror dating back to nearly drowning during an ill-advised swim one cold autumn evening.

As far as the unconscious mind is concerned, there is probably no difference between personal symbols and personal metaphors: an image attracts associations, just as a magnet attracts metal, whether that metal is in the form of a cross or a crescent or just amorphous iron filings. For the conscious mind and personality, however, it is meaningful that known symbols have a dual character: the personal and the received. The river symbol that holds the traumatic or bittersweet memory can be reinterpreted, bringing into greater awareness some of the more conventional associations, the 'language' of the symbol. Realizing and expressing the idea that time is a river that flows onwards and is never the same at any moment may be an important perception to register in a healing process. Talking or doing guided imagery or making stories with people known to have difficult associations with streams can help their own individual streams to unblock and flow onwards.

The symbol in its general sense may, thus, be meaningfully connected to someone's personal metaphor, which can then be thought of as a personal symbol. This image can become a sign in a unique and private language. Simply bringing the image to mind in its new, extended and imaginatively experienced sense can bring back the feeling and the power of change. The stream can go on being interpreted in new ways; new analogies can inform new feelings and thoughts.

Working with symbols

Symbols, to reiterate, are part of the fabric of many traditional oral stories, particularly fairy tales, myths and legends, whilst modern-day authors and poets may also consciously thread them into their work. A symbol with known associations or whose implications can be worked out with a little imaginative thought adds dimension to a story and is an important element of the kinds of multiple-meaning story touched on at the end of Chapter 4.

For example, 'The Wonderful Tapestry', the story told there, contains many metaphors, starting with the central multi-level metaphor of the tapestry itself. One could arguably call tapestry and weaving universal symbols,[3] analogous to the creating or weaving of consciousness itself. Every part of the story is full of symbolism, and we can get a taste of this even just by looking at one section: the stone horse that comes to life when it receives the third brother's two front teeth, eats the berries red as blood from the tree and is ridden by the young man.

The image of horse and rider has often been used in mythology and folklore, with a suggestion of various isomorphic relationships – mind to body, consciousness/self to unconsciousness, will to mind, and so on. In public statuary and official paintings, rulers and leaders have frequently been shown on horseback, typifying command and control. Muhammad, in his night vision, rode upon the winged horse Burak given to him by the Archangel Gabriel, symbolizing both control and inspiration. According to J.C. Cooper,[4] the horse itself can symbolize amongst other things intellect, wisdom, mind, reason, swiftness of thought, nobility and dynamic power.

When the third son, representing the part of the mind and being that is sincere and true and not distracted by 'gold', mounts the horse of stone and brings it to life by giving it his own front teeth, the image is powerfully symbolic of, among other things, trust and mutual respect – essential between rider and mount.

Stone is a metaphor likely to have at least some similar meanings across cultures. Stone is inanimate, inactive but also a strong foundation, as in bedrock. Stone can also be a symbol of the unchanging and of eternity. But stone is cold, unmoved and unmoving. People are turned to stone in the magical imagery of many universal folk tales. The process in this story is the reverse:

from inactivity and apparent death to life, from coldness to warmth and inspiration.

The horse eats the berries red as blood from the tree, berries and tree providing two more symbols associated with life. It then has the supernatural power of flight over the seas of boiling oil and ice and through the fiery mountain...

This is rather a rich mixture to take in at a go. To make sense of it, it is necessary to ponder and make connections, putting such imagery into context with the other images in the story, so that one image illuminates and makes sense of another. The associations I have pulled out are not intended to be either exhaustive or definitive, as would be the case if we were to decode the story according to a system such as Jungian archetypes. The meanings remain multiple, yet by no means chaotic and random because they are held within the meaningful frame of the story, which in turn reflects the meaningful frames of life and experience.

While few people would want to struggle with working out the implications of all the images in a story like this, it is quite possible that, as one becomes absorbed as a teller or listener, the metaphors communicate naturally on unconscious levels. Also, exploring a single symbol as part of a story can often be a useful means of talking about an area of concern to an individual, in a non-threatening, indirect way. For example, a suitable mount and rider symbol might be meaningful for people trying to develop skills or the will to overcome addictions or habit patterns or obsessions. Any experience of riding a horse or a donkey or a bike or a car or a wheelchair can be drawn on, as an illustration of control, of how much you have to make an effort to achieve that control and how much you have to trust to the 'instincts' of the mount.

The apparently dead tree that bursts into life is a motif that migrates between stories, cropping up in various folk tales and legends, and with good reason: a dead tree bursting into blossom is a very powerful image. I once told the story about the tree that burst into life when the man found his fortune underneath it (told in Chapter 6) to a woman who was in the grip of a severe depression. She had always loved her garden, though it had been neglected of late, and this one image stayed vividly within her mind, giving her much hope.

When working with symbols, just as with stories, it is important to keep in mind appropriateness. Is the image one that will work for this person, chime with their experience and temperament?

Some people who have always lived in cities may not respond to a tree image as well as someone who lives near a forest; other urban dwellers may relate very well to tree images, perhaps because a tree is one of the few natural features in some urban landscapes, or because they see forests and parks depicted on television and in films, even if they don't themselves walk in them. Equally, some country dwellers may be surprisingly unmoved by natural imagery, so it is important not to make assumptions based on stereotypes. To test the waters, it can be helpful to mention the image in passing before committing much time to it. For example, 'I was looking at an old tree the other day that I'd always thought was dead and, do you know, it was sprouting...' or 'I don't know whether you've ever ridden a bike or maybe even a horse?' A casual discussion might follow, from which you can glean some hints about the appropriateness of the image, and then you might leave it to sit for a while, before picking up on it in a story or in guided imagery at a later stage.

Here are a few questions that some people find help them in ordering thoughts and perceptions about symbols and their possibilities for practical story purposes.

1. What could be universal or primary 'natural' elements in this image?

2. How might its use and appreciation be culturally defined and limited?

3. How do I respond to this image emotionally, intellectually and through association? What, if any, obvious associations come to mind in relation to it?

4. Do I need to research this a little more, by looking in a dictionary, encyclopaedia or other reference work or simply by contemplating it for a while to see what emerges or by exploring it imaginatively through different senses?

5. How differently might someone else experience this symbol or image? What kinds of person can I imagine responding to it and why?

6. What could be wrong with this kind of image and how might it become frozen, fixed and unproductive?

7. Might this image in some way reflect an underlying general pattern or principle?

8. What else comes into my mind, however irrelevant?

The Morning Dew

A young man had inherited his rich father's wealth and decided to devote himself to tasting every kind of delicacy available in the known world. But the experience only left him stale and disappointed and deeply unhappy. He decided instead to seek a truly happy person and eat whatever he or she ate.

His servants scoured the world but were always told by seemingly happy people that they were not entirely happy. At last, however, an old woman was found who everyone agreed was the happiest person anywhere in the world because she was both contented and wise. What is more, when asked why, she attributed her state to a simple meal of bread and fruit she prepared each morning, the essential ingredient of which was the fresh morning dew.

The rich young man at once told his servants to bring him such a breakfast the very next day, which they did. Every day for a week, he munched his way disconsolately through this peasant food, getting no happier and none the wiser. At last, he set off himself to see the old woman and, when he found her, told her she was either a fraud or there must be some ingredient to the recipe she had left out.

'How exactly did you take this meal?' the old woman asked and he told her that his men had very carefully gathered the dew fresh each morning and baked the bread and picked the fruit, bringing it at once to him where he lay in bed.

'Ah,' said the old woman, 'there's the thing. For this recipe to work, you have to bake the bread and pick the fruit and, most especially, gather the fresh morning dew yourself!'

Five traditional symbols

What follows are some symbols commonly used in traditional narratives and other literature, plus some suggestions of exercises for working with them. You might find it helpful to jot down whatever associations, information, knowledge or imaginary pictures about each come to mind, and any more related words or adjectives. (I have included some jottings of my own at the end of the section.) It might also be helpful to look back at some stories in this book which contain these kinds of symbols, to see what use is made of them.

Symbol 1. Tree

Related: bush, plant, sapling, branches, thicket, wood, forest, copse, coppice, spinney...

Words to try with tree: tall, stunted, fruitful (apple, pear, cherry, etc.), abundant, leafy, bare, of knowledge, of life, of death, evergreen, deciduous, tropical, shady, fallen, stark, silhouette...

Exercise: Think of a tree to represent yourself. What would it be like? What kinds of trees (or aspects of trees) come to mind when you think of people you know well and/or deal with professionally? What uses spring to mind for the tree as a metaphor for personal growth and development or as a metaphor for change?

Symbol 2. Mounts and minions

For example: horses, donkeys, camels, elephants, dragons, unicorns, flying horses, lions, wolves, foxes, magical servants, genies, invisible helpers, magic carpets, bicycles, rockets, cars, motor bikes (especially sci-fi versions)...

Exercise: Choose a steed and/or magical helper and imagine developing a rapport with it/him/her. Imagine a symbolic adventure through obstacles that have a metaphorical meaning for you. What springs to mind for use as a metaphor for personal growth and development or as metaphors for change?

Symbol 3. The house

Related: castle, mill, hall, hut, palace, flat, apartment, villa, cottage, tent, fortress, hotel, shelter...

Words to try with house: open, closed, grand, tiny, red, blue, of cards, of ill repute, homely, vast, luxurious, stately, humble, gloomy, of possibilities, of fortune...

Exercises: As a visualization, try imagining the perfect house, the way you would have it in a perfect world. In casual conversation, persuade people to tell you a little about their imagined perfect houses. What kinds of things could this tell you about people? Observe actual houses and the way people live in them. What uses spring to mind as analogies with mental states, metaphors for personal change and growth or as metaphors for change?

Symbol 4. Gardens

Related: parks, plots, fields, groves, plantations, palaces, courtyards...

Words to try with garden: overgrown, over-tended, scruffy, tidy, beautiful, ugly, fussy, mysterious, designed, natural, of life, of truth, of pleasure, of love, of time...

Exercise: Mentally (or verbally through storytelling) design a garden just for yourself. What further uses spring to mind for gardens as analogies with states of being and awareness and/or social organization/effectiveness? What uses spring to mind as metaphors for personal change and growth or creative ways to think about change?

Symbol 5. Jewels and precious metals

Related: diamonds, rubies, pearls, amethysts, lapis lazuli, opals, gold, silver, platinum... rings, bracelets, crowns, tiaras, necklaces...

Words to try with jewels and precious metals: priceless, fake, stunning, fabulous, perfect, mysterious, ancient, flashy, valuable, beautiful...

Exercises: Develop a purposeful imagining involving as many sensory modes as possible (not just picturing mentally, but also feeling, touching, hearing and even smelling) of an individual jewel and/or a precious metal or valuable artefact (crown/ring/icon, etc.) that combines various jewels and precious metals. What uses might such a 'visualization' have? Make up a spontaneous story or a tall tale about a lost jewel or valuable artefact. What other uses spring to mind for jewels and precious metals as extended analogies with unusual experiences and states of mind, for ways of thinking about personal development and for images connected with change?

Some further traditional images that might be interesting to explore in this way include natural elements (fire, air, earth, water); weapon symbols (swords, bows, knives); receptors (cups, bottles, vases); natural environmental imagery (mountains, rocks, seas, islands); colours and shades; light and dark; planets; and animals (lions, tigers, fishes, snakes).

The promised jottings (not definitive)

TREES

Although rooted in the earth, trees 'aspire' upwards into the air, bridging two traditional elements and acting in various ways as a conduit for a third, water. How rooted do you feel? Would you like to branch out or blossom in new ways, or reap the fruit of experience? In myth, there is the Tree of Knowledge, as in the Garden of Eden, and the Tree of Life. In animistic religion/myth, trees have their own spirits. The Buddha attained enlightenment under a Bodhi tree; Moses heard the voice of God in the burning bush.

The branching pattern of trees is a visual metaphor for how knowledge (for example) develops. Perhaps because of the concentric (and eccentric) growth rings visible in a cross-section of the trunk, wood has been used as a metaphor for experience.

Sometimes we can't see the wood for the trees. Many heroes and heroines in traditional stories find their way into deep, dark forests.

MOUNTS AND MINIONS

In myth, legend and story, mounts may have their own special powers. Each of the magical creatures listed has its own extensive lore and is a separate symbol in itself. Riding a dragon or flying horse gives an extra dimension to the rider/mount metaphor. Such steeds are sometimes forms of the magic helper/minion, which also expresses itself in forms such as the genie, the man or woman with exceptional qualities, the devil, demon or angel. Each of these has been used in different traditions as metaphors for higher powers of mind and consciousness.

HOUSES

Images associated with houses, such as windows, rooms, staircases, basements, cellars, larders, etc., as well as houses themselves are widely used metaphors in cultures where people live in houses. Think of common phrases such as 'safe as houses', 'window on the world', 'door of opportunity', etc. One common use of the image of the house is as a metaphor for the mind. What would you be doing if you explored hidden upper rooms, tidied your attic or cleared out the basement? How symbolic might moving house be? Wouldn't it be nice to discover an extra room, just for you? Or to have the whole place sound, safe and sorted?

A darker side is that houses and associated structures, such as castles and towers, can be prisons, too. They may be enchanted or locked. But keys, ropes and ladders exist, and so do spell-breakers, whilst even the most solidly built wall might not last for ever, or could be breached.

A house can be possibility. Rooms can be redesigned and redecorated. Ruined houses may be rebuilt, whilst building a new house also has a special resonance.

GARDENS

These are places where growth is encouraged but controlled, focused, subjugated to an overall design. Weeds (perhaps defined as plants growing in the wrong place at the wrong time) can be removed and balance created. Imagery connected with gardens (flowers, bushes, fruit, leaves, herbs, vegetables, fountains, pools, wells, butterflies, bees, and so on) features in many myths and fairy tales. Inner experiences have often been symbolized using garden and flower imagery. Paradise is a garden or garden-like in some religions.

There is also a great deal of legend and lore concerning specific flowers and fruits. The rose and the lotus are frequently used esoteric symbols. Adam and Eve ate the apple of knowledge. In some stories, particular fruits that yield life, cause healing or help generate insight are sought, whilst others that enchant or destroy the will must be avoided.

JEWELS AND PRECIOUS METALS

Kings and queens are not given crowns of gold decorated with diamonds just because they look pretty. Just about every kind of jewel and precious metal has many layers of lore, myth and superstition attached to it. There is the gold standard, the heart of gold. All that glitters is not gold; but gold, because of its durability, may often symbolize eternity. The making of gold was the (perhaps metaphorical) objective of medieval alchemists, with the discovery of the Philosopher's Stone and the Elixir of Life. Diamonds can be rough and they are hard as well as beautiful, needing to be cut and faceted before they yield their dazzling qualities. Pearls start out as itchy little stones in oyster shells, gradually acquiring their unique beauty. Best that they are not cast before swine. Certain stones and crystals are held by some to have physically and even psychically active properties.

Jewels have been used in poetry and legend, myth and religion to symbolize vital and precious inner experiences, on different levels. It is perhaps no accident that many idols are made of gold and have jewels for eyes.

Two symbolic stories

Both of the following stories are versions of traditional fairy/wonder tales, which incorporate some of the symbolic images already explored.

The Tree of Jewels

The king of a far-off and ancient land needed to marry, and every influential person at the court had a notion of exactly who his bride should be. The difficulty was that these notions did not coincide, since each of

them promoted a girl who would advance their own careers and power
– daughters, nieces, wards and protégés, friends of dear friends... The
king eventually made a choice that unified all of them – in opposition.
He decided to marry a common young singer and teller of stories who
came to his court simply to entertain. Her tales and music, particularly a song she sang and a tale she told of a marvellous tree of living
jewels, awakened his imagination as it had never been awakened before, and he fell in love with her.

Ignoring advice, the king married the girl and, against expectation, was soon very happy. The new queen turned out to be clever and
shrewd as well as talented, and the servants at the court soon loved
her almost as much as the king did, since she treated them fairly and
with kindness and understanding, having been more or less a servant
herself. She and the king enjoyed their life together. The courtiers,
however, were secretly furious and continually attempted to poison
the king's mind against her.

Eventually they got their chance when enemies invaded and the
king had to lead the armies to repel them. Whilst he was away, the
young queen was left in charge and proved herself worthy of the king's
trust, ruling wisely in his place. Each day, she sent to her husband
messages of love, humble requests for advice and details of important
decisions she had been obliged to take. However, the courtiers who
were not themselves involved in fighting, with the help of those who
were, intercepted these and substituted cold, haughty missives full of
twisted self-justifications and misinformation. They also bribed the
messengers not only to deliver these forgeries to the king but also to
tell him stories of the evil doings of his wife. At first the king ignored
what he was told but, since he was unable to leave his troops and the
only proof he had was in the form of letters and rumours, his faith
in his wife was slowly undermined. Eventually a party of the most
important courtiers approached the king, begging that his tyrant wife
should be removed from office at once for the good of the realm. The
king, physically exhausted and emotionally drained following yet another battle, his judgement clouded by all that he had heard, gave in
and signed and sealed the fate of his wife. 'Send her away!' he said.
'This woman obviously cared only for power and never for me!'

With the precious paper in their hands, the courtiers went back
and those appointed took over the running of the country. They ban-
ished the queen at once and she was sent away with no more than she
had had when she arrived. Since the people of the towns and villages
had heard the rumours and didn't want to be seen to help someone

who had offended the king so badly, none would give her shelter and food and she was obliged to stagger for miles along rough tracks, away from that kingdom and into the wild lands beyond. She was particularly tired and confused, since what the courtiers had not told the king, what she indeed thought she had told him very clearly in her letters, was that she had conceived his child before he left and was now months into the pregnancy.

At length, she collapsed on the edge of the wild lands on the borders of the kingdom. When she recovered her senses, she was surprised to see an old woman beckoning her, a thin wisp of a woman with white hair, a twinkle in her eyes and a comforting smile on her very wrinkled face. The old woman led her into a nearby forest where she had a rough cottage. There she gave her food and drink and showed her a warm, dry place where she could rest properly. The queen ate and drank and then slept a long, exhausted sleep.

When eventually she awoke, she found that the old woman was sitting on a stool nearby, doing some fine embroidery. She was so absorbed in her work that she seemed not to notice the queen, who watched as she worked at what seemed to be a tiny tree, glowing and glimmering with silver and gold and yellow and white and blue and purple threads. Somehow it looked just as if it were made of jewels and seeming almost more real than the trees of the forest beyond the window. 'That's beautiful! Who is it for?' the queen asked wonderingly, as the old lady spotted her.

'I shall give this away to someone who needs it. Maybe they'll sell it and maybe they'll keep it – which could be better for them. But I get the interest of the making one way or another.' That's all the strange old woman would say about her work, that time or any other time.

The queen stayed there with the old woman, trying to make herself useful in whatever way she could. But the baby was due soon, and indeed it was born in that woodland cottage, a healthy little boy.

Now on the very evening of the birth, the king had a strange vision. He had by this time returned from the war, regretting bitterly the decision he had taken under pressure to send his wife away. He secretly wished he had had a chance to see her again, at least to verify the rumours he had been persuaded were true before sending her away. These doubts he had kept to himself, since he needed to appear strong and decisive as a ruler. But as he reviewed his feelings, he seemed to see, far off through a window of his own room, a beautiful tree of jewels such as the one of which his wife had sung in her songs. Standing beside it was a figure, very small from this distance, but he soon became convinced that it was his wife. She seemed to be calling out to him, but he could hear no words though he felt somehow gladdened. It all seemed very clear and very real, and yet suddenly everything about it vanished like a dream and there was only a darkened sky. In the morning, he commanded that soldiers should be sent out at once to search his realms and bring back his wife. But, after a time, they all returned to tell him that she was nowhere to be found.

A second time and a third the vision returned to him, but after that there was only darkness. It troubled him so much that he called the courtiers and asked them to explain it to him. 'It is only a dream, your majesty,' they said. 'A passing fantasy with no sense other than to remind you of your real need. To forget the woman who tricked and deceived you, you need the magic of art. We shall command the court painters and poets to go to work.'

But although the painters painted perfect pictures and the poets sang immaculate verses to the accompaniment of harp and lute, although each painting and each poem conjured up images of gardens and trees as wonderful in their own way as those in the king's vision, he only shook his head. 'Your art is good,' he said wearily, 'but it does not have the wonder and the truth of what I have seen.' He grew sadder and more depressed than ever until one day a wandering beggar woman insisted that she had news for the king. When she was admitted, she announced boldly, 'Your majesty will never know happiness nor will he have peace until he has found the tree of jewels itself and the garden in which it grows. For that he will have to leave his court and his crown and travel the world as a beggar like me, until at last he finds the object of his quest.' A moment later she was gone, though none saw her go.

The courtiers tried to dismiss the episode as the jape of some passing enchantress, not to be taken seriously, but the king knew that what she had said had the ring of truth. The very next day, he handed over the ruling of the kingdom to his most trusted adviser and put on beggars' robes and set off in search of the tree.

Far and wide he searched but, whenever he asked, people shook their heads and looked at him strangely. Trees of jewels! Who ever heard of such nonsense! Eventually, he came to a forest where an old woman greeted him outside a small house. There was something familiar about her, though he could not think why. From inside the house, he heard a baby crying and another woman soothing it. Again there was something familiar about the sound that he did not understand.

'What's your business, beggar?' said the old woman.

'Strange though it may seem,' the king said, feeling foolish after all the rejections and blank looks, 'I am seeking a certain tree, a tree that sparkles as if it were made of jewels and a marvellous garden in which it grows.'

'There is such a tree and there is such a garden,' the old woman said. 'If that's what you want, carry on walking. You must walk straight on through this forest, never turning aside from the path until you reach the mountain beyond. The jewelled tree and the garden are at the top of that mountain. But that mountain also spews out streams of pure fire all down its sides. You will not be able to climb past these.' She shook her head sadly.

'Is there no way at all?' said the king.

The old woman seemed to hesitate, before she continued, 'Only one way, but it is hard, for it will depend on you. You must put this cloak around you and wear these sandals as you climb the mountain and you must keep your thoughts on the tree and anything else that is truly precious to you, not following any distractions, otherwise the fire will consume you at once.' She held out a shabby and flimsy looking cloak and a pair of old sandals. On the corner of the cloak, the king spotted a beautifully embroidered image of a gleaming tree.

Well, he thanked the old woman for her advice, took the cloak and sandals and at once set off walking through that forest. It took time and patience and concentration, but he stuck to the path and reached the mountain. All down its sides he saw gleaming shafts he realized were streams of fire. For a moment he held back. It seemed so unlikely that the robe and sandals would protect him in any way at all and the mountain was steep with only narrow paths. But, keeping his thoughts firmly anchored to the tree and also to images of his wife and hearing within his mind strains of the strange song she had sung when first he saw her, he began to climb.

It was hard going, and it took time and courage. Sometimes the path appeared to be impossibly slight, and sometimes the fiery streams jetted out suddenly from under his feet without warning, but he went on climbing and the fire became somehow cool and soothing through whatever power the cloak and sandals had. Sometimes he seemed to hear the voices of his own courtiers reminding him of his responsibilities to the realm and warning him of the terrible danger he was in. He seemed to see them shaking their heads as he returned his mind to images of the wife he loved. Still he kept on climbing and the fire did not harm him. As he reached the top, his path disappeared into a glowing mist that looked hot and bright as the sun itself at its core, but he plunged onwards and upwards and presently found what the glow was, for he suddenly came out in a magical garden and was confronted by the awesome brilliance of the tree itself.

Now the king understood at once why his own painters and poets could never create anything even to hint at such beauties, despite all their finely honed skills. For this tree and the rainbow garden around it was different at each moment; they were living things that, with every instant, were entirely different yet strangely constant. He gazed long and hard at all he could see and sense around him and felt the life within him renewed and strengthened. Without knowing why, he stretched out his hand to touch the tree itself and found a small branch came away in his hand. Again not knowing why and almost despite himself, he turned away then and returned through the mist and down the mountainside, carrying the branch and walking back through the forest.

When the beggar king reached the house of the old woman, he took off the cloak and sandals and handed them back to her. 'My sincerest thanks for these precious things,' he said. 'I could never have completed my quest without them. You should know that I am a king and if there is anything I can do for you ever...'

'I know well enough who you are,' the old woman laughed, 'but I want nothing from you!' The king had again the strange sensation that he knew her and he suddenly recalled the beggar who had visited his court.

'As for these,' continued the old woman, 'just look at this!' She beckoned him into the house where she threw the robe and sandals into a fire she had burning there. At once, they turned to ashes. 'Remember, king, the worth of the garment is in the wearer. Now, meet someone you know well enough and have wronged badly!'

The king turned around and saw his wife and his own child and, perhaps (as he thought afterwards) because he was still holding the branch of the jewelled tree, somehow he knew and understood at once all that had happened. He went to her and knelt, begging forgiveness, which she immediately gave to him – maybe also because she saw the magical branch and sensed its power. The two of them smiled happily at the baby together.

As for the old woman, when they looked around she was nowhere to be seen.

There are those who say that the king and his wife stayed there in the forest, leaving behind their responsibilities and leading a happy and simple life, bringing up their son as a child of the wilderness. But a king is a king and has taken certain vows. Storytellers who know this tale well insist that he and his wife returned with their son to the court and, when they arrived there, took command again. They were able to establish authority at once since, when the branch from the miraculous tree was planted, it grew in an instant and became a wonderful tree, as fine and marvellous and magical as the one on the mountain, blossoming and making fruits that became earthly jewels.[5]

The Golden Bird

Beyond seven seas and thrice nine lands, there lived a king who had the three sons the kings in those times of long ago and far away always fathered, no more and no less. He also had a beautiful garden, and in that garden was a magical tree on which grew apples of the purest gold. These apples were a wonder to behold and restored the health of those who were given the merest sniff of them. But the sniffing and the tasting of them were both becoming difficult to do, since, as those golden apples grew to ripeness, something was stealing them away in the night. Although guards guarded them, a sleep always overtook them and the apples disappeared.

At last the eldest son volunteered to guard the apples himself, thinking to establish himself as the favourite to take his father's throne in due course, but he was no more successful than the soldiers. As the night went on, he slipped into slumber and, in the morning, the ripest apples were gone. The second brother also tried unsuccessfully to stay awake, so the third one took his turn. Unlike his brothers, he was genuinely interested in the tree and whatever might be stealing the apples, and so he easily stayed awake. Just as night was departing, with the first rays of the sun, he suddenly saw a dazzling golden bird come flying and then perching in the branches and eating the fruit. The bird was so astounding that the third son just stared. Then, realizing that he should do something, he leapt towards it but only succeeded in taking a long golden tail feather as the bird quickly flew away.

When everyone was awake, the third son showed the incredible feather and everyone admired it as he explained about the golden bird. But his father was angry. 'You bring me a mere feather. Where is the bird itself? That is what I must and shall have.'

'I'll find it!' said the first son, hoping to redeem himself. There and then he set out in quest of the golden bird. But, when he asked people, no one knew of such a bird until he came to the edge of a forest, where he saw a fox, which spoke to him. 'If you are looking for the golden bird, then follow the path along the edge of this forest until you come to a village where there is a crossroads and also a fine inn. But don't go into that inn, otherwise you will not leave it for a long time. Go instead into the bare hovel you will see opposite and take lodging for the night. In the morning you will see what you will see.'

'What business is it to you what I should and should not do?' said the eldest son angrily, as he threw a stick at the fox, which ran into the forest. Then he set out along the path and eventually reached the village and the inn. The inn was obviously the better choice as regards places to stay, so he went inside and there he stayed. And all that is more or less exactly what happened to the second son when he followed his brother on the quest, though he attempted, but failed, to shoot the fox with a gun. He joined his brother at the inn where they enjoyed themselves and forgot all about golden birds and trees.

When the third brother decided that he should seek the golden bird, just in case his clever and bold brothers failed, he of course also met the fox, to whom he spoke kindly and respectfully and whose advice he took. He passed an uncomfortable night in the hovel and, in the morning, there was the fox outside waiting for him. 'Climb on my back!' said the fox. The prince did so, greatly surprised that the fox was not only strong enough to hold him but could also carry him rapidly over the land. One hundred miles they went, until they came to an enchanted castle. 'The golden bird is inside that castle,' said the fox. 'There it perches by day on the branch of a tree in the gardens. Go into that castle and take the bird, paying no attention to the people there, for they are held in a magical trance. Put the bird into the rusty old cage you will find nearby and ignore any other cages.'

The prince did as he had been bidden and entered the castle, where he saw the strange sight of many knights and ladies and servants of all kinds living and yet frozen in enchantment, and a king and a queen upon thrones, also enchanted. He passed them all and went into the gardens where he soon saw the wonderful bird again, very tame, sitting on the branch. He persuaded the bird to sit on his arm and looked for the cage, but the sight of it filled him with doubt. It was old and rusty, scarcely any good at all. Beside it was a beautiful jewelled cage so he took that one instead and began to put the bird into it. At once there was a blaring of trumpets and the spell was broken. The servants and knights seized him and dragged him before the king and queen. 'Who are you and how dare you come here stealing our beautiful golden bird?' shouted the king.

Well, the third son explained all about his royal lineage and the business of the golden apples and how he needed that golden bird for his father, since it had, after all, stolen the apples. The king and queen reluctantly decided not to have him publicly flogged and then hung, drawn and quartered as they'd first thought to do and chose instead to send him on a second quest, to bring back for them a certain golden horse. If he brought that, he could take the golden bird.

The prince went out from the castle and found the fox. 'Oh dear, dear!' said the fox. 'Could you not get the golden bird?' The prince explained all about his mistake with the cage and the fox told him that mistakes can often be mended and invited him to climb onto his back again. This time they travelled 200 miles until they came to another enchanted castle. Again, the prince should ignore the entranced people within and this time he should make for the stables. There he would find the golden horse, which he should saddle and bridle, using the old worn tackle he would find nearby and ignoring anything else.

Again, there was a royal throne with a king and a queen, and knights and ladies and all. Again, they were stock still, through the power of the magic, and the prince found the stables easily enough and, in them, the miraculous golden horse, surrounded by transfixed grooms, like living statues. He patted the fantastic creature, the only thing moving in the place, and then he reached for the bridle and saddle. Near at hand was a beautiful silver saddle studded with rubies and pearls with a finely tooled and cunningly decorated, gold-trimmed bridle and, forgetting the advice of the fox again, he reached for them. At once there was a blaring of trumpets and the grooms jumped up and grabbed him. He was roughly manhandled into the castle and up before the king and the queen. 'Who are you to come here stealing a marvellous steed?' the royal couple, now also released from the spell, demanded to know at once.

Again the prince explained and they too abandoned their plans for punishment and sent him on a third quest. They wanted the golden princess from the golden castle. If he brought her to marry their son, then he could have the golden horse. So, once again, it was out to the fox, hanging his head in shame and confessing his failure, and once again the fox reassured him and told him that failure could be part of success. Soon they were speeding over the 300 miles to the golden castle where lived the golden princess.

This time the castle was not enchanted. The requirement was that the prince himself should do the enchanting – using the spell of love to enchant the princess. Every morning the princess would go walking down by the river to gather the early morning dew and thereby increase her beauty. The plan was that the prince and the fox would wait for her there and the fox would become an incredible golden pavilion into which the prince would invite the curious princess. Once she entered, the prince would woo her and persuade her to come away with him to be married, and the fox would then carry them back to the castle of the golden horse. On no account should the prince allow her to say goodbye to her parents.

Everything went according to plan to begin with. But the prince's heart was melted by the beauty of the princess and her sorrow at not saying goodbye to her parents and he accompanied her to meet them. 'Of course you may take our daughter,' they said. 'Why would we refuse such a fine young prince? All we need is for you to remove yonder mountain, which is spoiling our view. You may use this spoon and do it by tomorrow morning or you'll be leaving without that head of yours!'

Of course, the prince could no more move the mountain than he could fly to the moon, no matter how much he tried. But the fox could do it and in the night, the mountain was moved. Yet now the king and queen wanted a whole forest cut down and a river diverted by morning, with the same terrible penalty if the prince failed. Again the prince struggled but the fox succeeded easily in the night.

The third task was to take a golden ring of power from a dragon's nest in the hills nearby. If the prince failed, either the dragon would destroy him or the king and the queen would, as they'd threatened before, remove his head. But the fox carried him to the dragon and this time he obeyed the fox's instructions and lifted the ring out whilst the dragon was enchanted, not in the slightest distracted by the many other treasures he glimpsed there. He put it on his finger. When he returned, again following the fox's instructions, he asked the princess to mount the fox with him before he would give the ring up. The king and queen acquiesced in this but, before they could take the ring, the fox was away.

Reaching the castle of the golden horse, the prince confessed to the fox that he was unsure about the deal, since he now loved the golden princess and she loved him. The fox told the princess to hide and then became an exact likeness of her. The prince was to take this fake golden princess to the castle so that he could exchange her for the horse. The plan worked and the prospective bridegroom had something of a surprise that night when he went to kiss his intended and found only the wet nose of a fox and sharp teeth that bit him, before the fox ran away to join the prince and princess, who had already left on the golden mount.

What a fine horse that golden steed was and what a shame to give it to the cruel king and queen who just happened to own the golden bird! But again the fox had the answer. Turning himself into a perfect replica of the golden horse, he had himself delivered by the third son to the castle, whilst the golden princess hid with the real golden horse. The golden bird was duly given to the prince, who joined the princess and the horse to await the fox. He was not long in following, after he had dumped the king and the queen who had attempted to ride him in the middle of a convenient duck pond.

So now the prince galloped back with the golden ring of power, the golden princess, the golden horse and the golden bird. And all would have gone well for them had he not stopped at the village to say good-bye to the fox there. Just after he had thanked the magical creature for all his help and shed a tear or two as he left, he saw his two brothers, who had at that very moment been thrown out of the inn. They looked enviously at all that he had gained, and then they asked him if he wouldn't mind drawing a little fresh water from the well nearby, since they needed to clear their heads and were too tired to get the drink for themselves. As soon as he was leaning over the edge of the well, they upped his heels and threw him down into it. Then they threatened the princess, telling her it would be the worse for her if she ever breathed a word of what she had seen. After that, they all rode upon the poor golden horse, carrying the golden bird. When they arrived back, their father and all the court treated those two sons as great heroes, and the golden bird was given a fine golden cage in the palace gardens and allowed to eat some of the golden apples.

Meanwhile, the third son was lying in the well. He had not been drowned, since the ring of power had protected him, but he was stunned and had lost all memory of how he came to be there until, at last rubbing the ring, he found the fox peering down at him. 'Take my tail,' said the fox, and dipped it down into the well so that the prince could climb out. Then he carried him to the court of his father.

As soon as they saw him coming, the other two sons were off as fast as they could go. Once they were gone, the golden princess told the story of all that had happened, so that the king could understand and the third son could regain his memory. She and the third son were married and in time became rulers of that land. The golden bird often sang in the branches of the golden tree and the golden horse often carried them around the kingdom and the fox often came to advise them. And, if they are not dead yet, they are living to this day.[6]

Metaphor – the trap and the hidden treasure

He can do things for you, things you do not know –
with his stories.
– Informal guide, speaking of a rawi qissas
(public storyteller)[7]

The Queen, the Lost Crown and the Storyteller

Warriors and statesmen alike looked down on the queen's storyteller, a mere harlequin-coated entertainer telling worthless tales of idle fantasy. One day the queen was leaning over a pool in the palace gardens when the crown fell from her head and sank without trace, despite her frantic attempts to grab it. Warrior after warrior dived in to get it; ministers fished with net and line all to no avail. Queen and court were in a desperate panic – until the storyteller jumped up and told a powerful and fascinating story of crowns and jewels and the finding of secret treasures. They all fell under the spell of the tale and were very quiet as he concluded. Then, to their amazement, he leapt nimbly into the water and emerged seconds later with the crown – which he had been able to see easily now that the waters were undisturbed and still.

'Perhaps,' he said modestly, 'a storyteller and a story may have some value.'[8]

We are narrative-making, metaphorical beings. We do not and cannot have god-like, all-encompassing minds and therefore we are obliged to make stories about how things work, using the experience and the knowledge we have and applying it as best we can to explain that which we do not yet understand. Sometimes this works extremely well as, with the help of illuminating images, we grope our way to recognitions of potent patterns that recur at many levels. Sometimes an image flatters to deceive; the analogy is only apparent and passing. We may have a marvellous and insightful grasp of a segment or three of reality, but the rest is guesswork.

As a society, we are largely illiterate about metaphor. Our education and our culture does not equip us to use it well, to think and imagine it through thoroughly. When it flashes into our minds, we are caught just for a moment or dismiss it quickly as a case of this equals that or is a bit like the other. Yet in metaphors we are being given pictures, dreams, stories and constructions with greater or lesser closeness to a larger reality, with greater or lesser use in developing our understanding and extending our freedom or, conversely, with a greater or lesser power to enslave us. To repeat the maxim used in Chapter 2, that which we do not control may control us.

To add another maxim – as above, so below. Our habits and our uncertainty with metaphor resonate at all levels of activity. Take the example of Katherine. She and her husband David have branched out on their own in business following his unexpected redundancy but, after a year or two, are very much feeling the strain. There are problems in the family because their two children are not getting enough attention and have been misbehaving in various ways, whilst Katherine's parents have recently been ill and unable to help out with child care in the way they usually do. Both she and David have lately been developing physical problems – she often suffers from back pain and is seriously overweight, whilst he has mysterious tingling sensations in fingers and toes, which the doctor says may be stress symptoms. She goes to a counsellor and explains about the heavy feelings of guilt that are oppressing her – she says she feels 'like piggy in the middle' and 'as though she were tied between wild horses dragging her in different directions'. On the other hand, she knows she has to 'keep soldiering on' as it is a time when 'it's all hands to the pump' and 'you have to put your back into it'. As far as the business is concerned, as David says, 'it's dog eat dog out there'.

If her counsellor is perceptive, one of the things he might pick up is that she is telling a story that is strongly coloured and shaped both by her aroused individual emotions and by some dominant and very powerful 'myth-making' metaphors from the surrounding culture, which she is incorporating into her personal narrative. If he is literate in metaphor and story, perhaps he first will calm her down one way or another and then explore the story she is telling and how it can be told differently – how wild horses can be slowly and gently broken in and trained to pull in the same direction, how as a matter of fact it is very rare for dogs to eat dogs, how pumps sometimes operate better if one understands both the mechanism of the pump and the water source, and so on. Used well, these metaphors will have an almost magical effect; even though they may seem hackneyed phrases, she has somehow made them her own and hence been trapped by their limiting perspectives. She may take a long cool look at the bind she has been in and find intelligent ways to adjust the life she and her family are living. That is the ideal scenario, anyway, the goal that a suitably trained professional would surely have in mind and carefully negotiate with his or her client. At the same time, she or he shouldn't underestimate the power of those informing myths, so often enshrined in common catch phrases and popular clichés.

Take another case. Here is an extract from an address given by the chairman of The Purple Widget Company in the early 1990s.

> We are currently entering a new phase of development. The global market is opening up rapidly on the back of the communications revolution and there are, as all of you will be aware, many new opportunities for growth and expansion. We have already begun to exploit them but progress has still been less rapid than it could have been. As a result, some of our competitors have stolen a march on us. As an organization, we need to be more lean and hungry, fit and ready. People talk about the 'tiger economies' of South East Asia. They have been successful because they are lean and they are hungry and they aren't carrying all the baggage we're carrying. A tiger needs to hunt to stay alive; it's as simple as that. A tiger needs to be hungry to hunt. And a tiger doesn't have any respect for the rules. He just goes for it, straight for the jugular. Anyone in this company who is not hungry, anyone who is not ready to hunt, had better say so. If you can't stand the heat, keep out of the kitchen. If you can't stand the hunt, go find a nice comfortable cage and leave the killing to the big cats...

This chairman drew freely on the metaphorical clichés that were bandied around in his day. He was a hard-working man who lived on caffeine and adrenaline and pioneered many of the company's links with China, where much of their manufacturing is now done. He didn't tolerate fools or slackers gladly and there were many sudden redundancies and sackings. As a result, the company became what he called (using the language of the day) leaner and hungrier, if to some it seemed too often just callous. Sadly, he suffered with burnout in 1999 and spent some months in a deep depression, consulting some of the leading world experts on stress, one of whom was shrewd enough to advise him of what was likely to happen – and did. The young colleagues he had originally trained and promoted, following principles he had inculcated, used the excuse of his obvious weakness to oust him in his absence to make the organization even leaner and hungrier.

The interesting thing about the rhetoric this man drew on is that it is really only just coming to the end of its shelf life and, in fact, is still out there, jumping from mouth to mouth and brain to brain, a mythology influencing and shaping behaviour. Currently, it might be considered less fashionable in informed business-speak – you are more likely to come across images of mutually supportive, mutually advantageous networks, win-win scenarios and metaphors that reinforce ideas of co-operation, which some may consider a step in the right direction. However, when I put this fictional chairman's address in front of an international group of executives involved in running the European operations of a major multinational corporation recently, several of them said that it made sense and was at least 'real world', whilst most of them had to be prompted to identify the amount of metaphor and story-making involved. Reassuringly, however, they all laughed when I pointed out the fundamental illiteracy and inconsistency of that metaphor he develops, which was widely promulgated in the '90s – the comparison between tigers and economies and business practice. A tiger, I reminded them, spends 18 hours a day asleep.

Take one more example – and this time we'll visit the realms of science fiction (from a statement from the President of the secret World Congress of Rationalist Scientists):

Very soon we will know all that there is to know about human beings and the cosmos we inhabit. We understand and appreciate that human beings have arisen as accidents in a senseless, if magnificently complex, universe. Redundant and foolish belief systems have protected us from this knowledge in the past, but can do so no longer. It is time to be honest about what we are, to face up to the strengths and the weaknesses and the ultimate limitations of our rationality. We are small islands of what some have called consciousness in a world of unconscious pattern and algorithm. We are really far more unconscious than conscious; most of what we do is pure mechanism. It is better that the bulk of humanity should not appreciate the hopelessness of our predicament, though we cannot help it if our honesty as scientists obliges us to communicate some of the facts. The universe is a black-hearted and senseless whirl of selfish, self-replicating fragments. We as human beings are ultimately senseless self-replicating fragments, a mere function of our genes. There is no coherence. This is fact. Perhaps we should, then, encourage the illusions of the masses. The more courageous and outspoken amongst us are too often occupied in fighting a rearguard action against superstition and irrationality. It is quite plain that the majority prefer to believe in old-fashioned myths of creation and divine beings. It will take time to disabuse them of these unfounded and destructive notions whilst we build a sensible and intelligent model of reality as it is, based on the above ultimately sensible and rational principles. We need to be tough-minded in this endeavour, hard-nosed and unsentimental...

Now, as far as I know, there is no such world organization of scientists. Outside fiction, scientists subscribe to a fairly wide range of beliefs and philosophies, since science itself cannot be a belief system. This does not stop some people trying to make it into something of the sort in the name of rationalism, and quite a few of the phrases in this pastiche (which I confess I created myself) are taken from the writings of popular science gurus, from books you will find on the science shelves of any good bookshop where, inevitably, polemic rubs shoulders with information. Because these kinds of statements pose as fact rather than philosophical bias and are usually made by people with imposing credentials, it is easy to miss the amount of storytelling and shoddy metaphor that is involved in them. It is, for example, unlikely that we understand fully what human beings are and may be, let alone grasp the full complexity of the multi-dimensional universe of which we inhabit a tiny corner and view through restrictive lenses. It is also highly unlikely that these kinds of prematurely limiting and emotionally driven statements do anything other than cloud the actual scientific issues. Even worse, they create a climate of opinion in our everyday world in which many informed and intelligent people regard the universe that spawned us as fundamentally hostile and empty of meaning, a feeling that may well underpin this world of crazy consumption and desperate distraction in which many people too easily see their own lives as desperately brief chances to grab as much of the action as they can get – since, as they say, 'it's dog eat dog out there'; 'you only live once'; and you have to 'do it now'.

Our lives are made up of stories – and stories within stories. The implications of this central fact of human life can go on revealing themselves at deeper and deeper levels. This world we live in is no less made up of stories than the worlds of peoples of other eras. Our habits and our uncertainty over metaphor need to be replaced by a growing metaphorical literacy, if we are to avoid the traps of the false and empty metaphors we are so often offered by the media – and indeed by many people who should know better.

A culture literate in metaphor would look at its own organizations and institutions and individuals not through one metaphor at a time but through multiple metaphors. People would be encouraged to use metaphors and tell stories, to develop multiple perspectives on those stories, and always to test the strength and the appropriateness of their metaphors against the ever-emerging knowledge of what human beings may aspire to be. But this would only be possible if we could give up, at least for some of the time, the constant quest for novelty and sensation. As things are, how many people would consider thinking over again what is widely considered just a children's story? And yet there are some tales amongst the treasury of world oral and literary traditions that can always yield new depths to anyone who gives them serious attention, no matter how familiar they may have become, because they hold the essence of a universal and essential pattern. Those kinds of stories should be at the heart of the repertoire of any real teller of tales, not because they make wonderful performance pieces and vehicles for display, but because they are real treasures, which need to be constantly re-worked in ways that will make them penetrate the veil of habitual cynicism. Here, for interest and example, is such an ancient story, updated to utilize that very cynicism, since, after all, stories have always adapted themselves to new ages in new ways.

The Touchy-Feely Show

Learned delegates to the Fourth International Know-How Forum were in for a surprise yesterday when performance artist Ian Connor Klaus pitched his black marquee outside the conference centre. During the evening, they each received a separate invitation to the mysterious tent and quite a few availed themselves of the opportunity to satisfy their curiosity. Reactions were a little mixed.

'It really was a pleasant change from all the theory,' said Director of Performance Studies at Freemup University, Eek Lectic. 'Art is a great thing for asking questions and liberating feelings. I had a sensation of – how shall I put it? – largeness, roughness, incredible vitality. There were all sorts of resonances, all sorts of hints and allusions. It is an experience I shall value for a long time.'

Miranda Hootha, of the Institute for Human Confusion at Delvdeep Down, was less complimentary. 'It's quite clear to me that this man has some serious issues and I'm not sure that this kind of display is the way to deal with them,' she said. 'I don't really care whether it was a python or a very large phallus I was made to handle in the darkness, since I am trained to discount my own feelings. All I know is that he desperately needs the kind of extensive help we are able to give in getting in touch with his real feelings.'

Military experts at the conference were evidently intrigued by what they described as 'sharp, curved warheads', whilst two ecologists were convinced that Connor Klaus had managed to animate at least four trees as part of the display. Textile artist Paulya Legg was fascinated by the use of what she described as a piece of rope, whilst inventor Craig Potts speculated on the principle that drove two large flat fans he had sensed in action. Illusionist Garren Whyte, however, was less impressed. 'When you know how these tricks are done,' he said, 'you realize that it's just a matter of cleverly stimulating nerve endings through hypnotic electro-magnetic signals. There is, of course, nothing at all in the tent.'

At the end of the evening, with a lot of razzmatazz and fanfare, Connor Klaus revealed the contents of the hitherto entirely darkened marquee in the full glare of the spotlights: one large grey elephant.[9]

Stories within stories within stories

I had to drive to an engagement shortly before I wrote the first draft of this chapter. I duly loaded up the car and grabbed the directions I had been sent, registering with a groan that they were of the step-by-step variety available as downloadable printouts from some websites. There was always something about them that I found deeply irritating and unhelpful. This one looked bright and efficient, with its numbered and measured stages of the journey before me. It just about told me how to get out of bed and go downstairs, stir my tea and get out of the front door. It gave me precise measurements of the length of the motorway ramps and roundabouts and the distances, to the nearest metre, between turnings. There were road names and numbers and, you might think, all the practical details I would need. Except that it failed entirely to give me landmarks for the vital last stages of the journey, the only bit I didn't know at all – no parks nor pubs nor public statuary, just this turn, then that one, this number then that one. And certainly nothing about what to do if I missed one of those carefully quantified steps. A robot would have had no trouble – and that is the point. Those directions were mechanically made for machines, not for people.

A map is a form of knowledge and so are stories. Good stories are like maps – or, rather, like a series of interlocking maps on different scales, because you can, as it were, zoom in to find the detail you need or zoom out to look at the broader pattern. You are not stuck with the myopic disadvantages of that step-by-step printout, nor with the inch-by-inch gropings of sequential logic. Maps are not the territories they describe but, if they are done with a feel for who is to read them and with the right kind of detail, if they are linked one to another in intelligent ways, they can give you a virtual experience of at least some of it. Story maps, unlike paper ones, can be kept in mental storage, ready to refer to when you need them – which is handy since, in life, we are doing many things that are not unlike driving and it can be dangerous to take our eyes off the road.

In the 1980s, Ericksonian therapists Stephen and Carole Lankton reintroduced and formalized an ancient technique of using and combining story maps to heighten their effectiveness.[10] They based their technique on the one illustrated so extensively and marvellously in *The Arabian Nights*. This, as many people will know, is not just a series of separate stories but also one story – the story of Shahrazad, the clever daughter of the wazir (adviser) who volunteered to marry King Sharyar, a man with the unfortunate habit of cutting off the heads of his wives after just one night of marriage. This he did because his first wife had betrayed him, an occurrence that had thrown him into deep and bitter despondency, and he judged all women by her. But Shahrazad was able to stay his hand night after night simply by telling stories, telling them well and, very importantly, leaving those stories unfinished until the next day. So the king would say, 'By Allah! I will not slay her until I have heard the rest of this tale.' Each story was expertly spun and then stitched artfully and invisibly to the next and sometimes two or three or more stories remained unfinished, as story within story unfolded, giving the effect of a series of infinitely reflecting mirrors.

Shahrazad's technique is by no means unique in the classics of world literature, nor was she the first fictional character to use it. It was almost a convention of Eastern collections of tales to use frame stories. Somadeva's 10th-century Indian classic, *The Ocean of Story*,[11] already referred to in this book several times, uses the tales within tales technique, managing to include within those tales some still more ancient stories within stories revered and told in the India of its day, such as the *Panchatantra* and *The Vetala Tales*. In Persia, the *Panchatantra*, as already noted, became *The Fables of Bidpai* and *Kalila and Dimna*;[12] both include an additional frame. There are many other literary examples, all the way down to the writings of Boccaccio and Chaucer in the West. There are also many suggestions within the literature that the 'tales within tales' techniques were used by oral tellers of tales. Could all this be just literary artifice or a sales method used by story 'sellers' to keep their audiences on the hook? Both the Lanktons' method and the story of Shahrazad itself suggest that there is rather more to it.

Shahrazad may be teasing the king and manipulating his attention, but she does so with the important immediate purpose of saving herself and her younger sister, Dunyazad, who will be the sultan's next bride and victim if she fails, not to mention the countless other young brides who may follow. She is also gradually educating the king, telling him stories that will slowly show him that the world is not simply black and white, that there is a whole rainbow of colours and shadings to find and experience. She is slowly, slowly expanding the king's mind, lifting his depression, taking him into marvellous worlds with fantastic vistas, showing him ordinary and very earthy life from new angles, making him laugh and cry, but above all see and understand. The Arabic title *Alif Layla wa Layla* ('one thousand nights and one night') can, as Idries Shah points out, be translated through the widely known Arabic abjad code system, as the 'mother of records' or 'source of patterns'.[13] It was a pattern book for the public storytellers but, even more importantly, remains a book of the patterns of life, presented in fabulous form.

The Lanktons called their version the 'multiple embedded metaphor scheme'; it seems relatively simple by comparison with Shahrazad's virtuosity. It was introduced for use in therapy and it works well with people who are resistant to formal guided imagery or are inclined to be self-conscious. It can also usefully be applied outside the field of therapy. Its basic five-stage/three-story scheme is not difficult to master, though it requires some forward planning and thinking, whilst imagining through and the linking takes a little ingenuity. Three stories (or elaborated metaphors without an overt narrative structure) are chosen for their appropriateness to the client's situation. The stories can range from the traditional to the entirely modern, from fables to fantasies, from allegories drawing fairly obvious parallels to apparently rambling anecdotes. (The Lanktons themselves have published a book of mostly modern and suitably everyday tales that can be very useful in the scheme and elsewhere as ballast to traditional material.[14])

Of these three stories, two will be metaphorically related to the concern but the third will provide a direct matching of the concern to a solution revealed in its structure. Told straight out and unembellished, the story could evoke a negative response, maybe an instant rejection, classic mbala stuff. (Tell King Sharyar a fable about a lion who bites animals' heads off because he doesn't trust them and therefore never gets to appreciate any intelligence and perspective other than his own, but gives it all up one day and finds that he likes himself a lot better, and the king will probably have your head instantly trimmed for your impudence.) Told straight through but cunningly hidden inside two not-yet-completed stories that have established a pleasantly vague and relaxingly imaginative story trance with a strong feeling of expectancy, and the effect will be quite different and very direct. (First tell King Sharyar the beginnings of a tale about a man who has been cheated and how his feelings about that eat away inside him, but leave that unfinished and move on to a story told to that first man about a person who gained extraordinary power over others through a genie and how this power went to his head and he abused it, wreaking revenge and hatred... Then leave that tale hanging in the air too, whilst you introduce someone else who tells the second person the complete fable of the lion that mended its ways. Then come back to the story about the genie with a resolution in which he learns to use his power better, and then to the story about the cheated man, with a resolution in which he remembers what it is like to feel and act differently.) In summary:

1. Story 1, a metaphor that mirrors aspects of the concern, is begun.

2. On some pretext (perhaps someone tells a story within the story; perhaps you are just 'reminded' of another story which happens to compare; perhaps you just casually sidle into the second tale), Story 1 is left unfinished and Story 2 is begun. This mirrors other aspects of the concern.

3. Story 2 is also abandoned approximately midway (or as appropriate) and Story 3 (the tale with the most direct analogical description and solution) is told all the way through without interruption.

4. Story 2 is now returned to and told to its end, providing a satisfying resolution and linking back to Story 1.

5. Story 1 is told to its ending, which may also covertly or directly suggest an ending to the story trance.[15]

The multiple embedded metaphor scheme exemplifies two important principles of therapeutic effectiveness applicable to communication in general. The first is the creation of expectancy and the corresponding need for completion: once you arouse natural curiosity and the feeling that something is going to happen, then there is an equivalent need for something to happen to complete the circuit. The second is the principle of confusion: if you cheat the expectation of a logical conclusion and go off at a tangent, the critical mind begins to give up and allow a more receptive trance state to develop. Indeed, one way to handle the linking of tales is to ramble artfully in a way that seems just boring waffle, with each tale emerging as an island of welcome, if temporary, coherence.

The multiple embedded metaphor scheme, Shahrazad's method of mixing together stories, or story maps in general are, at the basic level of the technique itself, quite neutral. You can use them as distractions to distract from distractions; you can use them to increase a sense of confusion so that you can manipulate more effectively; you can use them to communicate information or lore you feel to be important; or you can use them with more holistic intentions. But there is a level at which what seems on the surface like confusion can give way to coherence and clarity, as one story combines to enhance another, as map links to map to make a more and more edifying vision of that territory and its possibilities. There is a potential integrity to storytelling because there is a potential integrity to human consciousness, a level at which something separate from our fragmented everyday superficial consciousness draws together the treasures of our disparate experiences and shows us the inner wealth we are so inclined to ignore.

Nigerian novelist and metaphor virtuoso Ben Okri has it that 'stories are one of the highest and most invisible forms of human creativity'. There are very practical, almost invisible uses for metaphor and story in all aspects of our lives, including the communication of every day. Say worthwhile things in a logical way and they may disappear into the ether. Use an image, tell a story, make an analogy and it wakes people up. There is suddenly something to stimulate the imaginative part of us that had gone to sleep. A story can make us see, feel and understand things much better. But it can also confuse and mesmerize, like the dance of the weasel in front of the rabbit. It is, therefore, the task of anyone working with stories for change to encourage and enhance inward coherence.

There is a vital and perhaps necessarily not quite so invisible use for metaphor and story in education, which is highly practical as well as idealistic. If you tell stories to children and tell them regularly, they are learning to listen closely, and not only to imagine but to control and focus their imaginations. You are giving them templates for all kinds of things, from the ways in which language in a particular culture and time can be shaped expressively, to the patterns of underlying experiences they have not yet had. You are teaching them ways of thinking, ways of empathizing, ways of developing insight, all sorts of incidental information, all sorts of small and large wisdoms; you are cultivating understanding that can go on growing throughout their lives. And if, alongside this, you teach them the making and telling and writing of stories as a way of finding and expressing and developing meaning for themselves, you will have given them an inexhaustible treasure.

There is a vital and essential and very much visible 'in-your-face' use for storytelling and metaphor in entertainment and in bringing people together. Those who start to think of stories as a kind of medicine and get all pious about them miss a lot. Listening and enjoying and imagining together, and being absorbed in the moment at the same time as 'seeing' far off and marvellous places, is a pleasure and a joy this culture may well need to find ways to rediscover. Whilst we have astonishing films that, at best, create all sorts of vistas and do the work of imagining for us in extraordinary ways, whilst we also have a burgeoning fiction industry with all kinds of genres catering to all kinds of tastes, there is something frantic about it all. The very words with which it is sold – 'must read', 'must have', 'sensational', 'thrilling' – betray the values that warp and destroy what integrity and value there is in the experience.

One of the worst things that could happen over the next decades is that stories and storytelling could be taken SERIOUSLY. Top storytellers would be regarded as very special and feted as celebrities; a whole field of story therapy would develop, with expert practitioners ready to tell stories old and new, entirely appropriate to whatever condition might be put before them. The problem when things are taken SERIOUSLY is that they become useless icons; people erect wonderful ideas and theories around them but the underlying message is 'Keep out and don't touch. We are the high priests and it is your job simply to admire and appreciate.' But admiration and appreciation, necessary though they may be at some stages, soon turn into quite stupid cult followings and the worst kinds of sycophantic behaviour. And then, certainly, nothing much changes.

Stories are part of everybody's life and there are no experts on our own stories beyond ourselves. Every life is made up of different private stories but also of many overlapping public stories. This is where there is room for real expertise; not everyone has the time or inclination to study the myths and stories of tradition or to familiarize themselves thoroughly with the ways in which metaphor can work; not everyone knows how to shape their own stories in new ways. But every life can, potentially, be touched and enriched by great stories both large and small and by the act of creating and re-creating stories.

Storytelling, in all the many ways we have looked at and some that we haven't, is a skill that, paradoxically, we have and yet do not have. Like many skills, it can be practised at the level of art. Like many skills, too, it can be learned and used in much more ordinary ways.

A coda – three interwoven stories in five stages

1a. The Storyteller

There was once a storyteller who decided to set down in writing what he had gleaned about the art of telling and using stories, to make a kind of manual from which other people might draw ideas and techniques and even inspiration. As he thought about this initially very reasonable-sounding notion, it seemed both very possible and completely impossible. It was possible because he was a storyteller and his business was words – and because when you tell stories, you know that you start at whatever beginning seems just about right and go on until you reach whatever end also seems just about right, taking whatever detours and loops along the way might enrich the journey, but not straying so far from the path that you get lost completely. You accept the compromise between the ideal and the practical. It was impossible because...well, there was so much to capture, far too much to set down in one book, or even several. It was impossible too because what he knew was really so little compared to what he could and should know; his experience had taught him, he realized, little more than the extent of his own ignorance. And as he turned the word 'story' over in his mind, it seemed to shift its sense constantly, to look different with each new angle from which he squinted at it. Sometimes it appeared to mean stories you could tell out loud and share with people and pass on or record on a CD or write down and print out and send around the world between the covers of a book. Sometimes it seemed to mean very private things like dreams and imaginations and visions and fleeting resemblances, impossible to fix in any kind of recognizable sign. Sometimes it condensed itself into short, bright, hard little pulsars of metaphor and symbol. Sometimes it spread itself out into sprawling, billowing yarns and anecdotes. Sometimes it grew even bigger until wherever he looked, there was story and all of life seemed to be only that. But then sometimes it seemed just a harlequin all made up of words, and pictures, or smells or tastes or feelings. Sometimes it was hard to believe that it was not some chimerical being masquerading as one unbelievable beast.

This storyteller thought of a story. A true story – but of course, not a true story, since time muddles things and blends events together and it is sometimes difficult to distinguish between what is memory of experiences long ago and far away, what is metaphor for experience here and now and what is simply now redundant imagination. It was a story that always came back first with the image of an old sailor's chest in an antiques auction hall...

2a. The Sandcastle and the Chest

As he recalled things, he would have been about 12 at the time, on the edge of being a teenager. His brother was ten. They were going to the seaside, a rare event in those far off sepia days before motorways. His mother would drive them. She was a good driver and she took her driving seriously, liked to concentrate on the road, on doing things well. The journey would take hours and car stereo systems and iPods were also in the future. There was time to think. Also to resent.

The sense of injustice is sometimes difficult to cope with, even for a grown man. In the gut of a 12-year-old who wants to be taken seriously, it burns like acid. His brother had been in the wrong and he had been in the right. It had been his turn to sit in the front and for once he had insisted. His brother had wangled the privileged berth the last three times they'd gone out and he'd been dumped in the back, so fair was fair. But the little sod, who had today been ordered out of the front seat sulking and pouting, was at his most dangerous when thwarted. He had chosen his moments carefully, when no one was looking. First a surreptitious poke in the neck and a wicked little giggle. Next an unexpected pull on the left ear lobe and a scarcely suppressed snigger, just when he had been dreaming of future fame and recognition. Finally, the coup de grace – a pinch, a nasty, tight little pinch that nipped like pliers on fuse wire. 'You bastard!' he had screamed, swivelling round to punch the evil little... Then his mother had screeched to a halt and he had been blamed for violence and for swearing and told to behave himself. Both of them had been lectured severely and told that the car would turn around and go back if there was any more of this. There would be no more argument. And there was not – except for these sharp, querulous little pangs that wouldn't leave off.

They had arrived at the sea. Here his memory was unclear. There would first have been that excitement at glimpsing it between the hills, that magical feeling, the wonder of it he'd always felt. No more land, just this vast water, huge and green or pigeon grey or sometimes even startlingly blue and shiny. They'd have been excited at the prospect, because they just about always were. But those were general memories, could have been any time, any age from four to 14. How they had driven down to the shore that day when he was 12, what they had seen as they swung around and drove along beside the sea walls he had no idea. It was as if the next little bubble of memory (or whatever it was) emerged complete, a living snapshot with him magically transported to the top of the sea wall clutching bucket and spade and looking back down at his mother and brother fiddling around with stuff from the car boot. 'It's stones, Mum!' he heard himself shouting crossly. And there, around the edges of the soundscape with the seagulls and the waves, was his mother saying that it was pretty and she wanted to do some sketching and they'd find sand later on.

There are moments of decision in a life, occasionally taken coolly, rationally, more often taken out of pure pique and puerile impulse. He recalled stomping off along the path on top of the wall, shouting back something about going for a walk. He supposed, now, that he had been in a bind not untypical of adolescents, since he knew what he had wanted, back then: to make a sandcastle. He had wanted to do that, but been unsure of whether it was an all right thing to do for someone getting older, more serious, more dignified, so he had also not wanted to do it. But now the choice of not choosing had been taken away and he was in an impossible place. He stomped and stamped his way along that path, thinking dark thoughts about families. He recalled almost watching his thoughts chuntering on despite himself, those thoughts of 40-odd years ago he could almost hear now, with the shriek of a gull and the sound of the waves sucking at the shingle. Also an image, presumably from some story in a book he had been absorbed in at the time, a stray picture which time had detached from its context...

3. The Ruined Palace

There was once a ruined palace beside the sea. It had been a glory, home to generations of wise and just monarchs. Now stone had fallen on stone and, though the towers still stood, the weeds trailed down from corners of the battlements and the seagulls nested in what had once been observatories used by men of science to study the heavens. As for the grand, ornately carved gates, they had long since crumbled to dust or been taken away to make the roofs of walls of the peasant buildings that littered the hills nearby.

Of course, such a building attracted legends. Over the many years during which its original purpose and meaning were being slowly worn away and finally erased from living memory, there was a growth of imaginings and suppositions about the place. It was haunted, home to evil spirits. A witch had lived there or a wizard or a prince under a curse. If you were foolish enough to go to the place at midnight, the ghost of this or that person would carry you off to hell and damnation. There were also rituals the local people performed to propitiate the spirits of the place or to bring themselves luck or to sanction this or that project. Hardly anyone had an inkling of what the castle was for. At least, until the minstrel came, a ruffian from some passing ship who happened to stop by for a while.

At first they just enjoyed the songs he sang, the jokes he told and the tricks he played on them. It was fun. They scarcely noticed how the legends he drew them into gradually became longer and more involved, how the imaginary world they entered with him slowly made the unfamiliar familiar and explained what had once been inexplicable – legends of knights and their heroic deeds and the strict codes they lived by, stories of wise women and learned scholars, of marvellous gardens and magnificent monarchs – and indeed of lofty castles and fabulous palaces.

When he left, these images seemed to linger in the air. They gave people ideas about what they could do. They began to restore and rebuild the palace. As they did so, gradually other travellers from passing ships, attracted by what they saw, decided to stop by and help, bringing new skills and new ideas from their own travels. Then one day, digging in the grounds to make new pools and fountains at the suggestion of one of these travellers, they found a buried box and in it a map that showed them the whereabouts of a wonderful treasure in a sunken galleon in the bay nearby. This they rescued and used to completely restore all the glories of the palace...

2b. The Sandcastle and the Chest

Another fog. Another picture. He had walked right around the headland now since the tide was out and was standing in another bay on a beach that was sandy – buff white sand, dry and fine in his memory but probably mixed with stones and seaweed and rubbish, of which he could recall nothing. People here and there crouched behind yellow and red and green and orange windshields you pitched like tents? Did they have those back then? Probably a later accretion... And he was looking at a box bobbing on the water near some rocks on the far side of the bay, just beyond where some boats were moored. Not exactly bobbing actually, half sunk in the water, but he could see enough to set his imagination working. He waded into the water and managed to drag it out onto the sand.

Without stories, perhaps there would be no such dreams. How would he have known about doubloons and pieces of eight and pirates and sunken galleons otherwise? But he did know, just as he knew that, as a matter of fact, there are actual treasures in the sea that are occasionally belched up and deposited on the shore by the tides. This kind of thing happened. It was known to happen. Perhaps, just possibly this was the day that would change his life, bring his fortune.

Of course, it was only a box, some sort of old trunk dumped in the sea somehow or other. When he prised it open, there was only the salt smell of rock pools and a hint of dead crab. But if he was disappointed, the feeling didn't last long, since he had learned then what as an adult he would forget too often: that fantasies are often empty, seldom realized, best diverted along different channels. He would cover the trunk over with sand, make it the keep of a castle, a particularly large and special castle he alone would make, there on the beach that he had discovered for himself...

More absorption in the moment. You do not need to recall every stage of the making, all of the effort. You do these things in a pleasant trance, thinking more of what will be than what it is. It emerges slowly, very slowly – you accept this when you are making a sandcastle, shaping the main structure, using the bucket and the wetted sand to tip out those towers and fashion those turrets, sticking in here a stick from an ice lolly or a bit of a crisp packet for a flag, poking the slits for the windows, maybe scratching in the pattern of the bricks...

His brother probably didn't need to sneak up on him. He'd have been wrapped up in the doing, living more in a royal country of imagination than on that strip of sand on the edge of England. So there he was, suddenly looming out of the backdrop, looking at him, at the castle. Or maybe this was just the filmic way his memory framed it, his brother appearing out of nowhere and telling him he had to go back soon... and then looking again at the castle, admiring it. Did he say something else? He couldn't recall.

Sometimes perhaps you don't appreciate your options, don't notice the opportunities. Revenge they say is sweet – but not as sweet as making a sandcastle. Children to whom he'd told this tale had seen the chance he had for getting his own back, getting his brother angry, getting him to kick the castle and stub his toe on the box. It had been a surprise to him even then, many years on; it just had never occurred to him. At the time he had simply been too much inside the making to recall any need for those kinds of tricks. The resentments had all burned out and any remaining hot ashes had been blown away by the new mood in which his brother had joined him, the two of them going on with the making for maybe half an hour or an hour or more, until there was not only a castle with wall inside wall inside wall but a whole town of turreted houses with channels around all of them, linking up in a complicated network, a little Venice of a place waiting for the water...which was of course getting closer with the turning of the tide...

Again a gap. Did he remember the water actually filling in the channels? Did the waves wash all around the castle whilst they watched, or was that some other castle some other time? He could not be certain. Of course it would eventually have been washed away completely as sandcastles always are and the box underneath would have been carried somewhere else, perhaps sinking somewhere deep under mud, perhaps breaking up on rocks. It was, however, the castle and the way it looked when they were finishing it and the feeling of having worked well together that he recalled, a rare moment of perfection in a world of imperfection.

1b. The Storyteller

The chest was in an antiques auction many years later. Something about that particular lot had prompted him to remember the old box in the water and the day of the perfect sandcastle, to recapture and dust off the little fragments of memory that had seemed important, to make them into a story. It was, he realized, the same kind of box. Or at least it seemed to be. It fetched £900 in bidding in which he took no part, a lot of money at the time. But he had lost interest in the sale, even though it seemed a marvellous irony that the box in which he had expected to find treasure might itself have been a treasure. The castle was more important and there it was, still there, an impermanent work of imagination with a permanent trace, a different kind of treasure much more like a story...

Perhaps it was both too personal and almost clumsily metaphorical, despite being based on his own real experience. There was a problem with taking stories too seriously anyway – people can be put off by the faintest whiff of real seriousness, not to mention embarrassed by seeing too much into the private world of the tale teller. If you are going to invoke images of the impermanence of life as we know it and the deeper patterns that might lie beyond it, best to do it tongue-in-cheek with a heavy dash of irony. Best to be light-hearted and to make jokes or simply to be practical. Storytelling and story making were practical crafts with practical purposes. You began at what seemed a beginning and you went on until you reached what seemed to be an end.

He decided to make a start on his project and he sketched some sentences: 'Stories are marvellous, magical things. They are also, paradoxically, mundane and commonplace – because they are everywhere. You can't live without stories, without telling them and making them. You yourself are a story...'

Notes

CHAPTER 1 THE NATURAL STORYTELLER

1. From *Birds of Heaven* (1996), p.24.

2. Berry (1988).

3. 'Limbic system' is a useful shorthand, though neuroscientists are evidently now a little wary of the term, pointing out that it is not a sealed and entirely separate self-organizing entity. For a very readable account of the emotional 'system', see Goleman (1996). See also LeDoux, Joseph (1998); Ornstein (1991). For a more recent general tour of the brain, reviewing the current state of knowledge about its functioning, see Bainbridge (2008).

4. A lucid and approachable account of aspects of brain functioning relevant here is given in Robertson (1999). See also Ornstein (1986) for a challenging and brilliantly written exposition of the consequences of this.

5. Rossi (1993).

6. Meme is a concept first introduced by Richard Dawkins in his influential 1970s book, *The Selfish Gene*. The Oxford English Dictionary defines it as 'an element of culture that may be considered to be passed on by non-genetic means, esp. imitation'. See Chapter 6 for a discussion.

7. Original source oral.

8. This function of stories, which is now being re-discovered (and indeed re-packaged) quite widely, is clearly very ancient – at least as old as Aesop or the mostly anonymous creators of even more ancient fables and exemplary tales, often incorporated into the earliest classics of world literature or into scriptures and the teachings of the founders of religions (see also Breakthrough Stories below – pp 61–64). The notion that traditional stories of many kinds enshrine potent practical wisdom about the self is not new. However, in relatively recent times, no one did more to re-awaken interest in and shed new light on the power of stories than the remarkable and extraordinary Sufi writer and teacher, Idries Shah, who used arresting modern metaphors to describe how stories are understood and used in the Sufi tradition as 'blueprints' or 'templates' which, apart from mirroring mistakes, could also prepare a person for experiences he or she had not yet had. (See also Chapter 4 p. 177.) A similar if perhaps less complex perception evidently underlay the highly influential work of Ameri-can psychiatrist and father of modern indirect hypnotherapeutic approaches Milton Erickson, who told his deceptively simple homespun yarns as part of uncannily effective therapeutic interventions and was doubtless a major source

of the burgeoning interest in stories and storytelling amongst brief therapy practitioners and many others concerned with change and development today. (See for example Rosen, Sidney ed. (1982) *My Voice Will Go With You – The Teaching Tales of Milton H. Erickson.* New York: W.W.Norton & Company)

9 Deikman, A. (1982).

10. From *Birds of Heaven* (1996), p.18.

11. See also Chapter 2, pp.85–86.

12. See Chapter 6, pp.246–247.

13. From 'The Web of Silence: Storytelling's Power to Hypnotize' (1988). This and other interesting and related out-of-print articles have been made available free online at www.healingstory.org.

14. The alternative explanation – that the lady was right and the events in the story had actually been acted out in Weybridge – has been suggested to me more than once by people to whom I've told this tale. That seems unlikely, though not impossible. Indeed, the fact that life sometimes imitates art and that people actually do act out fantasies from books and films, etc. is further proof of how dangerously real fiction can become.

15. For a succinct account of illusory memories and suggestibility, exploding many myths common in therapy, see the account of a seminar given by Dr Michael Yapko in Williams (1994).

16. Sturm (1999).

17. Stallings (1988).

18. Griffin and Tyrrell (2003), pp.72–73.

19. From Campbell, J. *The Hero With a Thousand Faces* (2008), p.101.

20. Borges (1976).

21. For a full discussion of metaphor in language, see Lakoff and Johnson (1980 and 2003).

22. *Homo metaphorica* might be an alternative to Ben Okri's suggestion at the head of the chapter – almost anything human beings do can be metaphorical.

23. Quoted in Gardner (1982), p.62.

24. From *Metaphor Therapy: Using Client-Generated Metaphors in Psychotherapy* (1995), p.173.

25. Griffin and Tyrrell (2004).

26. In *The Language Instinct* (1994).

27. Griffin and Tyrrell (2004).

28. See Griffin and Tyrrell (2003), pp.284–289. Also see Chapter 2, pp.86–88.

29. Claxton (1997), pp.168–9.

30. Narby (1998), p.137.

31. Damasio (2000), p.189. Used with the permission of the publishers.

32. Rossi (1993), p.163.

33. Retold here. First heard in 1985 orally from Prem Dhupa, a storyteller who told mostly Hindu legends in schools in the Medway towns in Kent (see also note 5, Chapter 7). There is a version in Kirin Narayan's *Storytellers, Saints and Scoundrels: Folk Narrative in Hindu Religious Teaching* (1989), a study of the storytelling of a Hindu guru that is well worth reading. Numerous other versions are in print.

34. In the double CD *How Stories Heal* (1998 and 2006).

35. Damasio (2000), p.188. Used with the permission of the publishers.

36. Damasio (*ibid.*), p.189, strongly asserts the centrality of storytelling in basic

brain processes, insisting that telling stories at a simpler, mapping level 'precedes language' – and is indeed a 'condition of language'.

37. See Griffin and Tyrrell (2003), pp.93–94 etc.

38. Damasio (2000), p.188 (including and continuing from the last sentence of the quotation which begins this section): 'A natural preverbal occurrence of storytelling may well be the reason why we ended up creating drama and eventually books, *and why a good part of humanity is currently hooked on movie theaters and television screens. Movies are the closest external representation of the prevailing storytelling that goes on in our minds....*' (italics added). Quoted with the permission of the publishers.

CHAPTER 2 THE SPANISH GAME: GUIDED IMAGERY AND STORIES

1. Chuang Tzu was a Taoist philosopher thought to have lived in the fourth century BCE. This is a widely quoted paradox. The great Japanese poet Basho wrote a famous haiku based on it.

2. Haley (1986), pp.29–30.

3. For an examination of mount and rider imagery, see discussion Chapter 7 pp.271–2 and 'Mounts and minions' (p.275 and pp.277–278).

4. Ty Boyd cited in Wubbolding (1991), p.39.

5. Robertson (1999), p.37.

6. *Ibid.*, p.39.

7. Information and publications list from www.thegraycenter.org. This site also gives guidelines for creating a Social Story™, for which quite strict rules have been developed – though there is common ground with methods used in narrative therapy, which in turn are developments of various kinds of story work in use for centuries. Gray's contribution seems to be one of application, especially to the specific needs of autistic spectrum learners and their particular needs – and, paradoxically, to their tendency to literalism and difficulties with metaphor.

8. Guy and Guy (2003).

9. Since January 2008, the human givens inspired charity Resolution (www. ptsdresolution.org) has been providing effective rewind treatment through therapists trained in the approach for many sufferers of severe military PTSD across the UK. Statistics concerning its startling effectiveness derived from this source should be available in due course.

10. See, for example, Griffin (2005). For a full description of recent research and thinking on the emotional system and fear conditioning, see LeDoux (1998).

11. This technique is learned by all trainee human givens therapists, as are the other techniques in this section, apart from 'the three things' technique, which is widely known. I am grateful to Mark Tyrrell and Roger Elliott of Uncommon Knowledge for introducing me to the version described here.

12. See for example my own CD *Just Imagine – Use the Power of Imagination to Relax and Create a Clear Personal Focus* (2005b).

13. This is summarized from my booklet *Imagine On* (2005a), which includes many other visualization techniques for use in story work with school-age pupils and is available from www.imaginaryjourneys.co.uk. The booklet is the second of four in the Natural Storytellers series. The fourth volume, *New Lamps from Old*, also includes some visualizing techniques for encouraging children to picture new versions of stories. At the time of writing, I am due to record a new CD of guided imagery for children called *The Golden Staircase and the Magic Door* for

production and release in late 2009 by Imaginary Journeys.

14. From the poem 'Vitae summa brevis spem nos vetat incohare longam'.

15. This is a version of a story that has become quite widely known in a range of different forms. In various oral traditions, the wolf becomes a different animal – for example, a lion in an African tale or a bear in a European analogue. Perhaps the best-known version is the Korean story about a tiger and a similar girl – I first heard it from traveller and storyteller Helena Edwards, who ran a branch of the College of Storytellers in the 1980s and told the tale often. I tell a version on my CD *Powerful Stories* (2003). The story can be adapted and transposed using some of the ideas in Chapter 6. In therapeutic work with both adults and children, incidentally, I have found versions of this tale extremely valuable in working with phobia and PTSD sufferers in conjunction with the rewind and special place picturing techniques explained in this chapter, usually much elaborated with many hidden suggestions for controlled calm and patience as explained in Chapter 3.

CHAPTER 3 THE WAY YOU TELL 'EM:
THE ART AND CRAFT OF ORAL STORYTELLING

1. 'Right' and 'left' brain functioning is used as a widely understood shorthand here, accepting that this is a simplification of actual brain processes. In this simplified model, the 'right brain', which controls the left side, works more with context and whole pattern than the analytical, sequential 'left brain'. For a review of this aspect of brain functioning, see Robert Ornstein's *The Right Brain* (1997).

2. This is a well-known and much-told tall tale. For a version with a location and other details, see Katharine Briggs's *A Dictionary of British Folk Tales in the English Language: Part A Folk Narratives* (1970).

3. Adapted from my *Tall Tale Telling – 24 Fun Games for Making and Telling Incredible Stories* (2004). This is Book 1 in the Natural Storytellers booklet series, available from my website (www.imaginaryjourneys.co.uk). This booklet includes more extensive protocols for using this game with workshop groups, plus a series of variations and developments.

4. Both Wicked Whoppers and Being Joe Bloggs are also from *Tall Tale Telling* (see note 3 above), where again various practical developments are suggested.

5. From my *Yarn Spinning – 24 Fun Ways to Stretch a Tale in the Telling* (2007b). This is Book 3 in the Natural Storytellers booklet series (see note 3 above).

6. Quoted in Rubin (1995), p.59.

7. This is my brief summary of the tale. For more detail, see David Thompson's *The People of the Sea* (1996), p.48 onwards.

8. Chatwin (1987).

9. For example, Buzan (1986).

10. See note 5 above.

11. My thanks are due to the remarkable American-born, France-based story-teller Sam Cannarozzi, who gave me permission to quote from his collection of over 600 standard openings and endings from storytellers around the world. The Society for Storytelling (www.sfs.org.uk) has since published a selection of these in Sam Cannarozzi's *When Tigers Smoked Pipes* (2008). Sam can be contacted at 76 Rue Neyret, 01600 Parcieux, France or by e-mail: scan.yad@ tiscali.fr.

12. From the 10th-century *Book of the Dun Cow* and reproduced in various books

of Celtic lore, including T.W. Rolleston's *Myths and Legends of the Celtic Race* (1985), pp.309–331.

13. Burton (1894), Vol. 3, p.223, 'The City of Labayt'. This story was retold by Jorge Luis Borges in *A Universal History of Infamy* (1975) as 'The Chamber of Statues'.

14. A slight exaggeration, since such books usually combine verbal and non-verbal approaches. For example, Jerry Richardson's *The Magic of Rapport* (2000), which summarizes many of the non-verbal techniques as well as verbal techniques of NLP (neuro-linguistic programming). A broader perspective is given in Roberto Cialdini's *Influence: The Psychology of Persuasion* (1984), which examines the very many techniques of influence.

15. One of the best manuals is Rubin Battino and Thomas South's *Ericksonian Approaches: A Comprehensive Manual* (1999). It includes an extensive summary of language techniques. Battino's other two excellent manuals, *Guided Imagery and Other Approaches to Healing* (2000) and *Metaphoria: Metaphor and Guided Metaphor for Psychotherapy and Healing* (2002), also cover language techniques.

16. See my *Three Angles on an Awakening Kiss* (1998). Also *Qualities of Moment*, a presentation to University of Cape Breton Annual Storytelling Symposium in May 2001; retrieved 13 September 2008 from www.imaginaryjourneys.co.uk/word_files/qualitiesofconsciousness.pdf.

17. Csikszentmihalyi (1990). Whilst Csikszentmihalyi does not use the terms 'hypnosis' or 'trance' (understandably, in view of controversies in the academic world over these terms), flow seems to be a kind of trance state as defined in Chapter 1.

18. Goleman (1996), p.91.

19. Goleman (1998). On p.166, Goleman quotes an experiment by Sigal Barsade, a professor at the Yale University School of Management, in which an actor planted in groups affected the group mood. Goleman says: 'The emotions did spread like a virus. When the actor argued with cheerfulness or warmth, those feelings rippled through the group, making people more positive as the meeting went on. And when he was irritable, people felt grumpier. (Depression, on the other hand, spread little, perhaps because it manifests as subtle social withdrawal – indicated, for instance, by little eye contact – and so has little amplification.)'

20. See Chapter 4 for a better definition and description of the role of the *seanachie*.

21. Foley (1979). There are other popular forms of *wayang* in Indonesia. The term is used for drama in general, for example the *wayang wong* (a form of masked drama playing scenes from the Ramayana) as well as for the various forms of puppetry – *wayang kulit*, for example, can refer to the leather puppets used in shadow puppetry.

22. Sutton (1996).

23. Usually defined as a 'gong orchestra', the gamelan is an ensemble that typically also includes large, elaborately decorated xylophones and drums plus one or two bowed instruments, flutes, etc. Its music is developed around complex interlocking, slowly developing ostinato patterns and tends to be hypnotic in effect. The *wayang* gamelan includes female singers who sing a narration.

24. See Federico Garcia Lorca's *In Search of Duende* (1998). Lorca wrote passionately and poetically about the *duende* (which comes from the Spanish *duen de casa* – master of the house) as a quality which flamenco players and singers as well as bullfighters and, according to Lorca, many other artists might have.

For example: 'The duende is a momentary burst of inspiration, the blush of all that is truly alive, all that the performer is creating at a certain moment. It manifests itself principally among musicians and poets of the spoken word for it needs the trembling of the moment and then a long silence.' For an exciting and engaging account of a more recent quest for this quality in Spanish Flamenco, see Jason Webster's *Duende: A Journey in Search of Flamenco* (2003).

25. Fadoists perform the *fado*. These are literally 'fate songs', a deeply emotional form of expressive poetry usually accompanied by a supporting player of the Portuguese guitar, which has a mandolin-like sound. *Fado* is considered typically Portuguese, but, like Spanish flamenco, has strong affinities with some forms of North African/Arab music.

26. Noted by Chuck Krueger in an article in *Storylines* (Society for Storytelling, Spring 1999), reporting on a workshop with Sheila at the Cape Clear International Storytelling workshop, 24–26 October 1998.

27. See for example 'A Sort of Monks' by John Grant, published in Shah (1972), pp.171–176.

28. There is an informative entry for *mana* available from Wikipedia, the free online encyclopaedia, whilst the online Encyclopaedia Britannica has a brief informative note about *wakan*. It is fair to point out that many anthropologists argue that these 'powers' might be better understood as dependent on social status, hence socially constructed. *Mana* has been a particular topic for debate in this field.

29. 'The Perfect Storyteller' was originally created for some workshop notes and is © Rob Parkinson 1986 and 1994 for publishing purposes, but in keeping with the point of the tale, of course anyone may tell it orally. It was first formally published in the Society for Storytelling's newsletter of June 1994.

CHAPTER 4 TRADITIONAL WAYS OF STORYTELLING

1. From *Illuminations* (1970), pp.89–90. This is from the famous seminal essay 'The Storyteller – Reflections on the Work of Nikolai Leskov', pp.83–107, in which Benjamin managed to say many important things about the oral storyteller whilst actually writing about a writer. Quoted with the permission of the publishers.

2. From an online article 'Word of skill', originally published 1995 (www.chalicecentre.net/wordofskill.htm). Thanks are due to Mara Freeman for permission to use the extract here.

3. It has been suggested by some scholars that Homer was not one historical personality but a legendary name that became associated with the Homeric epics. In this view, the epics would have been created by the 'shared genius' of the Homeric bards over time and with repetition.

4. A more prosaic and scholarly account of the development of this legend is given in John Southworth's *The English Medieval Minstrel* (1989), a very interesting and informative account of minstrelsy.

5. An account of this meeting was published in the Society for Storytelling's magazine, *Storylines*, in 1999 and is available free online in an extended version at www.imaginaryjourneys.co.uk/word_files/talkingtotherawi.pdf.

6. Dwivedi, K.N. (2000) 'Therapeutic powers of narratives and stories.' *Context* 47, 11–12. *Context* is the magazine for family therapy and systematic practice in the UK. Dr Dwivedi is a consultant psychiatrist who has written and lectured extensively on the subject of uses of stories in therapy; see for example Dwivedi, K.N. (ed.) *The Therapeutic Use of Stories* (1997) London: Routledge.

Thanks are due to the author for permission to include this quotation.

7. Shah (1971), p.137.

8. From Arthur Christensen's *Contes Persans en Langue Populaire* (1918), p.41.

9. Schwartz (1987), pp.78–81.

10. Temple and Temple (1998), Introduction by Robert Temple, pp.*xv–xvi*. Temple points out that some morals may equally have been added with more philosophical insight.

11. The boy's name, as I recall, was Darrius Coppen. My apologies to Darrius since, several years since we met during some school visits, I have no contact address to check his details and ask his permission to use his work.

12. Each of these fables has been retold from my repertoire, elaborated and adapted a little to make them a little more interesting, though in oral telling they could be extended further. Three of them (the first and the last two) are included in extended versions on my CD *Fabulous Fables – Witty and Wise Tales from World Traditions* (2008).

13. The oldest version of this Indian fable is one of the *Vetala Tales* (Tawney 1924), though there are many others in oral traditions. This shaping of the plot developed through telling. In oral telling, it is very useful to surprise and puzzle an audience for a moment; most can recall the mention of *four* wise men and wonder why you are talking about *three* fools.

14. I first heard this West African tale at a storytelling event many years ago and have since come across various different versions. Jane Yolen, in the introduction to her highly recommended collection *Favorite Folktales from Around the World* (1986), tells a version from the Nupe of Nigeria and points out that it has been widely told by different tribes in Africa and indeed migrated to the Americas on slave ships

15. The version here is freely adapted and extended from Aesop's version. The original can be found, for example, in Olivia and Robert Temple's *Aesop: The Complete Fables* (1998), p.65. There are several other versions of the motif of the frozen snake in world oral literature, including an Afghan and a First Nation American tale. The great 13th-century poet and fabulist Jalaludin Rumi tells a version in his *Masnawi*.

16. There are very many versions of this fable in world oral literature, for example 'The Traveller's Adventure' in *Folklore and Legends – Oriental* (1889), p.135. The Arabian Nights tale 'The Beasts and the Carpenter' is not dissimilar and there are affinities with the very well known genie in the bottle plot quoted elsewhere in this chapter. In more westerly traditions, the snake may be transformed into a troll or a dragon or an ogre, and the chain of animals with a grudge varies widely too, though the central trick remains more or less the same.

17. There are various fables amongst the Buddhist Jataka Tales. This one is transformed in one Eastern telling into a story that is about two pearl divers and a lawyer. It transposes easily to other settings using the techniques presented in Chapter 6.

18. The story is adapted from the *Panchatantra*. A full note on this collection is given on p.246–247. Though the story is strangely alarming and actually very adult in its underlying themes, children can enjoy it immensely.

19. As previously noted, this collection is included in Somadeva's *Ocean of Story* (Tawney 1924). Other translations include Richard F. Burton's *Vikram and the Vampire* (1870).

20. This is, of course, the story of Nzilla the tracker begun in Chapter 1. There is a different version of this widely known tale in Susan Feldman's *African Myths and Tales* (1970), p.217. This gives the story as belonging to the Bakongo

people and gives names to each of the wives. That version also has the husband favouring the third wife who restored his life whilst the women of the village disagree. Other versions leave the dilemma more open. See also 'The Princess Who Died', Story 2 of nine adaptable tales in Chapter 6.

21. I heard this one from a Hungarian storyteller very much as a European tale, though since then I've also found an African version in Jack Berry's *West African Folk Tales* (1961), pp.79–81.

22. A storyteller from Ghana told me this traditional West African tale, though in a simpler version involving only two wizards. It has been elaborated here somewhat as I tend to embroider it in public telling, so I should perhaps take responsibility for this shaping of the plot.

23. All three of these are new and original. The Aesop's fable 'The Ploughman and the Tree' with which the third can be compared is told on my *Fabulous Fables* CD (2008).

24. See www.petecastle.co.uk/fandf.

25. See Shah (1971), pp.191–195.

26. See for example in Idries Shah's *World Tales* (1979). This fascinating and rewarding collection of stories should be on the shelves of all storytellers. See also 'The Teaching Story' published in Robert Ornstein's *The Nature of Human Consciousness* (1973), pp.289–307.

27. Retold here from my repertoire, with assistance of a new working translation by Hooi Ling Smith. I first learned this story in my early days as a storyteller from the now defunct Anvil Cassettes series. It appeared as 'The Piece of Chuang Brocade' in *Folk Tales from China, Third Series*, (1958) – now out of print – and is included in Joanna Cole's *Best Loved Folktales of the World* (1982), pp.539–544, as 'The Magic Brocade'. There are various other published versions in existence, including a beautiful picture book – *The Magic Brocade: A Tale of China* – with a retelling by storyteller Aaron Shepard (2000). My thanks are due to Aaron for putting me on the right track when researching copyright on this and other stories.

CHAPTER 5 MARVELLOUS MINIATURES: MAKING SHORT METAPHORS

1. Battino (2002), p.196.

2. In the Arabian Nights, the king is Haroun al Raschid (see Burton 1894; Mardrus and Mathers 1962).

3. *The Languid Goat is Always Thin: The World's Strangest Proverbs* (2001) by Stephen Arnot.

4. 'The Destruction of Sennacherib' by Lord Byron, perhaps the best known of a series Byron called Hebrew Melodies, intended to express the feelings of the Hebrew people in their struggle with the pagan nations. Byron hence used what he conceived of as biblical/classical imagery. It is interesting to compare this with the technique of Middle Eastern poets in which a series of brightly multisensory images might begin a poem to effectively dazzle the reader/listener and draw him or her into the imaginative orbit of the poem – as for example in the well-known opening verses of *The Rubaiyat* of Omar Khayyam.

5. See Thomas Cleary's *Unlocking the Zen Koan: A New Translation of the Zen Classic Wumenguan* (1993).

6. See Chapter 3, pp.132–135.

7. See Griffin and Tyrrell (2003), pp.221–223 for a dramatic example of a healing allegory using this kind of structure to heal a patient with chronic verrucas.

8. de Bono (1973), p.119.

9. This is a very widely known little story. Like many 'jokes with content', it is to be found in the Mulla/Hoja Nasrudin corpus. I first came across this one in 1976 in a pamphlet of Nasrudin stories published in Turkey for tourists. The best Nasrudin collections in English are those by Idries Shah, published by Octagon Press.

10. Retold here from my repertoire, originally based on shorter versions in Somadeva's recension of the *Panchatantra* in *The Ocean of Story* (1924) and Arthur Mee's *The Children's Encyclopedia*.

11. See Chapter 3, pp.133–136.

12. Rosen (1982).

13. This story and no. 3 'The Optimist' are included with a series of other quick frames on my double CD *Powerful Stories* (2003).

14. Adapted from Somadeva's *The Ocean of Story* (Tawney 1924).

15. Chinese fable.

16. This story is, apparently, original. It was re-told to me in outline by my good friend Bryan Lester who tells me I made it up almost 40 years ago before his very eyes and bit by bit over a drink in a bar, as an example of how stories could be invented to challenge perceptions. I'd be proud of that had I not since forgotten it completely – an interesting example, perhaps, of how anonymous oral traditions might work.

17. This personal anecdote is included as an example of the way in which experience can be framed in a story to make a reframing metaphor.

18. 'The Emir's Robe' is an original story – I've used the plot in other settings but this one seems to work well.

19. One of the stories of Lieh Tzu, an early Chinese Taoist philosopher, thought to have lived in the 5th century BCE; though, as with Aesop, stories attributed to him were written down centuries later. This story is retold from my repertoire. There are versions in Hsiao Ch'ien's *The Harp with a Thousand Strings* (1944), p.156, and in Yong Yap Cotterell's *The Illustrated Book of World Fables* (1979), p.112.

20. This account was inspired by Alexander Waugh's *Time* (1999), pp.42–43.

21. Source: oral anecdote.

22. Retold here from my repertoire, originally based on shorter versions in Somadeva's *Panchatantra* (Tawney 1924) and Arthur Mee's *The Children's Encyclopaedia*.

23. Croesus was king of Lydia in western Asia Minor. Cyrus the Great ruled Persia. This legend of the two kings has also been told of other legendary heroes. Some other tales of Croesus put him in a better light than Cyrus – which bears out the truth of the old fable about the man who showed a lion a series of statues in which men conquered and subdued lions as proof of the superiority of man. 'If lions had made these images,' the lion observed, 'they might be a little different.'

24. This traditional Indian story is widely known in many different versions – there is even a children's picture book based on it.

25. Nos 22, 23 and 24 – more stories/jokes picked up from now unidentifiable and forgotten oral sources.

26. Retold here in brief form from my repertoire. There is a still shorter version in Yong Yap Cotterell's *The Illustrated Book of World Fables* (1979), p.45. Also in Hsiao Ch'ien's *The Harp with a Thousand Strings* (1944).

CHAPTER 6 NEW LAMPS FOR OLD: TRANSPOSING STORIES

1. Samples of Jung's diverse writings on archetypes have been published in single paperback volumes such as *Four Archetypes – Mother, Rebirth, Spirit, Trickster* (Jung 1972). Most people find Jung's autobiographical account *Memories, Dreams, Reflections* (1963) an easier (and perhaps seductive) introduction to Jung, though Richard Noll points out that this is a posthumous work which was primarily written and constructed by Aniela Jaffé, one of Jung's closest associates with 'contributions from C.G. Jung' and hence what Noll calls 'a product of discipleship' (Noll 1994, p.13).

2. See Neil Philip's *The Cinderella Story: The Origins and Variations of the Story Known as Cinderella* (1989) for a selection of the variants and a discussion of the pattern.

3. Blackmore (1999), pp.242–243.

4. *Ibid.*, p.244.

5. Interestingly, Chris Nunn (2007) has recently integrated a revised notion of archetypes, stripped of what he calls Jung's 'flummery', along with memes in an intriguing new theory based around attractors in the brain.

6. This game, with many others around changing stories, can be found in my *New Lamps from Old: 24 Games for Making New Tales from Old Plots* (2007a).

7. The climb can make useful guided imagery, as noted below. It is similar to an image used in psychosynthesis, for example, as described in Piero Ferrucci's *What We May Be: The Vision and Techniques of Psychosynthesis* (1982), pp.144–146.

8. Burton (1894), Story no. 351, Vol. 3, pp.401–402.

9. Deikman (1982), pp.155–156.

10. In Somadeva's recension (Tawney 1924) there are two stories that are analogues, the first ('The Story of the Three Young Brahmans Who Restored a Lady to Life', Vol. 7, p.179) being closest to the story of 'The Man Who Died' (Chapter 4, p.169). The second ('Somaprahba and Her Three Suitors', Vol. 7, p.200) is like this tale, as regards the three gifts or powers of the suitors, but the girl is abducted by a Rakshasha and rescued by means of their combined abilities.

11. Attributed to Aesop.

12. Included in Tawney (1924), Vol. 5, with full scholarly notes on the origins and very wide distribution of the book's many offshoots. The original Sanskrit model was lost and the book was later translated back into the language from already translated/altered models.

13. A very engaging and well-written modern version of part of *Kalila and Dimna* is Ramsay Wood's *Kalila and Dimna: Selected Fables of Bidpai* (1982).

14. In *Storytellers, Saints and Scoundrels*, pp.118–119, Kirin Narayan compares various different but similar versions of this tale from Indian folk and religious lore and goes on to discuss themes of the tale as they relate to celibacy and ascetic practices in the Hindu mystical tradition.

15. *The Book of the Thousand Nights and a Night* (1894), Vol. 10, pp.297–342 and (similar) Vol. 11, pp.58–67. Burton included these tales in his Supplemental Nights – the stories which have become associated with the Nights through the vagaries of translation or otherwise, but are not part of the 'essential corpus'.

16. *The Book of the Thousand Nights and One Night* (1962), Vol. 3, pp.439–459.

17. Calvino (1982), pp.315–322.

18. The term 'solution-focused' is used literally because the aim of working with the story is to find solutions, not to express, examine and amplify problems.

The association with the imaginative effect of the questioning patterns used in solution-focused therapy is described in note 21 below. Those unfamiliar with this method will find a very clear, approachable and extremely useful summary in O'Hanlon and Weiner-Davis (1989).

19. It has been pointed out to me that there are some coincidences in the frame method described in the following section with the six part story method used by drama therapists, following an outline developed by Alida Gersie, inspired by Vladimir Propp and Algirdas Greimas. The idea, was however, generated independently and has different emphases and uses.

20. C.S. Lewis, like many fantasy writers, used many traditional motifs in the Narnia series. Frame 5 also has elements in common with the plot of *The Lion, the Witch and the Wardrobe*, which can famously be read as a Christian allegory.

21. A comparison useful in seeing how this and the other frames can function in change work is with some of the questions used in solution-focused therapy (see also note 18 above). For example, the famous miracle question, in basic form, is: 'Suppose that one night, while you were asleep, there was a miracle and this problem was solved. How would you know? What would be different?' (de Shazer 1988). Another form is: 'Supposing this problem had disappeared, if I follow you around with a video camera, what will I see on the video footage? How will you be behaving differently?' Both questions ask the subject to clearly imagine a future free of the problem, to experience the feeling of a solution, as also do the frames. When this imagining happens, an expectation is set up in the mind that is likely to realize itself. The person knows on an imaginative level how change works.

CHAPTER 7 TRAPS AND TREASURES: SYMBOLS, STORIES WITHIN STORIES AND METAPHORICAL LITERACY

1. Semiology and semiotics have, of course, quite different origins. Semiotics is, theoretically, the more complete study of all signs. The term is derived from a Greek root, *seme* (sign). The American philosopher Charles Sanders Peirce (1831–1913) aimed to classify all types of signs in the universe; the modern discipline of semiotics, of which he was a pioneer, also traces its roots back to ancients, such as the medical physician Hippocrates and Galen of Pergamon. Semiology, on the other hand, came out of the work of Ferdinand de Saussure (1857–1913) and was developed in the following generation by semiologists such as Roland Barthes and Pierre Guiraud. In looser contemporary cultural studies, the two are often conflated and the generalization here applies to what is the most common 'received opinion' within that now very influential field.

2. Lakoff and Johnson (2003), pp.256–257. Lakoff and Johnson have pursued this theme in *Philosophy in the Flesh: The Embodied Mind and Its Challenge to Western Thought* (1999).

3. Arguably, since not all cultures have developed weaving and tapestry making as such, though most have an equivalent. The natural principle of weaving is universal enough, however, with plenty of examples of its exploitation by 'simpler' life forms – birds' nests, beehives, termite colonies, etc.

4. In *An Illustrated Encylopaedia of Traditional Symbols* (1978), p.85. This is an excellent reference work for looking at symbols, though it provides an almost too rich series of associations for each image it examines.

5. My first source for this haunting and beautiful version of a universal tale was an oral telling by a storyteller whose name I do not recall at a private gathering in 1982, when I was first involved in oral storytelling. This was reinforced by

another version I heard from the late Prem Dhupa, when I worked alongside her at the Medway Festival of Cultures in 1985. Prem was a charming older Indian lady who told mostly Hindu stories in the Asian community and in schools in the Medway towns in Kent (see also note 33, Chapter 1). She volunteered a story she had loved in her childhood that had many of the features of this version when I asked her whether she knew any Indian tales that were more like fairy tales. Parts of the plot are similar to Howard Schwartz's telling of 'The Golden Tree' in *Elijah's Violin and Other Jewish Folktales* (1987), pp.106–112, a retelling of a story from Indian oral tradition in the Israel Folk Archives (IFA 8181), and I acknowledge my debt to this telling from a superb collection of stories in clarifying and sharpening aspects of the story told here. The tale combines various folk-tale motifs and shares themes with many another story – amongst which are motifs and subplots commented on elsewhere in this book. Howard Schwartz suggests in his notes on the tale a convincing connection of the symbolism with Messianic myth, though as with most metaphors it is possible to look at the story in different ways.

6. There are very many versions of this universal pattern in world folk literature, from the famous Russian 'Firebird' to the Scottish 'Ian Direach and the Blue Falcon' and many more. This version is a distillation of various versions taken from my own repertoire, though it is most like the one in Grimm.

7. See Chapter 4, p.149.

8. This is a succinct version of a plot that appears to be widespread in world oral literature, concerning the value of storytellers. In another version, the storyteller again quietens the court with a tale, but this time he has spotted an assassin creeping into the court who also falls under the spell of his tale and whom he catches at the conclusion of it. The Irish *Vision of Maconglinne* has a poet luring a demon of gluttony that is inhabiting the King of Munster from its human lair through tempting imagery and tale telling. In one of the more extended and probably most ancient workings of this motif, 'The Legend of Far-li-mas', quoted by Joseph Campbell in *The Masks of God – Volume 1: Primitive Mythology* (1976), pp.152–161, from an oral telling by an Arab storyteller in 1912, the storyteller Far-li-mas rescues the ancient king of Kordofan from a customary and barbarous death at the hands of superstitious priests with his marvellous storytelling skills.

9. Many readers will recognize this story as the well-known tale 'The Elephant in the Dark' or 'The Blind Men and the Elephant', an ancient fable that dates back at least as far as the Jataka Tales of Gautama the Buddha and is also claimed by Jainists, Hindus and particularly Sufis – it has been much used by writers and teachers in that tradition. The great modern Sufi writer and teacher Idries Shah, referred to in Chapter 4, promoted the story extensively and indeed made a short film giving the tale a modern, science-fiction setting (see Shah 1970). In brief, the original story goes that, in a certain ancient city, no one had ever seen an elephant. The king relied entirely on the opinions and judgement of his advisers, who were, however, obliged to examine the beast in the dark (in some versions, the advisers are simply blind). Each grasped a different part of the elephant, one taking the trunk, another an ear, another a leg, another a tusk, and so on. Discussing their findings, they were unable to agree on what the elephant was, since each defined it in terms of the part he had experienced.

10. Lankton and Lankton (1984).

11. Tawney (1924).

12. See Chapter 6, p.247.

13. Shah, Idries (1982), pp.174–175. The code system is well established

– Arabic–English dictionaries typically give the number each letter can stand for at the start of each letter section.

14. *Tales of Enchantment* (1989). This book has a very useful diagrammatic representation of the three-story scheme on p.8.

15. For a further practical explanation of this technique with examples, see also Battino and South (1999), pp.325–340.

Bibliography

Aarne, A. (1961) *The Types of the Folktale* (translated and enlarged by Stith Thompson). Helsinki: F.F. Communications.

Arnot, S. (2001) *The Languid Goat Is Always Thin: The World's Strangest Proverbs.* London: Prion Books.

Bainbridge, D. (2008) *Beyond the Zonules of Zinn (A Fantastic Journey Through Your Brain).* Cambridge, MA: Harvard University Press.

Battino, R. (2000) *Guided Imagery and Other Approaches to Healing.* Carmarthen: Crown House Publishing.

Battino, R. (2002) *Metaphoria: Metaphor and Guided Metaphor for Psychotherapy and Healing.* Carmarthen: Crown House Publishing.

Battino, R. and South, T.L. (1999) *Ericksonian Approaches: A Comprehensive Manual.* Carmarthen: Crown House Publishing.

Benjamin, W. (1970) *Illuminations.* London: Fontana Press.

Berry, J. (1961) *West African Folk Tales.* Evanston, IL: Northwestern University Press.

Berry, J. (1988) *Anansi-Spiderman.* London: Walker Books.

Blackmore, S. (1999) *The Meme Machine.* Oxford: Oxford University Press.

Booker, C. (2004) *The Seven Basic Plots: Why We Tell Stories.* London: Continuum.

Borges, J.L. (1975) *A Universal History of Infamy.* London: Penguin.

Borges, J.L. (1976) *Doctor Brodie's Report.* London: Penguin.

Briggs, K.M. (1970) *A Dictionary of British Folk Tales in the English Language: Part A Folk Narratives.* London: Routledge & Kegan Paul.

Brodie, R. (1996) *Virus of the Mind: The New Science of the Meme.* Seattle, WA: Integral Press.

Burton, R.F. (1870) *Vikram and the Vampire.* London: Longmans, Green & Co.

Burton, R.F. (1894) *The Book of the Thousand Nights and a Night.* London: H.S. Nichols & Co.

Buzan, T. (1986) *Use Your Memory.* London: BBC Worldwide.

Calvino, I. (1982) *Italian Folktales.* London: Penguin Books.

Campbell, J. (1976) *The Masks of God. Volume 1: Primitive Mythology.* Harmondsworth: Penguin.

Campbell, J. (2008) *The Hero With a Thousand Faces,* 3rd edition. Novato, CA: New World Library.

Cannarozzi, S. (2008) *When Tigers Smoked Pipes*. Reading: Society for Storytelling.

Chatwin, B. (1987) *The Songlines*. New York: Viking Penguin.

Christensen, A. (1918) *Contes Persans en Langue Populaire*. Copenhagen: Andr. Fred. Høst & Søn.

Cialdini, R.B. (1984) *Influence: The Psychology of Persuasion*. New York: William Morrow.

Claxton, G. (1997) *Hare Brain, Tortoise Mind*. London: Fourth Estate.

Cleary, T. (1993) *Unlocking the Zen Koan – A New Translation of the Zen Classic Wumenguan*. Berkeley, CA: North Atlantic Books.

Coelho, P. (1995) *The Alchemist*. London: HarperCollins.

Cole, J. (1982) *Best Loved Folktales of the World*. New York: Doubleday.

Cooper, J.C. (1978) *An Illustrated Encyclopaedia of Traditional Symbols*. London: Thames & Hudson.

Cotterell, Y.Y. (1979) *The Illustrated Book of World Fables*. London: Book Club Associates.

Csikszentmihalyi, M. (1990) *Flow: The Psychology of Optimal Experience*. New York: Harper Perennial.

Damasio, A. (2000) *The Feeling of What Happens: Body, Emotion and the Making of Consciousness*. London: Vintage.

Dawkins, R. (1976) *The Selfish Gene*. Oxford: Oxford University Press.

de Bono, E. (1973) *Po: Beyond Yes and No*. London: Penguin.

de Shazer, S. (1988) *Clues: Investigating Solutions in Brief Therapy*. New York: Norton.

Deikman, A. (1982) *The Observing Self*. Boston, MA: Beacon Press.

Dennett, D. (1991) *Consciousness Explained*. Boston, MA: Little, Brown & Co.

Dennett, D. (1995) *Darwin's Dangerous Idea*. London: Penguin.

Dwivedi, K.N. (ed.) (1997) *The Therapeutic Use of Stories*. London: Routledge.

Dwivedi, K.N. (2000) 'Therapeutic powers of narratives and stories.' *Context 47*, February, 11–12.

Feldman, S. (1970) *African Myths and Tales*. New York: Dell Publishing.

Ferrucci, P. (1982) *What We May Be: The Vision and Techniques of Psychosynthesis*. London: Mandala.

Foley, M.K. (1979) *The Sundanese 'Wayang Golek': The Rod Puppet Theatre of West Java*. (PhD thesis, University of Hawaii, 1980).

Folklore and Legends – Oriental (1889). London: W.W. Gibbings.

Folk Tales from China (1958) Third Series. Peking: Foreign Languages Press.

Freeman, M. (1995) 'Word of skill.' Retrieved 16 January 2009 from www.chalice centre.net/wordofskill.htm.

Gardner, H. (1982) *Art, Mind and Brain: A Cognitive Approach to Creativity*. New York: Basic Books.

Goleman, D. (1996) *Emotional Intelligence*. London: Bloomsbury.

Goleman, D. (1998) *Working with Emotional Intelligence*. London: Bloomsbury.

Griffin, J. (1997) *The Origin of Dreams*. Worthing: The Therapist Ltd.

Griffin, J. (2005) 'PTSD: why some techniques to treat it work so fast.' *Human Givens 12*, 3, 12–17.

Griffin, J. and Tyrrell, I. (2003) *Human Givens: A New Approach to Emotional Health and Clear Thinking*. Chalvington: HG Publishing.

Griffin, J. and Tyrrell, I. (2004) *Dreaming Reality*. Chalvington: HG Publishing.

Guy, K. and Guy, N. (2003) 'The fast cure for phobia and trauma: evidence that it works.' *Human Givens 9*, 4, 31–35.

Haley, J. (1986) *Uncommon Therapy: The Psychiatric Techniques of Milton H. Erickson, M.D.* New York: Norton.

Hsiao Ch'ien (1944) *A Harp with a Thousand Strings: A Chinese Anthology in Six Parts.* London: Pilot Press.

Jung, C.G. (1963) *Memories, Dreams, Reflections.* London: Collins/Routledge & Kegan Paul.

Jung, C.G. (1972) *Four Archetypes – Mother, Rebirth, Spirit, Trickster.* London: Routledge & Kegan Paul.

Kopp, R.R. (1995) *Metaphor Therapy: Using Client-Generated Metaphors in Psychotherapy.* New York: Brunner/Mazel.

Lakoff, G. and Johnson, M. (1980 and 2003) *Metaphors We Live By.* Chicago. IL: University of Chicago Press.

Lakoff, G. and Johnson, M. (1999) *Philosophy in the Flesh: The Embodied Mind and Its Challenge to Western Thought.* New York: Basic Books.

Lankton, C.H. and Lankton, S.R. (1984) *The Answer Within: A Clinical Framework of Ericksonian Therapy.* New York: Brunner/Mazel.

Lankton, C.H. and Lankton, S.R. (1989) *Tales of Enchantment.* New York: Brunner/ Mazel.

LeDoux, J. (1998) *The Emotional Brain.* London: Weidenfeld & Nicolson.

Lessing, D. (1974) *The Memoirs of a Survivor.* London: The Octagon Press.

Lorca, F.G. (1998) *In Search of Duende* (ed. & trans. C. Maurer). New York: New Directions Bibelot.

Lynch, A. (1996) *Thought Contagion: How Belief Spreads Through Society.* New York: Basic Books.

Mardrus, J.C. and Mathers, P. (1962) *The Book of the Thousand Nights and One Night.* London: Routledge & Kegan Paul.

Matarosso, P.M. (1969) *The Quest of the Holy Grail.* London: Penguin.

Mee, A. (1956, etc.) *The Children's Encyclopaedia.* London: The Educational Book Company.

Narayan, K. (1989) *Storytellers, Saints and Scoundrels: Folk Narrative in Hindu Religious Teaching.* Philadelphia, PA: University of Pennsylvania Press.

Narby, J. (1998) *The Cosmic Serpent: DNA and the Origins of Knowledge.* London: Victor Gollanz.

Noll, R. (1994) *The Jung Cult: Origins of a Charismatic Movement.* Princeton, NJ: Princeton University Press.

Nunn, C. (2007) *Neurons to Notions: Brains, Mind and Meaning.* Edinburgh: Floris Books.

O'Hanlon, W.H. and Weiner-Davis, M. (1989) *In Search of Solutions: A New Direction in Psychotherapy.* New York: Norton.

Okri, B. (1996) *Birds of Heaven.* London: Phoenix Paperback.

Ornstein, R. (1986) *Multimind.* Boston, MA: Houghton Mifflin.

Ornstein, R. (1991) *The Evolution of Consciousness.* New York: Prentice Hall.

Ornstein, R. (1997) *The Right Brain.* New York: Harcourt Brace.

Ornstein, R. (ed.) (1973) *The Nature of Human Consciousness.* San Francisco, CA: W.H. Freeman.

Parkinson, R. (1998) *Three Angles on an Awakening Kiss.* Reading: Society for Storytelling.

Parkinson, R. (2003) *Powerful Stories* (double CD). Brighton: Uncommon Knowledge. www.uncommon-knowledge.co.uk

Parkinson, R. (2004) *Tall Tale Telling: 24 Fun Games for Making and Telling Incredible Stories.* Tonbridge: Imaginary Journeys Publishing. www.imaginaryjourneys.co.uk

Parkinson, R. (2005a) *Imagine On.* Tonbridge: Imaginary Journeys Publishing. www.imaginaryjourneys.co.uk

Parkinson, R. (2005b) *Just Imagine – Use the Power of Imagination to Relax and Create a Clear Personal Focus.* (CD). Tonbridge: Imaginary Journeys.

Parkinson, R. (2007a) *New Lamps from Old: 24 Games for Making New Tales from Old Plots.* Tonbridge: Imaginary Journeys Publishing. www.imaginaryjourneys.co.uk

Parkinson, R. (2007b) *Yarn Spinning – 24 Fun Ways to Stretch a Tale in the Telling.* Tonbridge: Imaginary Journeys Publishing. www.imaginaryjourneys.co.uk

Parkinson, R. (2008) *Fabulous Fables – Witty and Wise Tales from World Traditions* (CD). Tonbridge: Imaginary Journeys. www.imaginaryjourneys.co.uk

Philip, N. (1989) *The Cinderella Story: The Origins and Variations of the Story Known as Cinderella.* London: Penguin.

Pinker, S. (1994) *The Language Instinct.* New York: Morrow.

Richardson, J. (2000) *The Magic of Rapport.* Capitola, CA: Meta Publications.

Robertson, I. (1999) *Mind Sculpture.* London: Bantam Press.

Rolleston, T.W. (1985) *Myths and Legends of the Celtic Race.* London: Constable.

Rosen, Sidney (ed.) (1982) *My Voice Will Go with You: The Teaching Tales of Milton H. Erickson.* New York: Norton.

Rossi, E.L. (1993) *The Psychobiology of Mind-Body Healing.* New York: Norton.

Rubin, D.C. (1995) *Memory in Oral Traditions: The Cognitive Psychology of Epic, Ballads, and Counting-out Rhymes.* New York: Oxford University Press.

Schwartz, H. (1987) *Elijah's Violin and Other Jewish Folktales.* London: Penguin.

Shah, I. (1970) *The Dermis Probe.* London: Jonathan Cape.

Shah, I. (1971) *Thinkers of the East.* London: Jonathan Cape.

Shah, I. (1972) *The Diffusion of Sufi Ideas in the West.* Boulder, CO: Keysign Press.

Shah, I. (1979) *World Tales: The Extraordinary Coincidence of Stories Told in All Times, in All Places.* London: Allen Lane/Kestrel.

Shah, I. (1982) *The Sufis.* London: The Octagon Press.

Shepard, A. (2000) *The Magic Brocade: A Tale of China.* Union City, CA: EduStar Press.

Southworth, J. (1989) *The English Medieval Minstrel.* Woodbridge: The Boydell Press.

Stallings, F. (1988) 'The web of silence: storytelling's power to hypnotize.' *The National Storytelling Journal,* Spring/Summer. Retrieved 1 October 2008 from www.healingstory.org/articles/web_of_silence/fran_stallings.html.

Sturm, Brian (1999) 'The enchanted imagination: Storytelling's power to entrance listeners.' ALA Archives. Retrieved 26 August 2008 from www.ala.org/ala/aasl/aaslpubsandjournals/slmrb/slmrcontents/volume21999/vol2sturm.cfm.

Sutton, R.A. (1996) 'Interpreting electronic sound technology in the contemporary Javanese soundscape.' *Ethnomusicology 40,* 2, 249–268.

Tawney, C.H. (trans.) (1924) *The Ocean of Story: Somadeva's Katha Sarit Sagara.* London: Chas J. Sawyer.

Temple, O. and Temple, R. (1998) *Aesop – The Complete Fables.* London: Penguin.

Thompson, D. (1996) *The People of the Sea*. Edinburgh: Canongate Classics.

Thompson, S. (1955) *Motif Index of Folk Literature*. Bloomington, IN: Indiana University Press.

Waugh, A. (1999) *Time*. London: Headline.

Webster, J. (2003) *Duende: A Journey in Search of Flamenco*. London: Doubleday.

Whitfield, E.H. (translator/abridger)(1979) *Teaching of Rumi – The Masnavi i Ma'navi – The Spiritual Couplets of Maulana Jalalu-d-din Muhammad i Rumi*. London: The Octagon Press.

Williams, P. (1994) 'Suggestibility and illusory memories in the therapeutic setting.' *The Therapist 2*, 2, 24–29.

Williams, P. (1998 and 2006) *How Stories Heal* (double CD). Chalvington: HG Publishing.

Wood, R. (1982) *Kalila and Dimna: Selected Fables of Bidpai*. London: Granada.

Wubbolding, R.E. (1991) *Understanding Reality Therapy: A Metaphorical Approach*. New York: HarperCollins.

Yolen, J. (ed.) (1986) *Favorite Folktales from Around the World*. New York: Pantheon Books.

Subject Index

The Abyss 218
addictions 52, 53, 63
advertising 32, 33, 133
Aesop
  dilemma tales 174
  fables and short
    teaching tales
    158, 160
  transposing stories
    229, 245, 246, 247
The Alchemist (Coelho)
  239
Alexander the Great 20
Alif Layla wa Layla (Tales
  of the Arabian Nights)
  dilemma tales 171
  oral storytelling 123
  stories within stories
    within stories
    297–8
  traditional stories and
    storytellers 145,
    149
  transposing stories
    229, 239, 254, 255
allegories 36, 177,
  198–202
amygdala 87, 88
analogies 58, 176, 190–2,
  193, 202
Anansi-Spiderman (Berry)
  27
anecdotes 183–6
Animal Farm (Orwell) 198
Anwar-i-Suhaili (The Lights
  of Canopus) 247 see
  also Panchatantra
anxiety 49, 50, 70
aphorisms 187, 188,
  189–92, 193, 202

The Apprentice, the
  Honeypot and the
  Scissors 117–19
The Arabian Nights (Alif
  Layla wa Layla)
  dilemma tales 171
  oral storytelling 123
  stories within stories
    within stories
    297–8
  traditional stories and
    storytellers 145,
    149
  transposing stories
    229, 239, 254, 255
Arabic language 41–2
archetypes 226–8, 234,
  235, 272
ashiks 147
Attar 153
attention bargain 140–2
autistic spectrum
  disorders 85
The Axe 217–18

Baklava 206–7
Bandler, Richard 87
bards 147, 148
The Bean 215
biology of stories 45–50
The Blue Jackal 245–7
Boccaccio, Giovanni 145,
  298
body and mind 55, 56,
  57, 58
body language 126
body scan 90
The Boy Who Cried Wolf
  158
brain

biology of stories 48,
  49
healing stories 50
natural storyteller 65,
  67
oral storytelling 102,
  112
personal stories 29
symbols as shared
  metaphors 267
visualization 85, 87
Breaking the Diet 203
breathing 90, 203
Brothers Grimm 233, 234
Brown, Gordon 123
Bunyan, John 198
Byron, Lord George
  Gordon 194

cadence 128
Canterbury Tales
  (Chaucer) 144–5,
  149, 152
Castle, Pete 176
chaining images 194–5
'The Chamber of Statues'
  123
change
  change through stories
    17, 18, 19
  guided imagery 80, 81,
    82, 83, 84
  the Mbala effect 63, 64
Chaucer, Geoffrey 144–5,
  149, 152, 235, 298
children 92–4
A Chinese Fable 30
chosen peoples 155–6
Christ, Jesus 183, 190
Chuang Tzu 68

Cole, Keith 131
collective unconscious 227
compulsions 52, 63
confessionals 154
confusional language 133–4
consciousness
   natural storyteller
      biology of stories 47
      healing stories 56
      overview 26, 65
      personal stories 29, 30, 31
      trance-forming stories 37, 39
   oral storytelling 135–40
   stories within stories within stories 301
   transposing stories
      Jung's archetypes 227
      memes and fundamentals 231, 232, 233
      psychoactive stories 234, 235
Consciousness Explained (Dennett) 231
conundrums 134
conyach 140
cortisol 87
Cox, Marion Roalf 230
craic 139, 140
Crocodiles and Cares 212
culture 155, 156

Darwin's Dangerous Idea (Dennett) 231
Decameron (Boccaccio) 145
delivery, speed of 128
Delphic Oracle 27
Delusions 222
depression 50, 89
The Destruction of Senacherib (Byron) 194
The Devil's Trill (Tartini) 268
Dhonden, Yeshi 53, 54
dilemma tales 36, 168–75
Diogenes 20
Doctor Brodie's Report (Borges) 41
Dog Snuff 213–14
The Donkey and the Diet 205

doors, locks and keys 137
Dowson, Ernest 94
Dreaming Reality (Griffin and Tyrrell) 47
dreams
   natural storyteller 40, 47–8, 65
   the Spanish game 72
   traps and treasures 265, 267, 268
duende 140

education
   change through stories 18, 19
   fables and short teaching tales 161, 162
   guided imagery 69
   stories within stories within stories 301
Einstein, Albert 268
Elijah's Violin and Other Stories (Schwartz) 157
embedded and interspersal suggestions 132–3
embroidering stories 108, 116–17, 159
Emerson, Ralph Waldo 42
The Emir's Robe 215–17
emotional contagion 138–9
Emotional Intelligence (Goleman) 136
emotions 29, 56, 87
The Enchanting Bird 253–5
The Enchantress and the Animals 69
endings 125
energy 129
Enoch and the Cockerel 184
Erickson, Milton
   change through stories 18
   guided imagery 73, 74, 87
   personal stories 28
   quick reframing stories 211
   techniques for focusing attention inwards 131–5
   trance-forming stories 38
expectations 47, 48, 49, 267

eye contact 127

fables
   dilemma tales 170, 174
   fables and short teaching tales 157–68
   making short metaphors 191
   puzzling tales 176
   Social Stories™ 36
   transposing stories 229, 236, 245, 246, 247
The Fables of Bidpai 247, 298 see also Panchatantra
Facts & Fiction 176
fado 140
false memory 37, 38
false pattern matching 50, 51, 52
fantasizing 103–4
fast phobia cure 87
fear 50, 87, 94, 210
fibs 23, 103–4
fight or flight response 50, 87, 110
filidh 147, 149
First Nation Americans 155
flashbacks 30, 51
flight 137, 141
flow 136–7
focus 136
Ford, Henry 189
The Fortunate Dog 214
The Four Wise Men 162–3
The Fox in the Well 160–1
frames see solution-focused story frames
'Franklin's Tale' (Chaucer) 149
Freud, Sigmund 48
The Frogs and the Snake 167–8
fundamentals 231–3
The Furniture Van 61–2

gardens as symbols 276, 278–9
Gautama the Buddha 183
genes 231, 232
German Saying 218
Gestalt therapy 90
Goethe, Johann Wolfgang von 235

The Golden Bird 285–90
Goodman, Nelson 43
The Gorilla 208
Gray, Carol 85
Grimm, Brothers 233, 234
griots 147
group mood 139–40
guided imagery 68–99
  allegories and satires
    199
  four relaxation
    techniques 89–92
  healing stories 59
  how we know that
    visualization works
    84–9
  interpretations and
    misinterpretations
    78–84
  overview 68–71
  personal symbols 270
  seven visualizations
    75–8
  the Spanish game 71–5
  visualization and
    guided imagery
    with children 92–4
  visualizing for change
    94–9
Gulliver's Travels (Swift)
  198
Guru Nanak 183

habits 53, 63
haka 90
Hall, George 84
Hare Brain, Tortoise Mind
  (Claxton) 53
healers 149–50
healing stories 41, 50–61
Hebb, Donald 29, 112
Hebbian learning principle
  29, 112
hippocampus 87, 88
Hippocrates 50
The Hoe 213
holy man 154
Homer 148, 255
Horses in Alexandria
  195–6
houses as symbols 275–6,
  278
Howerd, Frankie 126
human givens approach
  87
Human Givens Foundation
  87
hypnosis

remembering and
  'fixing' stories 112
techniques for focusing
  attention inwards
  131–5
traditional stories and
  storytellers 149
trance-forming stories
  37, 38, 39, 40–1
The Idol 244–5
imagination
  false pattern matching
    52, 53
  guided imagery
    interpretations and
    misinterpretations 79
  overview 68, 69, 70
  special place
    visualization
    91–2
  the Spanish game
    72, 73
  visualization and
    guided imagery
    with children
    92, 93
  natural storyteller 67
  solution-focused story
    frames 264
instinct 46, 47, 48, 49
intelligence 29, 47
internal narrative 28, 29
internet 157
interspersal suggestions
  132–3
Italian Folktales (Calvino)
  255

Jataka Tales 183
Java 139
The Jester and the King
  185–6
jesters 185
jewels and precious metals
  as symbols 276–7,
  279
Jewish tales 155, 157
Johnson, Donald Alastair
  109
jokes
  fables and short
    teaching tales 157
  making short
    metaphors 183–6,
    210
  natural storyteller 23,
    24, 36

transposing stories
  236
jongleurs 148
journalism 32, 33
Jouvet, Michel 46, 47
Jungle Book 39

Kalila and Dimna 247,
  298 see also
  Panchatantra
kayif 140
Kekule, Friedrich August
  268
King Lear 159
King Vikram and the
  Vampire 168–9
Knowing Where the
  Problem Is 222
koan principle 196–8,
  232
Korzybski, Alfred 188

The Lachrymose Peeler
  191
La Fontaine, Jean de 229
Lakshmi and Vishnu 62–3
language 41–5, 49, 54, 65
language instinct 47
The Languid Goat is
  Always Thin 186
learning
  biology of stories 46,
    49
  fables and short
    teaching tales 160
  personal stories 29
  remembering and
    'fixing' stories
    109–16
Ledigo, Hugh 113
left brain 102
legends 271
Lester, Bryan 107
Lewis, C.S. 257, 263
lies 103–4
limbic system 29
The Lion, the Witch and the
  Wardrobe (Lewis) 257
list technique (pedal point)
  123–4
literacy 145
The Little Tailor and the
  Silkie Tale 111

mana 140
The Man on the Train 24,
  26

The Man, the Snake and
   the Fox 165–6
The Man Who Became
   Rich Through
   Dreaming 238–9
The Man Who Died 169,
   170–1
The Masnawi 247
maxims 186–90, 191, 193
Mbala effect 61–4, 299
media 32, 33, 70
medical diagnosis 53, 54,
   55–6, 57, 58, 61
meditation 90, 232
The Meme Machine
   (Blackmore) 231
memes 30, 231–3, 234,
   235
memory
   false memory 37, 38
   natural storyteller
      biology of stories 48
      overview 66
      personal stories 29,
         30
      trance-forming
         stories 37, 38
   remembering and
      'fixing' stories
      109–16
   visualization 88
Mesmer, Anton 39
metaphor
   definition 42–3
   fables and short
      teaching tales
      160–1
   making short
      metaphors
      182–223
      allegories and
         satires 198–
         202
      aphorisms to
         analogies to
         parables 190–2
      jokes and anecdotes

         183–6
      koan principle
         196–8
      overview 182–3
      quick reframing
         stories 211–23
      sayings and maxims
         186–90
      similes and smiles
         192–5
      vignettes 195–6

working with brief
   reframing
   stories 202–11
natural storyteller
   biology of stories
      46, 47, 48, 49
   healing stories 53,
      54, 55, 60
   language, metaphor
      and story 41–5
   Social Stories™ 35,
      36
   trance-forming
      stories 40
puzzling tales 177
traps and treasures
   personal symbols
   270
stories within stories
   within stories
   301
symbols as shared
   metaphors
   266–70
the trap and the
   hidden treasure
   290–6
working with
   symbols 271
visualization 85, 86
Metaphors We Live By
   (Lakoff and Johnson)
   267
The Milkmaid's Dreams
   228–9
mind and body 55, 56,
   57, 58
Mind Sculpture (Robertson)
   85
minstrels 148–9
morals 35, 36, 63, 158,
   159, 245
More Delusions 222–3
The Morning Dew 274
Motif Index of Folk
   Literature (Thompson)
   230
motifs 237
mounts and minions 275,
   277–8
Muhammad 183, 271
multiple embedded
   metaphor scheme
   299, 300
multiple-meaning
   allegories 177
multisensory imagery
   113, 131–2
myths 33, 36, 230, 271

My Voice Will Go with You
   (Erickson) 211

narrative
   natural storyteller
      healing stories 53
      overview 65, 67
      personal stories 28,
         29, 30
   oral storytelling 112,
      122
Nasrudin stories 177, 184
natural storyteller 23–67
   biology of stories 45–50
   breakthrough stories:
      the Mbala effect
      61–4
   healing stories 50–61
   language, metaphor
      and story 41–5
   overview 23–7
   personal stories 27–31
   Social Stories™ 31–6
   summary 65–7
   trance-forming stories
      37–41
neocortex 87
neuro-linguistic
   programming (NLP)
   87
neurons 29, 112
The Noisy House 249–51
The Noisy Neighbours 19
nursery tales 35, 177
Nzilla the Tracker 25, 26

observing self 31
The Observing Self
   (Deikman) 239
obsessions 52, 63
The Ocean of Story
   (Somadeva) 145, 298
Odyssey (Homer) 255
openings 119–21
The Optimist 212
oral storytelling 100–42
   attention bargain
      140–2
   extra signals 125–31
   fibbers and fantasists
      103–7
   overview 100–3
   remembering and
      'fixing' stories
      109–16
   storytelling and
      consciousness
      135–40

oral storytelling *cont.*
stretching stories
108–9, 116–19
techniques for focusing
attention inwards
131–5
techniques from
traditional telling
119–25
trance-forming stories
40–1
The Origin of Dreams
(Griffin) 47
Orwell, George 198
The Other Room 248–9

pacing devices 124
Panchatantra 36, 145,
229, 246, 247, 298
parables 190–2
parasympathetic nervous
system 90
The Pardoner's Story
152–3
Paving the Streets 221
Pearls 221
pedal point (list technique)
123–4
The People of the Sea
(Thompson) 110
The Perfect Storyteller
115–16, 119, 129,
135, 142
personal stories 27–31
personal symbols 270
Pert, Candace 56
Petrarch, Francesco 145
phobias 52, 70, 94
pilgrims 144, 145, 152
Pilgrim's Progress (Bunyan)
198
Plato 190, 226, 227
plots 225, 228–31, 256
The Ploughman and the
Snake 164–5
politics 32, 33, 133, 151
post-traumatic stress
disorder (PTSD) 51–2,
86–7, 88
Powerful Stories
(Parkinson) 243, 249,
250, 254
preachers 150–1, 154
preamble 121–2
priests 150–1
The Princess Who Died
239–41
psychoactive stories
233–5

psychotherapy *see* therapy
PTSD *see* post-traumatic
stress disorder
pundits, pilgrims and
plebs 144–6
puzzling tales 176–81

The Queen, the Lost
Crown and the
Storyteller 290

ramai 139, 140
rapport skills 126
rawi qissas 148, 149
reframing
making short
metaphors
jokes and anecdotes
184, 185
overview 182–3
quick reframing
stories 211–23
sayings and maxims
189
working with brief
reframing
stories 202–11
personal stories 28
relaxation exercises
89–92, 199–201
religion 150–1, 183, 185
remembering and 'fixing'
stories 109–16
reminiscence work 156
REM (rapid eye movement)
sleep 46, 47, 49
The Republic (Plato) 190
resistance and confusional
language 133–4
rewind technique 87, 88,
92, 94
The Rich Woman and the
Hat Maker 109
right brain 102
Robert the Bruce 189
The Robinson Crusoe
Island 199–201
Romanies 155
Roof and Walls 211
Rowe, Doc 142
The Ruined Palace 305–6
rule of three 122–3, 124
Rumi, Jalaludin 247
runs 124–5

Saddam Hussein 42
The Saddhu's Loincloth
251–2

saints 151–5
The Sandcastle and the
Chest 304–5, 306–8
satires 36, 191, 198–202
sayings 186–90, 191, 192
science 55, 294
The Scientists 174
Scott, Sir Walter 189
scoundrels 151–5
seanachies 139, 146–7,
149
Selchie legends 110–11
Self-Diagnosis 204
The Selfish Gene (Dawkins)
231
Selzer, Richard 53, 54
semiotics 265
Semitic languages 41
sensory awareness
(the 'three things'
technique) 90–1
The Seven Basic Plots
(Booker) 225
Shakespeare, William 36,
159, 235
shamans 55, 149–50
shaping the meaning
117–19
Silkie legends 110–11
similes 42, 192–5
Simple Arithmetic 213
Snap! 57
Social Control 219
Social Proof 219–20
Social Stories™ 31–6, 85
solution-focused story
frames 255–64
Somadeva 298
The Songlines (Chatwin)
112
songs 112
space 126–7
Spanish game: guided
imagery and stories
68–99
four relaxation
techniques 89–92
how we know that
visualization works
84–9
interpretations and
misinterpretations
78–84
overview 68–71
seven visualizations
75–8
the Spanish game 71–5

visualization and guided imagery with children 92–4
visualizing for change 94–9
special place visualization 88, 91–2
speed of delivery 128
spin-doctors 32, 33
spirited occasions 139–40
The Spotted Snake 162
standard openings 119–21
Stewart, Sheila 140
stories
 making short metaphors 182–223
  allegories and satires 198–202
  aphorisms to analogies to parables 190–2
  jokes and anecdotes 183–6
  koan principle 196–8
  overview 182–3
  quick reframing stories 211–23
  sayings and maxims 186–90
  similes and smiles 192–5
  vignettes 195–6
  working with brief reframing stories 202–11
 natural storyteller 23–67
  biology of stories 45–50
  breakthrough stories: the Mbala effect 61–4
  healing stories 50–61
  language, metaphor and story 41–5
  overview 23–7
  personal stories 27–31
  Social Stories™ 31–6
  summary 65–7
  trance-forming stories 37–41

oral storytelling 100–42
 attention bargain 140–2
 extra signals 125–31
 fibbers and fantasists 103–7
 overview 100–3
 remembering and 'fixing' stories 109–16
 storytelling and consciousness 135–40
 stretching stories 108–9, 116–19
 techniques for focusing attention inwards 131–5
 techniques from traditional telling 119–25
 overview 17–21
Spanish game: guided imagery and stories 68–99
 four relaxation techniques 89–92
 how we know that visualization works 84–9
 interpretations and misinterpretations 78–84
  overview 68–71
  the Spanish game 71–5
  visualization and guided imagery with children 92–4
 traditional ways of storytelling 143–81
  dilemma tales 168–75
  fables and short teaching tales 157–68
  puzzling tales 176–81
  traditional stories and storytellers 143–56
 transposing stories 224–64

Jung's archetypes 226–8
 the many forms of universal plot 228–31
 memes and fundamentals 231–3
 nine adaptable tales 237–55
 overview 224
 psychoactive stories 233–5
 repeating patterns 225–6
 solution-focused story frames 255–64
 transposing a story 235–7
traps and treasures 265–309
 metaphor: the trap and the hidden treasure 290–6
 overview 265–6
 personal symbols 270
 stories within stories within stories 296–302
 symbols as shared metaphors 266–70
 three interwoven stories 303–9
 two symbolic stories 279–90
 working with symbols 271–4
The Storyteller 303–4, 308–9
stress 52, 87
stretching stories 108–9, 116–19
stringing 130–1
Sufism 20
suggestions 132–3
The Sweet Merchant and the Peasant 154–5, 176–7
Swift, Jonathan 198
symbols
 dreams 48
 traps and treasures five traditional symbols 274–9
 overview 265, 266

personal symbols 270

symbols as shared metaphors 266–70

working with symbols 271–4

sympathetic nervous system 90

The Tailor's Cloth 44–5

Tales of the Arabian Nights see The Arabian Nights

The Talisman 242–4

Talleifer 148

tapestry 130

Tartini, Giuseppe 268

teaching stories 157–68

therapy

change through stories 18, 19

false memory 37

guided imagery 69, 78, 86

healing stories 56

making short metaphors 183, 194

personal stories 28

reframing 183

techniques for focusing attention inwards 131–5

traditional stories and storytellers 154

trance-forming stories 37, 38

Thought Contagion (Lynch) 231

The Thousand and One Nights see The Arabian Nights

The Three Artists 174–5

The Three Girls' Veils 34–5

Three Hairs from a Wolf's Chin 94–9

the 'three things' technique 90–1

The Three Wizards and the Tree 173

The Times 32

timing 129

Tolstoy, Leo 36

Tom and Yesterday 209–10

torque 138–9

Torture 218–19

To Them that Have... 214–15

The Touchy Feely Show 295–6

traditional ways of storytelling 143–81

dilemma tales 168–75

puzzling tales 176–81

traditional stories and storytellers 143–56

bards, ashiks, griots and all 147–8

fables and short teaching tales 157–68

overview 143–4

preachers, priests and politicians 150–1

pundits, pilgrims and plebs 144–6

scoundrels and saints 151–5

seanachies 146–7

shamans and healers 149–50

storyteller in the marketplace 148–9

travellers and chosen peoples 155–6

trance

guided imagery 86, 89

natural storyteller

biology of stories 49

healing stories 51

Social Stories™ 36

trance-forming stories 37–41

oral storytelling

overview 102

remembering and 'fixing' stories 110

stretching stories 108

techniques for focusing attention inwards 135

techniques from traditional telling 122, 125

traditional stories and storytellers 149

transposing stories 224–64

Jung's archetypes 226—8

the many forms of universal plot 228–31

memes and fundamentals 231–3

nine adaptable tales 237–55

overview 224

psychoactive stories 233–5

repeating patterns 225–6

solution-focused story frames 255–64

transposing a story 235–7

traps and treasures 265–309

five traditional symbols 274–9

metaphor: the trap and the hidden treasure 290–6

overview 265–6

personal symbols 270

stories within stories within stories 296–302

symbols as shared metaphors 266–70

three interwoven stories 303–9

two symbolic stories 279–90

working with symbols 271–4

trauma 87, 88, 110

travellers and chosen peoples 155–6

The Tray 31

The Treasure Hunter 212

The Tree 175

The Tree of Jewels 279–85

trees as symbols 275, 277

Two Disciples and One Guru 207

Two Existential Riddles 212

The Two Otters and the Jackal 166–7

The Two Thieves and the King 172–3

The Types of the Folktale (Aarne) 230

The Ugly Servant 59–60
unconscious
  dreams 49
  Jung's archetypes 227
  personal symbols 270
  resistance and
      confusional
      language 134
  symbols as shared
      metaphors 267
  visualization 86
urban legends 37, 61–2
use of space 126–7

Vetala Tales 169, 241,
  298
The Vicar and the
  Grindstone 103
vignettes 195–6
Virus of the Mind (Brodie)
  231
visualization
  how we know that
      visualization works
      84–9
  interpretations and
      misinterpretations
      78–84
  overview 68, 69, 71
  seven visualizations
      75–8
  special place
      visualization 91–2
  the Spanish game 71–5
  visualization and
      guided imagery
      with children 92–4
visual kinaesthetic
  dissociation technique
  (VKD) 87
vocal tone and cadence
  128
'The Voyage of Maeldun'
  123

wakan 140
wandering minstrels
  148–9
The Way You Tell 'Em
  102–3
The Wealth of Kings
  220–1
Williamson, Duncan 229
Wine Lover 223
The Wise Men of Schilda
  229
The Wonderful Tapestry
  178–81, 27

The Wooden Bayonet 157
Words 163–4
Wumenguan 196

Yarn Spinning (Parkinson)
  117

Zen 20, 196, 197, 232
Zoroaster 183

Author Index

Aarne, Antii 230

Battino, Rubin 182–3
Benjamin, Walter 143
Berry, James 27
Blackmore, Susan 231,
   232, 233, 234
Booker, Christopher 225,
   226, 231
Borges, Jorge Luis 41,
   235
Brodie, Richard 231
Burton, R.F. 254, 255
Buzan, Tony 114

Calvino, Italo 255
Campbell, Joseph 41, 228
Chatwin, Bruce 112
Claxton, Guy 53, 54
Coelho, Paolo 239
Cooper, J.C. 271
Csikszentmihalyi, Mihaly
   136

Damasio, Antonio 56,
   65, 67
Dawkins, Richard 231
de Bono, Edward 202
Deikman, Arthur 31, 239
Dennett, Daniel 231, 232
Dwivedi, Kedar Nath 154

Foley, Kathy 139
Freeman, Mara 146

Gardner, Howard 43
Goleman, Daniel 136
Griffin, Joe 39, 40, 47, 49,
   88, 267

Haley, Jay 73–4

Johnson, Mark 267
Jung, Carl 226

Kopp, Richard R. 45

Lakoff, George 267
Lankton, Carole 297, 298,
   299
Lankton, Stephen 297,
   298, 299
LeDoux, Joseph 87
Lessing, Doris 234, 263
Lynch, Aaron 231

Mardrus, J.C. 255
Mathers, P. 255
Mee, Arthur 246

Narayan, Kirin 252
Narby, Jeremy 55

Okri, Ben 15, 23, 31, 301

Pinker, Steven 47

Robertson, Ian 85
Rossi, Ernest 30, 56

Schwartz, Howard 157
Shah, Idries 177
Stallings, Fran 37, 38
Sturm, Brian 38, 40
Sutton, R.A. 139

Thompson, David 110
Thompson, Stith 230

Tyrrell, Ivan 39, 40, 47

Williams, Pat 64